Poverty Politics

POVERTY POLITICS

Poor Whites in Contemporary Southern Writing

SARAH ROBERTSON

University Press of Mississippi / Jackson

The University Press of Mississippi is the scholarly publishing agency of the Mississippi Institutions of Higher Learning: Alcorn State University, Delta State University, Jackson State University, Mississippi State University, Mississippi University for Women, Mississippi Valley State University, University of Mississippi, and University of Southern Mississippi.

www.upress.state.ms.us

The University Press of Mississippi is a member of the Association of University Presses.

Copyright © 2019 by University Press of Mississippi
All rights reserved

First printing 2019

∞

Library of Congress Cataloging-in-Publication Data

Names: Robertson, Sarah, 1976 October 2– author.
Title: Poverty politics: poor whites in contemporary southern writing / Sarah Robertson.
Description: Jackson: University Press of Mississippi, [2019] | Includes bibliographical references and index. |
Identifiers: LCCN 2019003996 (print) | LCCN 2019006270 (ebook) | ISBN 9781496824349 (epub single) | ISBN 9781496824356 (epub institutional) | ISBN 9781496824363 (pdf single) | ISBN 9781496824370 (pdf institutional) | ISBN 9781496824325 (cloth) | ISBN 9781496824332 (pbk.)
Subjects: LCSH: Southern States—In literature. | Rural poor in literature. | Whites in literature. | Poverty in literature. | American literature—Southern States—History and criticism. | Literature and society—Southern States—History—20th century. | LCGFT: Literary criticism.
Classification: LCC PS261 (ebook) | LCC PS261 .R52 2019 (print) | DDC 810.9/975—dc23
LC record available at https://lccn.loc.gov/2019003996

British Library Cataloging-in-Publication Data available

*For Rob, and my family,
especially my parents,
Reuben and Dorothy*

Contents

Acknowledgments ix

Introduction xi

Abbreviations xxiii

CHAPTER ONE 3
Locating Poor Whites in Contemporary Travel Narratives

CHAPTER TWO 25
Photo-Narratives and the Poor White Self since the FSA

CHAPTER THREE 63
"What I Am Here for Is to Claim My Life": Life-Writing and Reclaiming the Poor White Self

CHAPTER FOUR 89
"A Whitegirl Helped Me": Locating Poor Whites in Literature

CHAPTER FIVE 113
"Culture Springs from the Actions of People in a Landscape": Poor Whites and Environmentalism

CONCLUSION 147

Notes 153

Works Cited 161

Index 181

Acknowledgments

This book has been a long time in the making, and I am very grateful to my department at the UWE, Bristol, for awarding me two periods of research leave that gave me time to develop and refine the project.

I also want to thank all my colleagues in the English literature department at UWE who supported me along the way. In particular, my thanks go to Robin Jarvis, Zoe Brennan, and Mariadele Boccardi, who each read parts of the book and provided me with invaluable feedback. Additionally, my thanks go to Andrew Crooke, who also read part of the book and cheered me along with wonderful insights. For their generosity in offering to be readers for the book, I am thanking Michael P. Bibler, Martyn Bone, Suzanne W. Jones, Owen Robinson, and Brian Ward. Some broader thanks go out to those colleagues who shared ideas and feedback with me when I delivered papers on poverty and poor whites at the Society for the Study of Southern Literature, Southern Studies Forum, and British Association for American Studies conferences.

Finally, I am indebted to the love, support, and patience of Rob and my family, especially during the completion process.

Introduction

If nothing else, the rise of populism in recent years, notably marked by Brexit in the United Kingdom and Donald Trump's ascendancy to the White House in the United States, has shone a light once again on class. Naomi Klein terms such populism "the new shock politics" but makes a convincing argument that "Trump is *not* shocking" because he "is the entirely predictable, indeed clichéd outcome of ubiquitous ideas and trends that should have been stopped long ago" (*No Is Not Enough* 10). Although fully aware of economic inequalities and global poverty, when Klein acknowledges the impact of activist movements prior to Trump's election, she draws attention to gains for gender rights campaigners and environmentalists but does not cite any significant labor wins, probably because the movements she outlines have made tremendous inroads in bringing about change for an array of marginalized groups but have often sidelined labor and the inherent inequalities of capital. Those inequalities, as Noam Chomsky observes, have intensified since the late 1970s with the turn to a neoliberal financial model that ensures corporate wealth by the creation of a "low-wage economy" that spreads uneven development across the globe (24). Acknowledging such class inequalities makes the current turns to populism no less palatable, but certainly as unsurprising as Klein contends.

As neoliberalism became hegemonic, the silence around class and poverty increased to the point that, as Terry Eagleton notes, "[c]lass struggle is now embarrassingly passé, whereas the affirmation of cultural identity is not" (26), or as bell hooks reflects, "[c]lass is the pressing issue, but it is not talked about." Instead, she argues, considerations of class were displaced by concerns with racism and sexism that "were easier to identify and challenge than the evils of classism" (5). If hooks worries that identity politics renders class unseen, Walter Benn Michaels addresses the problem of what happens when class is viewed through the lens of identity politics. "We have," he argues,

> started to treat economic difference as if it were cultural difference. So now we're urged to be more respectful of poor people and to stop thinking of them as victims, since to treat them as victims is condescending—it denies them their "agency." And if we can stop thinking of the poor as people who have too little money and start thinking of them instead as people who have too little respect,

then it's our attitude toward the poor, not their poverty, that becomes the problem to be solved, and we can focus our efforts of reform not on getting rid of classes but in getting rid of what we like to call classism.... The trick is to think of inequality as a consequence of our prejudices rather than as a consequence of our social system. (*The Trouble*, 19–20)

While identity politics offers a balm against the seemingly insurmountable task of changing the real sources of inequity, it is just another form of distraction.[1] For Slavoj Žižek, such distraction has a profound cost because "[t]he ideological stakes of such individuation are easily discernable: I get lost in my own self-examination instead of raising much more pertinent global questions about our entire industrial civilization" (87). Even postcolonial studies, Eagleton argues, "has been on the whole rather stronger on identity than on the International Monetary Fund, more fascinated by marginality than markets" (26), so the brief turns to postcolonial theory throughout this book serve to illuminate my approach to class, arguing that the exploitation of workers under neoliberalism aligns poor whites in the US South with poor people of all ethnicities across the globe. Certainly, for Christian Marazzi financial capitalism, or neoliberalism, acts as a contemporary form of empire; he suggests:

> The globalization of capital has internalized peripheral economies, forming ... an empire in which the same logic of exploitation rules, even if articulated in different forms.... Today, the relationships between North and South, center and periphery are *inside* accumulation processes, every "outside" is already "inside" the processes of capitalist growth. (111)

Following Marazzi's logic, to discuss the US South today is always to discuss the global North and South because neoliberalism is the structuring dynamic that coheres them all, regardless of regional and national differences.

This book explores a range of genres and texts to expose the tendencies to overlook or sideline economics, often when nostalgia and preoccupations with authenticity take precedence, and to examine more concerted efforts to illuminate class from within and without. Although the sweep of the book encompasses travel writing, photo-narratives, life-writing, literature, and eco-writing, it is not a survey of writing about or by poor southern whites since 1970. This study is not intended to offer any comprehensive account of contemporary southern white poverty but rather to work with a selection of authors and texts that help to build a picture of the challenges in recognizing and addressing poverty, and I am less concerned with what they reveal about the US South than what they reveal about the region's place within global financial markets. As this book is not about southern poor white culture but about the economics of poverty and how socioeconomic policies are reflected through various narrative forms, it embraces the aim of new southern studies as laid out by Jon Smith and Deborah Cohn in their edited collection, *Look Away! The U.S. South in New World Studies* (2004). Smith and Cohn seek to "trouble essentialist narratives both of global-southern decline and of unproblematic global-northern national or regional unity, of American or southern exceptionalism" (13), a line I take as I critically engage with the distinctions drawn between the US South and the rest of the nation, as well as the binaries of Global North and Global South. To that end, the writers in this study might not always be those the reader expects. As the book explores narratives about the US South, in the latter chapters it dwells on authors who promote forms of communitarianism, including John Biguenet, Toni Morrison, Ann Pancake, and Janisse Ray, rather than works by Barry Hannah, Lewis Nordan, Chris Offutt, or Tom Franklin. In his book *American Hungers* (2008), Gavin Jones aims to "redress the neglect of poverty as a category of critical discourse in the study of American literature and culture" (xiii), and this study plays a part in the wider attempt to open up discussions about the ways literature and other narrative forms contribute to knowledge about class and economics.

The hesitancy to engage with class has certainly been a defining aspect of much recent literary criticism. For Fred Hobson, "[c]ontemporary literary scholars, of course (including those of the American South), hold forth magisterially on that critical triumvirate—race, class and gender—but, in fact, it is clear that of the three, class has been the least openly and honestly addressed" (*But Now* 134). Such an observation might seem at odds with the democratization of the American literary canon brought about by the civil rights and feminist movements, which, in conjunction with greater educational resources for the poor implemented during the 1960s in the last great hurrah of the welfare system in the twentieth century,[2] meant that, as Robert Rebein and others have observed, "by the mid-1980s, American literature was being authored increasingly by just the sorts of people who once only appeared as characters" (72).[3] Hobson, too, is attuned to the fact that in recent years "any number of plain and poor white southerners ... have spoken for themselves" (Introduction 6). In conjunction with the emergence of writers out of poor white backgrounds, the ongoing literary preoccupation with this class, bound up in attempts to categorize such writing under labels such as Grit Lit and Rough South (which I explore in chapter 4), makes it seem improbable that class remains underexplored in southern criticism. Yet just as Jones focuses on poverty in American literature from 1840 to 1945, southern literary criticism, as I have written elsewhere, tends to focus on the years leading up to World War II, and in those works where contemporary poverty is discussed, it is often considered within the parameters of its southernness rather than its reflection of broader socioeconomic shifts.[4]

Preempting a question that this book is bound to generate, I focus solely on southern poor whites for several reasons. In part, white poverty remains underacknowledged. As hooks notes, "[p]overty in the white mind is always primarily black. Even though the white poor are many, living in suburbs and rural areas, they remain invisible" (4), and the rise of whiteness studies in the 1990s has done little to fully expose the destructive economic models that continue to widen class divides.[5] Whiteness studies too often results in identity politics and notions of white culture, as evidenced in popular publications such as Jim Goad's *The Redneck Manifesto* (1997). Of course, several white studies scholars dwell at length on the economic plight of the poor, including Matt Wray, Annalee Newitz, and John Hartigan Jr., and their work is important in countering the fear expressed by Helen Taylor, who regards "white studies" as an "academic challenge to multiculturalism" that coincides with the rise of "reactionary movements such as the League of the South" and "with neofascist groups in many European countries" (62). My own focus on poor whites emerges not out of whiteness studies but out of an interest in the inequalities of neoliberalism and how they are reflected through contemporary forms of writing about the US South.

The book also focuses on southern poor whites because when they are seen, such recognition typically happens at the level of stereotype and takes the form of comedic jokes about inbred, illiterate "hillbillies" and "rednecks." As long as it is acceptable to laugh at poor whites, their actual condition is unlikely to be fully recognized or eradicated. As Nancy Isenberg observes, "the popularity of the 'reality TV' shows *Duck Dynasty* and *Here Comes Honey Boo Boo* in recent years" reveals that "white trash in the twenty-first century remains fraught with the older baggage of stereotypes of the hopelessly ill bred" (xvi). Before turning to Isenberg's wider argument, it is worth pausing here to reflect on depictions of southern poor whites in contemporary TV and film culture. Not all representations perpetuate stereotypes; for instance, in *The Walking Dead* (2010–), Daryl Dixon, played by Norman Reedus, initially embodied the "redneck" stereotype, heightened by his loyalty to his racist, bigoted brother in the first season. However, Daryl's character arc has seen him emerge out of stereotype to become an integral member of the group, and he has become a fan favorite.[6] While such examples show how depictions of poor whites do not simply depend on the caricatures that numerous shows and films propagate, Isenberg rightly observes that pseudo-documentaries in particular, including *Moonshiners* (2011–), do little to draw attention to poverty.

In her ambitious work *White Trash: The 400-Year Untold History of Class in America* (2016), Isenberg seeks to redress America's "narrow and skewed understanding of white trash" (xiv), but across her extensive study only fifty-two pages are dedicated to American society since the 1960s. While Isenberg devotes time to Jimmy Carter's presidency and his prejudices against poor whites despite championing his own "cracker" heritage, her work on the Ronald Reagan administration is cursory at best. This book dwells at length on the years since 1970 to consider the shift to neoliberalism and its wider impact on everyday lives. What I share with Isenberg is a concern with exploring the nuances and complexities that shape the lives of the poor that are typically drowned out by

> [a] corps of pundits ... whose fear of the lower classes has led them to assert that the unbred perverse—white as well as black—are crippling and corrupting American society. They deny that the nation's economic structure has a causal relationship with the social phenomena they highlight. They deny history. If they did not, they would recognize that the most powerful engines of the US economy—slaveowning planters and land speculators in the past, banks, tax policy, corporate giants, and ... politicians and angry voters today—bear considerable responsibility for the lasting effects on white trash ... and on the working poor generally. (309)

Like Isenberg, I pay attention to economic structures and history, although I depart from Isenberg in relation to nomenclature. While she utilizes the term "white trash," I use the terms "poor white" or "working" or "lower-middle class," because terms including "white trash," "cracker," and "redneck" not only serve, as Robert Brinkmeyer summarizes, to position poor whites on "the margins of culture, on the outskirts of society where trash is generally dumped, buried, and forgotten" (226) but also distract from the political and economic policies that shape and determine the lives of working-class people. Despite the reclamation of "trash" by writers such as Dorothy Allison, the term remains one to be overcome if poverty is to be recognized as societal rather than a result of the supposed behaviors or characteristics of specific individuals and groups.[7]

The problematic, distortive use of derogatory labels came to the fore during the 2016 US election campaign: as Trump stirred up hatred toward Muslims and immigrants, the leftist media often fell back on terms such as "white trash," "hillbilly," "cracker," and other designations as shorthand for right-wing extremism, populism, and Trump's ascendancy.[8] For instance, in the *Irish Times* Simon Carswell, in a piece entitled "Hipsters and Hillbillies Clash as Donald Trump Calls," states that Trump's "unsophisticated message" fell on receptive ears in Asheville, North Carolina, with its equally unsophisticated "hillbilly" audience. The tendency to vilify poor whites and categorize them with decidedly southern labels peaked because Trump supporters were widely assumed to be disenfranchised, working-class, poor whites. Yet, despite Carswell's assessment of the Trump rally, Buncombe County, of which Asheville is the county seat, actually voted 56 percent for Clinton and 41 percent for Trump, which is why Christine J. Walley suggests that "there is a pressing need to untangle election commentary around class" (231). Indeed, while many of Trump's supporters were from lower-income families, voting data revealed that Hillary Clinton won a greater percentage of the votes of those earning less than $30,000, so representations of Trump voters were highly distortive.[9] As Hugh Gusterson notes: "Particularly overlooked in media framings is the petty bourgeoisie. If one reads media accounts of Trump rallies carefully, one often finds quotes from small-business owners, accountants, and pharmacists, but they are buried in the prose rather than headlined" (212). Despite the fact that millions of Americans across the nation voted for Trump, rich and poor, and across racial lines, the loaded term "hillbilly" continually connotes the South and vilifies poor white people. For Walley,

> [w]inning the war of interpretation over growing economic inequality requires a resurgence of civic debate that links such inequality back to its origins in neoliberal ideology and policies. Doing so depends on countering the hatred and divisiveness Trump has fostered by working across racial, gender, religious, and other lines ... in order to create an explicitly multiracial form of class politics. (235)

Part of winning that war must involve a rejection of labels such as "white trash" that denigrate and rob people of what Avery Gordon terms "complex personhood." She writes: "It has always baffled me why those most interested in understanding and changing the barbaric domination that characterizes our modernity often ... withhold from the very people they are most concerned with the right to complex personhood" (4). She goes on to explain:

> Complex personhood is the second dimension of the theoretical statement that life is complicated. Complex personhood means that all people ... remember and forget, are beset by contradiction, and recognize and misrecognize themselves and others.... Complex personhood means that even those called "Other" are never never that. (4)

Regarding everyone as complex is, for Gordon, "about conferring the respect on others that comes from presuming that life and people's lives are simultaneously straightforward and full of enormously subtle meaning" (4–5). According to Alice O'Connor, such an approach is missing from contemporary, government-commissioned poverty research; she argues that "a more culturally aware poverty knowledge would demand a more accurate but also a more humanistic and less distancing language that respects how poor people think of themselves—as citizens, workers, parents, and neighbors rather than as benighted, deviant, or somehow deficient 'other' Americans" (293). To best explore the complex personhood of the poor, this book turns to several authors who have emerged out of poor backgrounds. Their reflections on the broader socioeconomic systems that shaped either their own lives or those of their characters reach out beyond stereotype to give a fuller account of poverty and its ramifications. For instance, in her essays on sex, class, and literature, Dorothy Allison notes:

> I was born into a world that despises the poor. The need to make my world believable to people who have never experienced it is part of why I write fiction. I know that things must be felt to be understood, that despair, for example, can never be adequately analyzed; it must be lived. But if I can write a story that so draws the reader in that she imagines herself like my characters, feels their sense of fear and uncertainty, their hopes and terrors, then I have come closer to knowing myself as real, important as the very people I have always watched with awe. (*Skin* 14)

Across Allison's body of writing, the need to humanize rather than romanticize or demonize the poor comes to the fore, and to begin outlining the wider economic shifts that are crucial to this study, it is pertinent to turn to Allison and fellow poor white writer Rick Bragg and their reflections on their early educational experiences.

In an interview with Michael LeMahieu, Allison reflects on the class structures taught to children as the simple, irrefutable facts of life, claiming:

> I was the child of a waitress and a truck driver. I was also the smartest damn kid in my school. I had the highest grades, and when they gave me an IQ test, they made me take it again because they thought I cheated. But where did they take me when I was ... where did they take us? They took us to tour the J. C. Stevens

mill.... they took us to tour the mill because that's where we were gonna work. It's a feudal empire, and it was when I was a girl. That has shifted, some. But it still is. (670)

Instilling the notion of class boundaries within the education system merely cements the structural inequalities of capitalism. Stanley Aronowitz argues that "[c]lass fatally shapes the relation of children to schooling" (67), but while that may often be the case, there are clearly exceptions, and Allison reveals not how class shaped her attitude to learning but how schooling sought to instill class-based limitations. Bragg similarly attends to education and class in his first memoir, *All Over but the Shoutin'* (1997), in which he observes that "white Southerners are not the same and symmetrical, like the boards in a white picket fence" (62). Although Bragg refers here specifically to the different levels of racism among whites in the South, he repeatedly explores class as the factor that distinguishes whites from one another. Bragg attributes his first conscious understanding of class systems to starting school in Alabama. As he recounts his early education, Bragg moves from a description of the run-down "two-story farmhouse with big, square columns in front" where the family lived for a time during his childhood (52), to the teacher who divided her first-grade class into Cardinals and Jaybirds: the Cardinals being "the children of the well-to-do who studied from nice books with bright pictures" and the Jaybirds being "the poor or just plain dumb children" who "got what was left after the good books were passed out" (55). Even though the teacher instantly recognized Bragg's abilities and temporarily propelled him into the Cardinal group, she quickly rectified this class transgression by demoting him back to the Jaybirds, telling him he "would be much more comfortable" with his "own kind" (55). Despite the teacher's best efforts to enforce class boundaries, Bragg would eventually work his way into a successful career in journalism.

Reflecting back on his teacher's prejudices, Bragg recalls that she was an "aristocrat ... dusted with white powder," a member of the "gentry, the old-money white Southerners who ran things" (55), and he compares her with the attic in the family's decaying home, which is also "covered in a fine gray powder of dust" (53). Both the house and the teacher are depicted as part of a dying South, yet the teacher desperately tries to cling onto the past in which poor whites knew their place, with Bragg noting how the gentry "treated the rest of the South like beggars with muddy feet who were about to track up their white shag carpeting" (55). Bragg nods here to William Faulkner's short story "Barn Burning" (1939), in which poor white tenant farmer, and arsonist, Abner Snopes deliberately steps in horse droppings and drags the muck across Major de Spain's "pale," "blond rug" (11). Where Snopes dirties the white rug with the boot of labor, Bragg's turn to Faulkner takes the form of writing back against the teacher and those of her class. Yet, if parts of the Old South were dying out during Allison's and Bragg's childhood during the 1950s and 1960s, they were only to be replaced with an economic system that increased divisions between the affluent and the poor.

Intrinsic to the New, or Sunbelt South, is, as Numan V. Bartley notes, "the need to subordinate social relations to the requirements of the market and the bottom line" (450). In short, Bartley continues, "[t]he effect was to liberate individuals ... and to sustain a commitment to self-fulfillment, self-achievement, and self-advancement" (450). Bartley's study of the New South depicts a region changing under the sway of broader global shifts. The collapse of the Keynesian economic model in the early 1970s brought about a neoliberal agenda whose new "regime of accumulation" intensified class divides and ensured that poverty would either continue to be recognized intermittently at times of economic crisis and thereby out of context, or conveniently overlooked since it is an uncomfortable reminder of neoliberalism's inherent inequalities (Harvey, *Spaces of Global* 29). As the economic crises of the 1970s gave way to the shared Western politics of Ronald Reagan and Margaret Thatcher, the tax breaks awarded to corporations and the rich brought about what David Harvey refers to as "the momentous shift towards greater social inequality and the restoration of upper class power" (*Spaces of Global* 18).

The advent of neoliberalism, or financial capitalism, saw the rise of the Sunbelt South as the region embraced free-market capitalism that "stressed individual self-interest, material acquisitiveness, and the commodification of people as paid labor" (Bartley 456). While the rhetoric of the New South promoted the region as a haven for business and research entrepreneurship, exemplified by North Carolina's Research Triangle, the region attracted new industrial and manufacturing businesses because of its wealth of cheap labor. So, despite the rise of an increasingly affluent, urban South since the 1970s, as Jacqueline Jones states, "[i]n the late 1980s, with one-seventh of the [Mississippi] Delta's people receiving food stamps (three times the national average) and more than one-quarter without work, the area rivaled any Northern city in terms of its deep and persistent (if not geographically concentrated) poverty" (287). Such comparisons with the North can usefully be opened out since the neoliberal agenda that shaped the New South and its pursuit of excessive profits and cheap, expendable labor became, Mary E. Frederickson explains, "the model for expansion" across "the Global South," a model that "sustained and fostered persistent patterns of corporate control, low wages, and an anti-union climate reinforced by state and local governments" (3). In the US South it was, as Robert D. Bullard claims, "[t]he large pool of docile and nonunionized labor" that constituted "the so-called 'good business climate'" of the region, so as the South basked in the warmth of corporate confidence, those who did not "have the requisite education" often became "part of the region's expanding underclass" (28).

This book focuses on poverty among southern whites from 1970 not merely because this decade witnessed the failure of Keynesian economics, out of which neoliberalism emerged as the New World Order, but because concomitant with those broader economic shifts was the gradual but persistent erosion of welfare provision. Despite Lyndon B. Johnson's War on Poverty in the 1960s and his notion of a Great Society, from the middle of that decade onward the public perception of poverty and welfare recipients dramatically altered. As Alyosha Goldstein outlines: "Since the demise of the War on Poverty, a bipartisan majority of US policymakers has contributed to the upward redistribution of wealth, increasing economic polarization, fiscal insecurity, and mass destitution" (245). If in the early part of the 1970s, as Alice O'Connor explains, "despite Richard M. Nixon's avowed determination to dismantle the War on Poverty . . . the economic stagnation, unemployment, and inflation that plagued the 1970s" meant that "social spending rose steadily—particularly for social insurance and 'in-kind' transfer programs such as Food Stamps," moves to reduce welfare spending that were thwarted in the 1970s became a defining feature of Reagan's two terms in office throughout the 1980s (213). Within his first year in office, Reagan's "administration struck its first major blow with OBRA, or the Omnibus Budget Reconciliation Act of 1981, which slashed federal antipoverty budgets and severely restricted eligibility rules to eliminate aid for all but the 'truly needy'" (A. O'Connor 242). Since the 1970s, both Republicans and Democrats have abandoned the idea of supporting the economically vulnerable, both parties now endorsing the demonization of welfare recipients and cuts to welfare spending. Indeed, it was the Bill Clinton administration that repealed Aid to Families with Dependent Children (AFDC) in 1996, which was "the principal government public assistance program providing monetary assistance to poor families" (Asen 7). If AFDC had "promised aid until all children in a family reached the age of maturity," its replacement, Temporary Assistance for Needy Families (TANF), "makes no such promise. The title articulates finite duration . . . and grants may be withdrawn before the age of maturity or dispensed to families only sporadically" (Asen 166). Neither Republican nor Democratic administrations in this period actively worked to better the lives of the poor; Jodi Dean writes in particular about the failure of the "American left" in its response "to the attack on the welfare state, collapse of Keynesianism, and emergence of a neoliberal consensus" (35). It "responded," she suggests, by forfeiting its historical solidarity with workers and the poor, retreating from the state, and losing the sense that collective solutions to large-scale systemic inequalities are possible and necessary. The failure of solidarity was manifest perhaps most acutely in President Bill Clinton's destruction of welfare guarantees.... Republicans didn't eliminate welfare; Democrats, the party associated with the interest of the poor and the working class since the Depression, did. (35)

In addition to overseeing the significant erosion of welfare provision, in 1994 Clinton signed the North American Free Trade Agreement (NAFTA), which resulted in mass unemployment as businesses, in the search for higher profit yields, relocated their manufacturing plants to regions with cheaper production costs, undermining the idea that the New South brought widespread prosperity to the region.[10] Indeed,

> as rural sociologist Thomas A. Lyson notes, "the so-called free-market, supply-side microeconomic policies during the 1980s have generally exacerbated the economic woes of families and communities in the rural South," putting them "into direct competition with the Third World countries for footloose industries," a competition southern communities could not win. (Carr 12–13)

The Left's commitment to the neoliberal policies implemented during the 1980s would eventually come back to haunt it during the 2016 presidential campaign, when Trump capitalized on the desperation of the poor, critiquing, among other policies, NAFTA and its betrayal of working-class Americans. It seems to matter little that Trump embodies the business class or that he filled his cabinet with, as Klein outlines, "a team of individuals" who "had a staggering combined net worth of $14.5 billion" and "made their personal fortunes by knowingly causing harm to some of the most vulnerable people on the planet" (*No Is Not Enough* 19). The failure of the Left to provide meaningful opposition left people so desperate for an alternative that it was easier to ignore Trump's contradictions, and also explains the popular appeal of Bernie Sanders during the Democratic presidential primaries in 2016: Sanders's commitment to democratic socialism gained traction with voters but not with the Democratic Party and its economic vision, which is shaped more by big business interests than social responsibility.

As this book unfolds, it explores both writers and texts that struggle to fully recognize the economics of poverty and those that pose a series of alternatives to neoliberalism and its mantra of greed and self-interest. Particularly in chapters 1 and 2, where I consider travel writing and photo-narratives, I focus on how both genres often reproduce heavily romanticized and dehistoricized notions of poverty. In the latter chapters of this book, I turn to writers who propose various forms of communalism and communitarianism, and, however idealistic such notions may be, in a world where neoliberalism holds sway, at least they provide ideas of how to swing the pendulum to a position of greater equality. In these writers' work, communitarianism is often framed as a response to neoliberalism, and, although they do not espouse formal, theorized communitarianism, they dwell on aspects of its three key principles as outlined by Henry Tam: "co-operative enquiry, mutual responsibility, and citizen participation" (12). The contemporary communitarianist movement grew, Daniel Bell argues, out of the neoliberal turn in the 1980s, which partly explains the prominence of such thinking across literature since the adoption of financial capitalism (9). Félix Guattari sums up the fear of such writers by suggesting: "It is not only species that are becoming extinct but also the words, phrases, and gestures of human solidarity. A stifling cloak of silence has been thrown over the emancipatory struggles of women, and of the new proletariat: the unemployed, the 'marginalized,' immigrants" (44). So while this book focuses on poor whites, the argument rests not on seeing that group as distinct and separate but as intricately connected to other poor communities regardless of race, ethnicity, or nationality. As hooks maintains, "Solidarity with the poor is the only path that can lead" the United States "back to a vision of community that can effectively challenge and eliminate violence and exploitation," both at home and abroad (49). In short, this book is about neoliberalism, poverty, and hope, with writing about the US South and its poor whites as a case study, and on more than one occasion it turns more specifically to the southern mountains and Appalachia to examine the resistance that grows in exploited places and among exploited people. While literary narratives might not form the requisite "poverty knowledge" that Alice O'Connor claims is necessary to reformulate policies and attitudes toward the poor (293), as is certainly the case with many of the travel writers explored in chapter 1, a growing body of writing about the South and poverty does more than simply reflect the condition of poverty. Alternatives might never be realized, but they are posed in several ways in writing about the US South, opening up debates about how society regards the poor and what could be done not merely to change those attitudes but to eradicate poverty itself.

Abbreviations

AFDC: Aid to Families with Dependent Children

AMI: Appalachian Media Institute

CRMW: Coal River Mountain Watch

FSA: Farm Security Administration

MTR: mountaintop removal

NAFTA: North American Free Trade Agreement

OEO: Office of Economic Opportunity

PARC: President's Appalachian Regional Commission

TCJA: Tax Cuts and Jobs Act

Poverty Politics

CHAPTER ONE

Locating Poor Whites in Contemporary Travel Narratives

If the United States proves fertile ground for travel writers, then the South is a particularly abundant region that continues to propagate the pages of travelogues. From colonial days to the present, there is a long history of travelers surveying, sashaying, and sauntering throughout the US South. The contemporary travel books of Brits abroad Jonathan Raban, *Old Glory* (1981) and *Hunting Mister Heartbreak* (1990), and Martin Fletcher, *Almost Heaven: Travels through the Backwoods of America* (1998), are prime examples of the peculiar fascination travelers have with the South. Although Fletcher's narrative begins and ends outside the region, he devotes over half his chapters to southern states, rendering the South decidedly more boondockish than anywhere else.

So while Terry Caesar argues that Latin American countries "make possible strange, distinctive experiences of squalor, dissoluteness, and dissimulation" (151), travel writers often do not find it necessary to traverse the borders of the United States to validate their conceptions of strangeness. Indeed, for British academic Nick Middleton in *Ice Tea and Elvis: A Saunter through the Southern States* (1999), the South is "the Heart of Darkness in the USA" (5), a sentiment echoed in Fletcher's consideration of Appalachia as a place "where all manner of dark and peculiar things still go on" (23). In Pamela Petro's *Sitting Up with the Dead* (2001), northern friends remind her to "[b]e careful down there" in a region where they assume "it's still pretty rural" and "[a]ll kinds of things go on" (xvii). "Down there" implies the descent into a hellish place, what Middleton terms a "Heart of Darkness" and Petro refers to as an "Otherworld" (xix). While these horror-filled ideas of the South stem in part from its violent history of slavery and segregation, they also emerge out of earlier cultural narratives including travelogues and movies, perhaps none more so than John Boorman's 1972 adaptation of James Dickey's *Deliverance*, which looms large in the popular imaginary.[1]

If the US South is horror show, it is also a place that evokes varying degrees of nostalgia. Nostalgia is a commonly recognized thread running through contemporary travel writing, as, in the face of a world saturated with the banality of globalization, the past becomes a site of "discovery" where "real" or "authentic" values are resurrected to give meaning to contemporary lives rendered vacuous by the onslaught of capitalism.[2] Discovery was obviously a key preoccupation of the genre during the height of empire, when there was still a sense that the world was not yet fully knowable. Today, however, satellite technology and apps such as Google Maps suggest that the world is not only knowable but an easily charted, consumable entity. To counter this prevailing sense of knowability and uniformity, there has been a marked turn in recent years to the promotion of localized traditions and practices that make discovery possible once again.

Under the auspices of localism, the US South remains a place of interest, with travel writers continuing to seek out encounters with "distinctive" or "authentic" figures, thereby underlining the genre's continued desire "to venture into the world of others" (Islam 121). In particular, they reveal peculiar preoccupations with the region's poor whites, who are regarded as tantalizing others.[3] As Peter Hulme and Tim Youngs suggest, such searches for primitive or untouched spaces and peoples emerged during the eighteenth century when many travelers "under the sway of Rousseau and Romanticism, were in search of various forms of 'the primitive'" (6). Even today, as Dean MacCannell outlines, "primitive and peasant peoples" are "among the most popular types of tourist attractions" (xix). So travel writers are still searching for "real" and "authentic" experiences, to become, in V. S. Naipaul's words, discoverers of a world "beyond the uniformity of highway[s] and chain hotel[s]" (222). To this end, romantic traces still abound: Naipaul celebrates his romantic view of the region, outlining as he does "the great pleasure I had taken in travelling in the South. Romance, a glow of hopefulness and freedom, had already begun to touch the earlier stages of the journey" (221). In a similar vein, Petro claims: "I went there as a Romantic, looking for a relationship between soil and history and stories" (391). Their romantic outlooks determine both what they expect and what they want to find in the South.

In their accounts of the region, both Petro and Naipaul promote the idea of a distinctive, or what Smith and Cohn define as an essentialist South in *Look Away!*—their important contribution to new southern studies. Naipaul's idea of the South, they write, "is precisely the vision we wish . . . to *avoid*" (11). While new southern studies saliently rejects Naipaul's South, outside the academy his books are commonly found on coffee tables, in coffeehouses, and on reading group lists.[4] The popularization of the genre and the mass readership of his work mean that his ideas about the US South carry cultural capital and ensure the proliferation of stereotypes.

The distinctive South that Petro, Naipaul, and others describe emerges more from preconceived ideas than the South they actually encounter. In his assessment of Tony Horwitz's *Confederates in the Attic* (1998), Scott Romine argues that Horwitz "wants the South that the South wants, not the South that it actually is" (*The Real South* 80). However, it may not simply be the South that the South wants, since ideas of the Old South were developed in part by northern travelers during the years after the Civil War, making it more widely a South that the rest of the nation also wants. Yet, as Romine suggests, travel writers often see the South they desire, and poor whites are central to those ideas of the region.

Throughout history, travelers have been fascinated by poor southern whites, either in the mountains of Appalachia or in the agricultural lowlands, as exemplified by William Byrd's accounts of the "Indolent Wretches" he encountered when surveying the boundary line between Virginia and North Carolina in 1728 (54). Since Byrd's venture, travelers and their readers have demonstrated an insatiable curiosity about the region's poor whites.[5] Yet to this end, travel writers do not simply "venture into the world of others." As Debbie Lisle explains: "Travel writers still need *other* places and people to visit and write about—which means that travel writers must always engage in the production of difference" (24). The idea that travel writing is complicit in the perpetuation of otherness forms part of the following discussion, which examines the representation of poor whites across a number of contemporary travelogues.

For Lisle, the "production of difference" lies at the heart of both neocolonial and cosmopolitan approaches.[6] She argues that while neocolonial perspectives overtly impose a sense of cultural superiority over places and people, cosmopolitan perspectives are also flawed, with cosmopolitan writers "smuggl[ing] in equally judgemental accounts of otherness *under the guise* of equality, tolerance and respect for difference" (10). Lisle proposes that it is difficult for contemporary travel writers to escape or write against a tradition of othering because "contemporary travel-writing operates in a contested, antagonistic and uncertain political terrain that is haunted by the logic of Empire" (16). In the case of many contemporary travel narratives that depict the US South and its poor whites, the "logic of Empire" is laden with the logic of capital. On one hand poor whites, for whom the designations of "lazy" and "shiftless" abound, are regarded as living unfit lives antithetical to processes of modern capitalist exchange. Conversely, their lives on the economic fringes of society are hailed as a last stalwart against the increasing pressures of capital, which continues to erode free will. These competing narratives mark this group as both frightfully other and preciously authentic, and they have a long history emerging out of the antebellum period.[7] In the years before the Civil War, travelers typically presented poor whites as degenerate, but with the surge of northern travel to southern states in the post–Civil War era, when northerners sought escape from their hectic urban lives, the South and its mountains were presented as havens, and the once degenerate poor whites were now considered homely and quaint. As Rebecca Cawood McIntyre summarizes, northern traveler Charles Lanman, "[t]he man who had written about miserable drunkards and haggard women living in wretched hovels in 1848[,] was twenty years later claiming his affection for the simple-hearted people who lived amid the grand scenery of the southern mountains" (45). Poor whites rarely escape the imposition of these preconceived narratives that represent them as either violent threats to the social order or as the last link back to a way of life free from the restraints of a late-capitalist world. So, while Middleton worries about being out in the swampy Attoyac River in East Texas as darkness approaches, since he finds it "easy to imagine unpleasant situations involving depraved rednecks, like in a Hollywood movie" (240), in *A Turn in the South* (1989), Naipaul regards the rednecks that he happens upon near Jackson, Mississippi, as "a threatened species" (213). Threatening and under threat, violent and passive: these oppositional readings of poor whites have a long history in travel narratives.

These dominant if shifting ideas about poor whites clearly continue to influence contemporary travelers who carry with them a preestablished set of ideas about the US South and its people. It is common, as Harvey explains, that reading about a place "will likely affect how we experience that place when we travel there even if we experience considerable cognitive dissonance between expectations generated by the written word and how it actually feels upon the ground" (*Spaces of Global* 131). While the intertextuality of daily life renders it almost impossible to see and experience a place without the weight of previous narratives, Harvey's point about the discrepancy that emerges between preconceptions and the actual place, "on the ground," is pertinent to my consideration of the ways that certain travel writers struggle to move beyond embedded ideas of both the South and poor whites. Complex layers of preconceived place-knowledge are certainly apparent in Petro's *Sitting Up with the Dead*, which is aptly subtitled *A Storied Journey through the American*

South. In her prologue, Petro cites fellow travel writer Horwitz's *Confederates in the Attic* as well as native Mississippian Willie Morris's memoir *North toward Home* (1967), meaning that she not only looks for stories in the South: her very idea of the place emerges out of a heavily narrativized notion of the region. In a similar vein, Paul Theroux, in his recent *Deep South: Four Seasons on Back Roads* (2015), comments at length on how he first came to understand the South through literature, referring to both previous travelogues and the impact of writers such as Faulkner, to whom he dedicates an entire chapter. Even before "Interlude: The Paradoxes of Faulkner," the influence of Faulkner's ideas about the southern landscape seep into Theroux's writing. In his reflections on the Mississippi Delta, Theroux writes about "the *alluvial* sprawl that stretches northward" (109), and just a few pages later he quotes the first line from Faulkner's "Delta Autumn": "The last hill, at the foot of which the rich unbroken *alluvial* flatness began . . ." (113; my emphases). Not only does Theroux employ Faulkner's language, he even rereads Faulkner during one of his visits back to his family home on Cape Cod. In effect, the southern representations of travel writers such as Theroux and Petro are heavily mediated representations of representations.

So, before focusing specifically on the representation of poor whites, it is important to spend some time examining the ways that these travel writers present the US South. To greater and lesser extents, contemporary travel narratives about the region engage with ideas about the Old and New Souths. Particularly interesting is their negotiation of Atlanta. In Martin Fletcher's narrative, Atlanta seemingly operates as absence as he travails Georgia in pursuit of its backwoods. Of course, cities are not part of his remit, yet they form the center against which Fletcher reads the backwoods. He drives through southern Georgia to Plains, Jimmy Carter's hometown, a small town no longer inundated with the tourists who flocked there during Carter's presidency, and now a place where Fletcher "spent a delightfully tranquil two hours wandering around in the late afternoon sun" (89). The only reference to Atlanta in the Georgia chapter comes at the mention of Carter's continued good works, including "building low-cost housing for Atlanta's poor." Yet the harsh realities of urban poverty don't hold much sway for Fletcher, who prefers to attend Carter's "adult Sunday school class" (91).

For those writers who venture into Atlanta, readers encounter familiar histrionics: Atlanta is depicted as the hellish embodiment of the New South. Horwitz describes it as "the anti-South: a crass, brash city built in the image of the Chamber of Commerce and overrun by carpetbaggers, corporate climbers and conventioneers" (283), and Middleton situates his experiences of Atlanta in a chapter entitled "Going Global," writing of a place that "didn't look particularly Southern. With its tall glass buildings, concrete expressways, corporate headquarters and suited executives, it just looked like big cities look anywhere in the US" (189). Atlanta is encountered as sameness, as a horrifically recognizable locale replete with the signs of global capital.[8]

Petro defines her own New England home as "the heartland of the American communications industry that daily beams a facsimile of itself to the world" (xvii), so when she arrives in Atlanta it does not provide a sense of southern distinctiveness; it is, instead, a place "saturated with signs of familiarity" (Islam 133). Petro regards Atlanta as a commercial hub, defining it as a "work-ethic driven, live-and-die-by-the-dollar, *Northern* kind of city, noisy and fast and flush with money" (5). In a temporal sense, as the embodiment of "now," Atlanta does not offer writers the sense of difference that is so fundamental to the genre: readers, they surmise, will find nothing new in Atlanta, and if Atlanta, as a hub of global capital, cannot produce the new but only the same, then newness and/or difference must be found elsewhere, most notably in the past.

At the outset of Petro's journey, she leaves these nightmarish New South areas of Atlanta to attend a performance in Abernathy, a neighborhood she describes as a "conduit," a window into an area that is "a little ramshackle, but pleasantly quiet"—an area that she classifies as "the Atlanta anomaly, more Old South than New, where time was to be had in greater quantities than money" (6–7). Petro's desire to uncover a "real" "Old" South follows the common pattern found in the narratives of "travel writers [who] use strategies of temporalisation to perpetuate the myth that certain places are 'stuck' in the past and untouched by modernity" (Lisle 209). Petro's alignment of the New South with money and the Old South with time completely erodes the inherent connectivity between the South's cotton economy and modern capitalism.[9] She reads the Old South as premodern and pastoral and imagines that poverty offers a "real" route back to that past. When she later drives through the countryside in South Carolina, she encounters a "deep" level of poverty that "wrenched modernity right out of the air," leading her to make "comparisons" with "the Depression, and ... past centuries" (146–47). Petro's comparisons highlight her attraction to poverty as an escape from modernity, and her dependency on understanding the poor via earlier narratives, such as Depression-era photography or photo-essays such as James Agee and Walker Evans's *Let Us Now Praise Famous Men* (1941).

Indeed, such dependency also appears in Horwitz's *Confederates in the Attic*, when he spends time toward the end of his journey visiting the only living Confederate widow at the time, Alberta. Alberta's son Willie drives him around to visit her relatives and her house. Out on the road, he writes:

> We wound back to Elba, pausing by the crossroads where Alberta was born and raised.... The landscape looked straight out of a Walker Evans photograph of Depression Alabama. I realized, too, that Alberta or Lera might easily have served as models for one of Evans's most famous portraits: a sharecropper's wife in a plain cotton dress, her prematurely worn features starkly framed against the rough wood siding of a tenant's shack. (348)

In a manner oddly reminiscent of Joseph Jastrow's duck-rabbit, Horwitz cannot look at Alberta in the present without imagining her as a figure from the past. Similarly, Douglas Kennedy in *In God's Country* (1989) struggles to see present-day Nashville without the distortive lens of Farm Security Administration (FSA) images. Kennedy writes: "Looking at the gaunt, unshaven drifters who loitered here—all possessing that haunted aura of men who realized that they had come to the end of the line—was like looking at one of those famous Walker Evans photographs of the 1930s which so bleakly delineated the monochromatic realities of life among the underclass of the American South" (139). This reliance on earlier narratives and images implies that these writers fail to see not only beyond dominant narratives but also beyond the past. Comparing the landscape, the buildings, and the people with the Depression renders contemporary economic issues null and void. If FSA photography and the images captured in photo-essays such as *Let Us Now Praise Famous Men*, and Erskine Caldwell and Margaret Bourke-White's *You Have Seen Their Faces* (1937), brought the plight of the Depression-era poor to the nation's attention, they also crystallized notions of who the southern poor are and how they live.

The FSA images generated a key narrative about the South: at the exclusion of almost everything else, the FSA Southern Series told a story of poor, stoic southerners living in rural and small-town locales. As Stuart Kidd notes: "Only a scattering of images of the comfortable classes exists in the Southern Series and privately owned, prosperous farms and housing for the affluent form a small portion of the file" ("Visualizing" 111–12). A narrative of southern poverty dominated, and those FSA images became an integral part of "the visual legacy of southern culture: a legacy that helps to constitute the very notion of 'the South'" (Henninger 1). Kidd further problematizes the FSA collection, suggesting that for the photographers, the images they captured were "as much a product of their imaginations as their experiences" ("Visualizing" 112). So, if contemporary travel writers depend as much on the "visual legacy" of the South as they do upon their own experiences, then any thought of discovering a "real" South is fundamentally flawed. This is perhaps nowhere more obvious than in Theroux's *Deep South*, where the narrative opens with a black-and-white photograph of an old, seemingly abandoned house set against the starkness of winter's bare branches. Longtime friend of Theroux Steve McCurry took the photographs that appear in the collection, and while they capture the South and its people in vivid color, the opening black-and-white shot could have been taken straight out of the FSA archives. While Theroux is concerned with detailing the levels of abject poverty that blight the rural South in the twenty-first century, the opening image implies that poverty has all the same markers of the Depression, forgoing the socioeconomic and political shifts that have radically altered the region since the 1930s. The problematic legacy of the FSA's work is a point to which I return in my discussion of photo-narratives in chapter 2.

Here, it is clear that travel writers continue to seek out the "real," and as they do many find relief from the vulgar commodification of contemporary American life among the poor or in poverty-laden landscapes. As MacCannell notes, "Modern Man has been condemned to look elsewhere, everywhere, for his authenticity, to see if he can catch a glimpse of it reflected in the simplicity, poverty, chastity or purity of others" (41). Naipaul certainly falls into this trap, repeatedly exulting in the decayed buildings that he passes on his journey, writing about North Carolina: "It was a landscape of small ruins. Houses and farmhouses and tobacco barns had simply been abandoned. The decay of each was individual, and they were all beautiful in the afternoon light" (10). His romantic outlook problematically comes to the fore again: in beautifying decay, Naipaul forgoes the economic realities that result in farm foreclosures and abandoned homes. As discussed in the introduction, in the 1980s massive levels of inequality abounded even in the New South, where, as Jacqueline Jones explains, many "[s]outherners endured hardship brought on by new kinds of industries that engaged in old forms of exploitation—low-wage service, tourism, and nonunion manufacturing jobs" (286–87). Naipaul's ruminations, like those across a number of contemporary southern travel narratives, fail to offer clear insights into the actualities of poverty, preferring instead to romanticize decay and deprivation.

In his work on the supposedly "real South," Romine argues:

> The worlds of the redneck, the tobacco farmer, Civil War reenactors, country music singers, and rebel flag warriors provide access to a foundational culture story, but they do so only because they filter out disorganized data as white noise. In particular, recovering the South's deep structure requires the filtration of

global market pressures, a preliminary move that allows the narrative digs to proceed in excavating a real South. (*The Real South* 62)

In ways similar to Naipaul, Petro and Fletcher blank out the white noise of contemporary economics in order to "excavate" the "real" South that they want to encounter—one effectively untouched by neoliberalism and the New South. Both displace class and economic issues in their searches for the "authentic." Petro begins a long search for Ray Hicks, a renowned Appalachian storyteller who became a National Heritage Fellow in 1983, while Fletcher spends time searching for a moonshiner.[10] Although Fletcher's search is thwarted, he writes:

> I felt I'd been hunting an endangered species. Moonshiners were making moonshine long before the practice was deemed illegal.... They were craftsmen keeping a tradition alive.... There was something almost romantic about these old rogues, and America would be a less colourful place without them. (68)

Here, Fletcher descends to the romantic, rendering moonshiners authentic and, by way of their elusive nature, awarding them mythical significance. Popular culture still depends on this idea of moonshiners as law-breaking renegades, with the Discovery Channel finding a receptive global audience for both its show *Moonshiners* (2011–) and its attendant merchandise. One widely available official T-shirt boasts the logo: "Made in America: Keep Tradition Alive—*Moonshiners*, 180 Proof." Like many, Fletcher has drunk the Kool-Aid, or perhaps the moonshine, and presents moonshiners as adding some much needed authenticity and local color, even though moonshining is now just another commodity, its renegade qualities vanquished by capital.

Like Fletcher, Petro searches for the "authentic," claiming that Hicks is difficult to track down despite the fact that he is a nationally renowned figure. She presses his exclusivity to bolster her own belief that Hicks is an authentic orator. Before finding Hicks, Petro encounters his cousin Orville, who is also a local storyteller. While Petro is fascinated by his storytelling voice, she is aware that his "storytelling betrays a very modern self-awareness" and that "[h]e is conscious of his own exoticism, of how the 'mountain man' image is perceived and valued—and ridiculed—in the world at large" (91). His self-consciousness is most obvious when he offers to sell Petro "his latest tape and CD." This offer should make Petro aware that the hills and their people are not quite what she expected: many of the locals, now surrounded by "condos and tourists," are conspicuously aware of what tourists expect and have cashed in on the market for "authenticity" (91). As Harvey suggests: "Through the presentation of a partially illusory past it becomes possible to signify something of local identity and perhaps to do it profitably" (*Condition* 303). Petro fails to look beyond the sign as she refuses to engage with the actualities of Orville's self-promotion, and her continued desire to seek out Hicks underlines her desperation to locate the "real."[11]

Orville's capitalist awareness certainly opens up a wider issue concerning poor whites, tourism, and authenticity in the region.[12] As Martin Brenden outlines:

> Facing grim economic prospects in the region, many indigenous entrepreneurs willingly embraced and exploited the hillbilly theme for economic gain. To give the people what they wanted and make more money, many mountaineers played the part of a hillbilly to validate the preconceptions of their visitors. (258)

There are certainly numerous performances and commodities that confirm travelers' and tourists' stereotypes of the region's poor whites.[13] From Civil War battlefields to Hatfield and McCoy–themed restaurants, southern history is packaged and sold as part of the heritage industry.[14] As Gareth Shaw and Allan Williams argue, at its worst the heritage industry turns history into "a commodity—a tourist spectacle" as people "search for authenticity" (121).[15] "White Trash" T-shirts, mugs, hats, and other paraphernalia proliferate in the global marketplace, and those journeying in the South can stop at all manner of dining establishments that champion "real" southern food alongside a slice of "authentic" down-home living. However historically inaccurate and degrading the fetishization of local people and practices may be, local businesses and entrepreneurs are compelled to trade in such commodities, because, as Patrick Huber explains in his work on the "Horny Hillbilly souvenir," such consumables "provided these regions with a distinct and marketable identity of authenticity and local color that proved highly profitable" (74).[16] While these travel writers attempt to distinguish themselves as travelers and not tourists, thereby going beyond tourist souvenirs, shows, and themed eateries to discover a "real" South, the South they want to find actually often depends upon, and confirms, those already existing stereotypes.

Even after meeting Orville, Petro, for instance, continues to place her belief in an untouched life. She dedicates an entire part of the narrative to eventually finding Hicks, and when she discovers his mountain home, it fulfills all that she desired:

> At last I came to a bend in the road protected by a hedgerow of junk: old bicycles, tires, wheelbarrows, flower pots, bits of torn tarpaulin. Leaving the car, I peered down a steep incline, and through a tangle of bushes and trees saw a large,

unpainted wooden house at the bottom of the holler. Aluminum pie plates tied to sticks—modern scarecrows—flashed and shone in the sun. (220)

His home is far from the gated communities of Atlanta's New South. This contrast increases Petro's delight and reinforces her idea that Ray's life is more "authentic" than that of the people of Atlanta. She gleefully describes Ray's clothes and odor—"his denim overalls were ancient, and soil-caked" (221)—and recalls that "[w]henever he shifted I could smell sweat from a hundred ancient exertions" (226). Her repeated use of "ancient" underscores her unrelenting belief in Hicks as foundational. Petro's narrative, like those of Naipaul and Fletcher, is neither exactly self-conscious nor self-ironizing. Patrick Holland and Graham Huggan suggest that "[t]ravel writing, like tourism, generates nostalgia for other times and places, even as it recognizes that they may by now have 'lost' their romantic aura.... Contemporary travel writing tends to be self-conscious—self-ironic—about such losses: it is both nostalgic and, at its best, aware of the deceptiveness of nostalgia." However, during Petro's visit with Hicks, TV show representatives call by to interview him, and she learns that groups of people often travel to his home to hear him speak, making Hicks far from elusive—yet Petro perseveres in representing him as an "authentic" link back to the past (8). MacCannell offers a useful insight into the problems surrounding "authentic" experiences, as he suggests that "it is very difficult to know for sure if the experience is in fact authentic. It is always possible that what is taken to be entry into a back region is really entry into a front region that has been totally set up in advance for touristic visitation" (101). Since Petro refuses to dwell on the possibility of artifice, her narrative lacks the exacting levels of irony that Holland and Huggan believe rescue much travel writing from the mire of nostalgia.

Instead, her narrative, and those of writers such as Naipaul and Fletcher, are involved in what Harvey terms "the cultivation of nostalgia" for a supposedly idyllic and lost or disappearing way of life (*Spaces of Hope* 168). In doing so, they overlook the economic imperatives that shape the lives of poor whites and instead regard the class as helping to fill the hollowness of contemporary life. In his review of Fletcher's book in the *Independent*, Rupert Cornwell defines it as "[a] gourmet's guide to the boondocks." This casual play on consumption actually offers a useful insight into Fletcher's desire and hunger for a "real" America, one that he fulfills through "backwoods" people. To that end, and following Holland and Huggan, what we see in these texts is the "commodification of place; what travel writers offer in this context is not an insight into the 'real,' but a countercommodified version of what they take to be reality" (3).

Indeed, novelist Kennedy's foray into travel writing in *In God's Country* completely dispels any attempt to represent the actual lives of the region's poor whites. At the outset of his journey through the Bible Belt, Kennedy claims that he will "attempt to approach a terrain with something of a mental tabula rasa—tossing aside all preconceptions and allowing the happenstantial aspects of the journey to shape the narrative" (x–xi). Kennedy spectacularly fails in this attempt and simply reproduces a South that is highly dependent upon well-established stereotypes. This is particularly troubling, since Kennedy states early in the narrative that

> any Yankee like myself who grew up in a northern state during the 1950s or 1960s was generally schooled in the idea that "down South" was America's Neanderthal neighbourhood—a baroque landscape of unparalleled ignorance and bigotry. A place peopled by illiterate poor white trash, good ole boys driving pick-up trucks with gun racks, and overfed cops who wore reflector sunglasses, referred to the black population as *nigras*, and turned a blind eye to the occasional lynch mob. (14)

He implies that his travelogue will dispel these culturally dominant ideas, yet rather than seeing the region through fresh eyes, Kennedy falls into the trap of "many travel writers" who "seek after the 'truths' they imagine they already have in their possession" (Holland and Huggan 11).

Before Kennedy's venture southward, he meets religious convert Sheila in New York but states that Sheila's account of her conversion "was a story that I might have bought had it come from, say, the archetypal toothless mouth of some semi-literate, mountainey woman living in a Tennessee shotgun shack. But not from the carefully painted lips of a seemingly worldly New Yorker" (7). It is clear that before embarking on his journey Kennedy has a distinct set of ideas about the people he is likely to encounter, but once in the South he never offers a "mountainey woman" the opportunity to speak, thereby allowing this preconceived idea to solidify as truth. In exploring the Bible Belt, he visits a range of churches and ministries, but mainly those attended by middle-class congregations. In the penultimate chapter, entitled "Going to Extremes," Kennedy, however, narrates his journey into "the Carolina hinterlands; the real backwoods centre of the state" (212). If this is the "real," then Kennedy wants none of it.

Kennedy's foray into the backwoods of North Carolina is worth dwelling on at length to expose his difficulty in moving beyond stereotype. He writes:

> Up ahead was an "unincorporated" town called Complex, beyond which was a stream with the name of Sweet Water Creek. It was a world of shotgun shacks

and decrepit trailers, this parish; of 15-year-old cars and rusted discarded vehicles with grass growing out of their bonnets. I pushed on, sauntering down an empty, virginal road with swamp on either side until I saw a tiny white Church of God set back from the road, with a trailer parked next to it (presumably acting as a presbytery). A few crippled cars were parked out front—a hint that a service was in progress. So I pulled over and wandered into a curious scene. (213)

Kennedy presents himself as an intrepid traveler ready to take the reader into this new, "virginal" space—indeed, before he departs Complex, Kennedy claims to have "stumbled upon a New World" (214). Proud of his off-the-beaten-track adventure, Kennedy feels like a discoverer; however, he presents this "New World" through already established conventions. In addition, Kennedy's employment of the word "curious" is loaded with the role curiosity played in early travel writing.[17] In his study of the emergence of curiosity in travel writing, Nigel Leask focuses on "antiquarianism" (48) and argues that many eighteenth-century travelers often used "[c]lassical or feudal tropes . . . (in a more imperialist vision)," which privileged "modernity" over "oriental stasis and 'underdevelopment'" (49–50).[18] In Kennedy's narrative, an "imperialist vision" emerges as he describes Complex as a place apart: with his emphasis on the "crippled cars" and "decrepit trailers," he defines Complex as aged, infirm, underdeveloped, and out of sync with the economic progress of the nation. Nevertheless, he feels drawn to this out-of-the-way church and cannot help but revel in the "curious scene" he finds inside.

Interestingly, while the scene inside may be "curious," Kennedy lacks any inquisitiveness in his approach, immediately labeling the congregation "deeply redneck" (213). I quote again at length:

> There were two girls for whom the word "fat" would have been a compliment, since they had long since gone beyond the obese point of no return. There were two old guys with big red faces and thoroughly malevolent eyes. There were two jailbaity teenagers, snapping gum. There were a couple of tough, leathery-skinned women who looked like they'd experienced and survived a great deal of life's innumerable deprivations. There were two Down's syndrome children. And up on the altar were a pair of guys with guitars, who were supposed to provide musical accompaniment. The problem was, they couldn't play their instruments. They simply strummed discordant chords while a young woman stood at the pulpit, screaming hymns at the top of her lungs. (213)

The judgments flow more freely here than anywhere else: whatever dubious ministers or shady believers Kennedy has met up to this moment, he saves his most searing critique for this group with whom he never converses. Duane Carr reminds us that "since few urban dwellers ever strike up an acquaintance with an 'outlander,' 'observations' made from whatever distance are, more often than not, derived from preconceived notions based on past experience, not with life in the hills, but with literature, the movies, television" (4). Such a distanced perspective is even more damning in Kennedy's text, which is, after all, an "investigation" into southern religion. Unlike his visits to other churches, where he actively seeks out interviews, it is clear that in Complex he does not need to speak to the congregation to know it. To this end, Kennedy's curiosity gives way to fetishism. Laura Mulvey argues:

> While curiosity is a compulsive desire to see and to know, to investigate something secret, fetishism is born out of a refusal to see, a refusal to accept the difference the female body represents for the male. These complex series of turning away, of covering over, not of the eyes but of understanding, of fixating on a substitute object to hold the gaze, leave the female body as an enigma and threat, condemned to return as a symbol of anxiety while simultaneously being transformed into its own screen in representation. (64)

While Mulvey focuses on women's bodies, her argument provides a useful gloss on Kennedy's account of the service. He promises the reader an investigation into this curious scene, but his failure to engage with the worshippers is tantamount to a "refusal to accept ... difference." His focus on the physiology of the locals only perpetuates a sense of otherness and denies any contemplation of the socioeconomic factors that shape the lives of people who live in remote communities. In short, Kennedy reverts to type when describing the local people: they might have just stepped out of the pages of Erskine Caldwell's *Tobacco Road* (1932) or Dickey's *Deliverance*.

Homi K. Bhabha reminds us that

> the stereotype requires, for its successful signification, a continual and repetitive chain of other stereotypes. The process by which the metaphoric "masking" is inscribed on a lack which must then be concealed gives the stereotype both its fixity and its phantasmatic quality—the same *old* stories ... *must* be told (compulsively) again and afresh, and are differently gratifying and terrifying each time. (111)

Kennedy certainly provides his readers with comfortable stereotypes that require little engagement. Here, in this world of "poor white-trashdom," Kennedy recalls all of the stereotypes of poor whites to confirm the reader's preconceptions of these "forgotten swampy corners" (214). For Lisle, this is a common problem in contemporary travel writing, in which, she argues, "[t]he unwillingness . . . to address the difficulties of representing others reveals the genre's reproduction of power most explicitly," and means that travel writers "rarely bother to examine the history or reproduction of those stereotypes" (270). An instance is Kennedy's judgments about the obese women. In an earlier encounter in Nashville, Kennedy meets working-class Shirley, "a seriously fat woman" who eats "two stacks of blueberry pancakes, each capped with two scoops of vanilla ice-cream and drowned in a small lake of maple syrup" (135–36). Despite Shirley's insatiable appetite and large waistline, she is saved from his rancor. He spends time getting to know her, learns about her two jobs, and informs readers that Shirley "simply accepted the fact that the price of doing something worthy like helping emotionally disturbed children was spending every Friday to Sunday on the night shift at the International House of Pancakes" (138).

Later on in Complex, the "two girls for whom the word 'fat' would have been a compliment" have no opportunity to tell their stories: they too may work long hours, they too may help the disenfranchised, or they may spend their lives inactive, idling their way to ever increasing degrees of obesity. Even if the latter is the case, Kennedy's failure to engage with the congregation in Complex is based on a series of judgments about people who live "beyond the pale" (214). His use of this loaded phrase exposes his neocolonial stance. Holland and Huggan explain that "the *neocolonial*" includes a "process by which cultural 'otherness' is assimilated, reproduced and consumed," so that whether Kipling's "Beyond the Pale" was in Kennedy's mind or not, Trejago's costly knowledge of what happens when the lines between self and other are crossed is clearly a lesson Kennedy has absorbed and taken heed from in this place that makes his "flesh creep."[19] He abandons the investigative nature of his journey and relies instead on the security of timeworn stereotypes (48).

This is perhaps nowhere more obvious than when Kennedy describes crossing the border into Alabama. For him, this meant that he had "moved across a major American frontier and into the true epicentre of the deepest Deep South. For Alabama is a state with a *reputation* . . . being the nation's leading repository of old-time racial prejudice: South Africa with a poor-white-trash drawl" (85). Here, Kennedy aligns the Jim Crow segregation laws with poor "trash" southerners, a sleight of hand that dehistoricizes the sociopolitical aspects that shaped southern life after the Civil War. Kennedy lays southern racism at the foot of poor whites, scapegoating this class in a manner all too comfortable and familiar.

As Joel Williamson explains, the move from radical to conservative Reconstruction in the years after 1865 saw the "recapture of political control of their states by the Southern elite" (79). While many poorer whites certainly held similarly conservative values and played an active role in reestablishing and maintaining the racial hierarchy that perversely restricted their own opportunities for economic advancement, the southern elite was a leading force in the creation of the segregated South. Kennedy's claim that segregation was instigated and propagated by those with "a poor-white-trash drawl" is highly distorted, reinforcing the myth propagated by elite whites. Williamson usefully reminds us that "[t]he Ku Klux Klan of the Reconstruction era was at first organized and headed by upper-class whites" and that

> [t]he whole idea of a specially vicious attitude towards blacks prevalent among lower-class whites is an upper-class myth. It was primarily a technique that the elite used to divorce itself from unflattering deeds no longer productive, and thus to arm itself to take the lead in peacefully putting things in a lasting order with itself at the top. (295)

Kennedy simply overlooks the origins of this organization, preferring instead to believe in the stereotype that all poor white people are intrinsically racist and bigoted.

So far, the writers considered have skirted around neocolonial perspectives in their approaches to poor whites, so it is useful to turn to travel narratives that display more cosmopolitan approaches. Best-selling, satirical travel writer Bill Bryson has tackled the South in both *The Lost Continent* (1989) and *A Walk in the Woods* (1997). In *The Lost Continent*, having crossed the border from Kentucky into Tennessee, Bryson comments on his welcome in a Burger King as the "girl at the counter said, 'Kin I hep yew?,'" which brings the stark realization that he "had entered another country" (54). Although Bryson claims a sense of "foreboding" as he ventures "to the Deep South," he consciously addresses the degree to which this fear arises out of popular culture by referring to films such as *Deliverance* that "depict Southerners as murderous, incestuous, shitty-shoed rednecks" (*Lost* 55). Yet, despite Bryson's overt engagement with stereotypes, he comes under Lisle's gaze as she examines cosmopolitan approaches that create "a new hegemonic position" (24). While writers such as Bryson are ironically self-referential, their brand of humor, Lisle argues, is shared by author and audience but is "not necessarily extend(ed) to the others being written about" (105). Lisle's observation is underscored by responses to *A Walk in the Woods* in the *Journal of Appalachian Studies*. *A Walk* is Bryson's account of hiking the Appalachian Trail from south to north with friend Stephen Katz; Ken Kwapis turned the book into a 2015 movie starring Robert Redford as Bryson and Nick Nolte as Katz. Charles Thompson writes of Bryson's Appalachian travelogue: "I have the sickening feeling that the destructive hillbilly image from Hollywood is what's been 'rediscovered'" (126); in her discussion piece on the book, Mary Herzog argues that "Bryson buys and sells stereotypes as if they were the truth" (124). She lists a number of moments in the book in which Bryson promotes stereotypes of Appalachian people, but for Herzog the problems do not solely rest with his representation of locals: she also comments on Bryson's "lack of respect for the mountains" (125).

While it is clear that Thompson and Herzog believe Bryson has created "a new hegemonic position," *A Walk in the Woods* resists such easy categorization. Yes, Bryson presents the South as a backward region, so backward in fact that he and Katz skip part of the trail to escape from the depths of the South and advance to the Blue Ridge Mountains in Virginia. He also overtly begins *A Walk* by playing on the culturally dominant ideas of Appalachia, stating:

> The woods were full of peril—rattlesnakes and water moccasins and nests of copperheads; bobcats, bears, coyotes, wolves, and wild boar; loony hillbillies destabilized by gross quantities of impure corn liquor and generations of profoundly unbiblical sex. (13)

This is the first of numerous references to potentially dangerous "hillbilly" types that provide readers with a familiar narrative about the southern mountains, yet Bryson and Katz never actually encounter any such threats. Indeed, after escaping out of the "backward" South to the apparent sanity and serenity of Virginia, Bryson and Katz rest overnight at Rock Spring Hut in the Shenandoah Valley, where, as Bryson states, "just over a month later" two women were murdered in the same spot (204). Bryson refrains from making humorous jokes about isolated rural areas and rampaging "hillbillies," and when he asks an information specialist at Harpers Ferry about the murders, he surmises that "[y]ou are more likely to be murdered in your bed in America than on the AT." At Harpers Ferry he also buys a book about an earlier murder on the AT in Pennsylvania, underlining the fact that the dangers hikers face are not restricted to the US South (220).

While Herzog takes issue with Bryson's depiction of drunken and overtly sexualized Darren and Donna, two local Georgians heading to "some desperate-sounding community" to get married (88), who give Bryson and Katz a ride to Hiawassee, Bryson notes at the end of the journey that the two "stoutly refused" their offer to pay for the ride (90). Darren and Donna's stout, charitable refusal undercuts the advice that Bryson and Katz received from "a pair of seasoned hikers" a day earlier. These hikers recount that "sometimes in the South drivers will swerve at AT hitchhikers, or run over their packs, for purposes of hilarity" (87). Darren and Donna may satisfy a stereotype of drunken, sexually carefree locals, but they also serve to challenge the idea that southern mountain people are dangerous and intent on tormenting travelers.

Despite Herzog's claim that Bryson also shows neither interest nor care for the landscape, he actually points out throughout the narrative that local residents have been systematically removed from the rural areas around the Appalachian Trail. At one point, he writes of the local population in the Blue Ridge Mountains that was removed to make space for Shenandoah National Park:

> Sixty years ago, there were almost no trees on the Blue Ridge Mountains. All this was farmland. Often in the woods now the trail would follow the relics of old stone field walls and once we passed a small, remote cemetery—reminders that this was one of the few mountaintop areas in the entire Appalachian chain where people once actually lived. Unluckily for them they were the wrong kind of people.... [T]he Blue Ridge Mountains were sensationally beautiful and conveniently sited for the benefit of a new class of motoring tourist. The obvious solution was to move the people off the mountaintops and into the valleys, where they could be poor lower down, build a scenic highway for people to cruise ... and turn the whole thing into a great mountaintop fun zone. (196)

This observation is significant in a number of respects. It shows that for all of Bryson's humorous jokes about the local population he is aware that poor Appalachians have long existed at the will and whim of the federal government. Additionally, the observation forms part of the ecocritical nature of Bryson's narrative. While he problematically bypasses issues such as strip-mining, which continues to devastate parts of the Appalachian Mountains, he does lament the man-made destruction of the ecosystem, from acid rain to the unrestrained killing of wildlife that has rendered many species extinct. Yet this observation also reveals a mourning for a premodern, pastoral South that is apparent in more overtly neocolonial travel narratives. Bryson may show concern for the displaced poor, but his interest is not in how to improve poor lives today but in imagining how life was then and wishing for a return to that idealized state. Later in the narrative, he states: "I would have been pleased to be walking now through hamlets and past farms rather than through some silent 'protected corridor'" (258). Poverty is again the order of the day as Bryson imagines retreating from gaudy displays of modernity such as those he encounters in Gatlinburg, Tennessee, a tourist hotspot with a host of alternating attractions including, at the time of Bryson's stay, "a Mysterious Mansion, Hillbilly Golf," and "a Motion Master ride" (140).[20] Yet for all his nostalgia for a lost way of life, after their trials on the AT Bryson is as delighted with "the large, brightly lit, coloured signs of roadside restaurants and big motels" as he is with any of the natural sights that he and Katz encounter along the way (169). Real hunger pangs at least remind Bryson that nostalgia does not fill stomachs, as he embraces modernity once again. To be sure, Bryson depends on in-jokes with his readers, but beyond the bluster and hyperbole rests a genuine concern with land management and the devastation of ecosystems. His approach to poor whites both depends on and rejects many of the labels that haunt this group, and throughout *A Walk*, bears and other predatory animals are presented as the greatest threat to personal safety.

If Bryson's cosmopolitanism is flawed, then among the more reflective travel narratives detailing the South are Eddy L. Harris's *Mississippi Solo* (1988) and *South of Haunted Dreams* (1993), which chart the complex relationship that black Americans have with the region.[21] Across the body of his work, which crosses the lines between travel and life-writing, Harris repeatedly reflects on his own subjectivity. If for Lisle "travel writers cannot and will not address the ethico-political problems of encounter if they are unwilling to question the authority of their own subject positions" (270), then at the very least Harris projects an unsure self that seeks wholeness through encounters with places and people.

In *Mississippi Solo*, a record of Harris's canoe trip down the length of the great river from its starting point in Minnesota to New Orleans and the Gulf of Mexico, he is more acutely aware than Naipaul and Petro of the strains of romantic nostalgia that hover at the edge of his consciousness. Early in his journey down river he reflects, in one of the italicized lines that he uses to demarcate present-tense thoughts during the journey from the retrospective past tense of the rest of the narrative, "*I hope to God I'm not out here because I miss the Good Old Days*" (29). Such acute self-awareness permeates Harris's travelogues and produces a series of ruminative and contradictory statements about his own identity and his relationship with the South.

The very fact that Harris offers contradictory notions of the region testifies to his struggle to understand it. If at the start of *Mississippi Solo* he professes to have not initially thought about how dangerous the South might still be for a black man, by the start of *South of Haunted Dreams* Harris describes the tight hold the region has on him. It is a place, he writes, that "still owns my nightmares and haunts my memory" (13), a response I also discuss in relation to Colson Whitehead's novel *John Henry Days* (2001) in chapter 4. After a violent encounter with "rednecks" in *Mississippi Solo* and with a newfound consciousness about being a black American, in *South of Haunted Dreams*, Harris anticipates that on arrival in the region he

> will find a bunch of big-bellied rednecks sitting around an old wood-burning stove. They will be chewing tobacco and wearing caps advertising seed corn, tractors, and transmission companies. And they will be drinking beer, of course, telling stories and dreaming about the good old days, dreaming about lynching niggers. (24)

Yet the South that Harris encounters challenges these assumptions. Indeed, just a few pages later he reflects on the debilitating nature of stereotypes when he remembers a poor white family he lived near growing up.[22] He recalls that the children "were the butt of our jokes.... Our prejudices were shallow.... [W]e had our stereotypes too" (*Haunted Dreams* 34–35). Harris realizes that in stereotyping another poor group, he has fallen into the trap that divides poor people along racial lines and prevents them from joining together to forge a significant political voice. So when Harris describes the "dirt farmers" and their families whom he sees at the side of road throughout the South, there is no hint of nostalgia. Interestingly, Harris does not specify the farmers' race—what matters is that they all share the same levels of deprivation. Indeed, he recognizes that the "soiled gingham" and "torn undershirts" are a direct result of their poverty. "There is," he states, "surrender in the soft smiles of all of them, and something akin to resignation" (39).[23]

In *Mississippi Solo*, as Harris moves deeper south he begins to notice poverty on a different scale. Of Helena, Arkansas, he writes:

> Dirt and squalor all around, it looked like Mexico. I had thought out-houses had all been replaced by indoor toilets a long time ago. I had thought even the most impoverished parts of this country were a zillion steps ahead of Third World poverty. I was wrong. This *was* the Third World. And I was wrong too when I thought that *my* luck was bad, and wrong again if I ever considered a man's fate to be entirely his own choosing and making. Wrong and naïve. (200)

Unlike Petro, Naipaul, and even to an extent Bryson, Harris does not find such poverty a quaint route back to simpler times. The analogy he draws with "Third World" poverty links the United States with global economics, and in this way Harris avoids the trap of southern exceptionalism. At the same time, though, by comparing Arkansas with Mexico, Harris forgoes the fact that such degrees of poverty exist within the borders of the United States. Similarly, in *Deep South*, despite concerted efforts to read southern poverty as a by-product of American society, Theroux repeatedly likens the poverty he sees across the region with that of developing countries. In his concluding remarks, Theroux simultaneously blames neoliberal policy makers and corporations who allowed jobs and aid to go overseas, leaving people inside the borders of the United States in dire poverty, while also claiming that "[t]hough America in its greatness is singular, it resembles the rest of the world in its failures" (440). While Theroux aligns American poverty with global poverty, in linking its failures to those of other countries he denies the idea that abject poverty might be an intrinsic by-product of the US economy, both within and, in some cases, beyond American borders. The sleight of hand that turns Arkansas into Mexico in Harris's work, and Allendale, South Carolina, into Africa or Asia in Theroux's narrative, tells us that poverty belongs there, outside the United States; both writers assume that the only point of reference for such poverty comes from the "Third World" and not other parts of the United States. Similarly, Jennifer Greeson asks us to "consider the national news coverage surrounding the aftermath of Hurricane Katrina" and to note that

> [a]s if by magic, the term "Third World" was resurrected from the dustbin of outmoded parlance, as aghast onlookers and media commentators made the diagnosis again and again.... To have put this observation into correct contemporary development parlance, the commentators would have had to say, "It looks like the South down here." And, of course, it did. (12)

Yet to assume that the South is different from the rest of the United States and more like regions in developing countries displaces the responsibility for both the high levels of poverty predating Katrina and the poor relief effort after the hurricane. Surely the observation should really be, "It looks like the United States down here": a statement neither Harris nor Theroux want to make.

It is clear, then, that travel writers struggle to engage with the socioeconomic realities of poverty. Slavoj Žižek, writing about the 2008 banking collapse, argues that when we fail to see the dereliction of free-market capital, "we end up in a naïve progressivism that ignores the mad dance of the opposites" (21). Such ignorance leads to a failure to see both sides of the coin, to see and understand that "the obverse of breathtaking capitalist dynamics is a clearly recognizable order of hierarchic domination" that keeps the poor in place (128). The travel writers explored in this chapter all strive to offer cultural insights, to delight readers with "new" places and people, but somehow the genre demands that they do not probe too far into the "real." Some, like Naipaul and Kennedy, have no appetite for the "real," but even those who do ask more challenging questions stop short of offering any searing insights into the monetary systems that order the lives of the poor. Perhaps Harris comes the closest, most notably in his memoir, *Still Life in Harlem* (1996). In a conversation with local resident Wilma Bishop, she tells him that Harlem is a prison, that "[i]t doesn't matter whether we live in Harlem or in the backwoods of Kentucky somewhere. We are all caught up in the same prison, but they can't—none of them—see it" (*Still Life* 245). While Bishop is referring primarily to the black American citizens of Harlem, her point is applicable to citizens of all races and ethnicities mired in poverty, East and West, North and South.

CHAPTER TWO

Photo-Narratives and the Poor White Self since the FSA

In the wake of the 2008 banking crisis and its ensuing recession, media outlets repeatedly showed images of the newly homeless, long lines for food banks, and the general desperation of those at the bottom of the economic scale hit hardest by the banking irregularities and illegalities carried out by individuals in the financial sector. From front-page stories to documentaries, images of the nation's poor came into sharp focus, yet the desire to visually document American poverty is hardly a new phenomenon. Ever since Jacob Riis and others scoured urban tenements at the end of the nineteenth century to capture downtrodden immigrants, poverty has fascinated Americans and fueled both sociopolitical initiatives to alleviate inequality, and feelings of contempt for people regarded as solely responsible for their misfortune.

Since the 1980s, the successive antiwelfare, neoliberal regimes of both Republicans and Democrats have resulted in widespread urban decay in predominantly working- and lower-middle-class neighborhoods in industrial towns and cities across the nation, where residents struggle to stay above the poverty line. For Christian Marazzi, neoliberalism, or financial capitalism, results in "social regression under the pressure of a growth model that, in order to distribute wealth, voluntarily sacrifices social cohesion and the quality of life itself" (44). So, in dying industrial communities, "[w]age deflation . . . worsening social balances and the irreparable deterioration of the environment are the effects of financial logic and of company delocalizations typical of global financial capitalism" (44). Despite the fact that neoliberalism has a profoundly detrimental impact on the working and lower-middle classes, several deindustrialization photobooks privilege infrastructure over people.[1] Here, aesthetic beauty is found in rusty, Gothic remnants rather than redundant workers, marking a crucial shift from an obsession with the lives of the poor to a fascination with the ruins of industrialization. A by-product of America's manufacturing decline is the market for "smokestack nostalgia" or what is also termed "ruin porn" (Strangleman 23). Like preceding images of poverty, the fascination with photographs of America's crumbling Rust Belt raises questions of aestheticization and what happens when poverty becomes art. W. F. Haug reminds us that "[w]herever there is a want, a need, a demand, there is a producer who offers his 'labour of love'... and presents the bill" (17). There is little doubt that poverty sells: from primetime television documentaries to glossy coffee-table books, poverty is big business, but often in the commercial domain art presides over action, and aestheticization over activism.

There are, of course, notable interventions into the deindustrialization genre, including Oraien E. Catledge's *Cabbagetown* (1985), and Dale Maharidge and Michael Williamson's collaborations *Journey to Nowhere: The Saga of the New Underclass* (1985) and *Someplace Like America: Tales from the New Great Depression* (2011). I will return to consider *Someplace Like America* toward the end of this chapter, but here it is useful to briefly turn to Catledge's work. Mississippian Catledge was propelled to record the lives of the working poor in Atlanta's eastside district Cabbagetown after watching news coverage in May 1980 of local residents pitted against real estate speculators (18). The next day, Catledge visited Cabbagetown, and five years later he published *Cabbagetown*, a collection of his black-and-white photographs of the community. Despite the opening pictures in the collection detailing an industrial landscape bereft of workers, it is not long before the community comes into sharp focus. These vibrant photographs, many of them family photographs, including several shots of men with babies and children, detail the private lives of workers and underscore the humanity of the laboring body.

Yet these powerful images were not enough to halt the gentrification of Cabbagetown. Novelist Richard Ford discovered Catledge's work on a friend's coffee table in Cabbagetown, a place where by 2008 factory buildings had been "refurbished ... into pricey 'loft space'" and "[t]he mill people" were "long gone" (viii). Captivated by Catledge's work, Ford sought him out, and the pair met in February 2009; their collaboration resulted in *Oraien Catledge: Photographs* (2010), which includes images from *Cabbagetown* and some previously unseen work. Ford compares Catledge with Walker Evans, claiming that "where Evans's rural Alabamians seem ready to recede into the sociopolitical woodwork, Catledge's Cabbagetown inhabitants—who don't, by the way, seem especially 'southern' to me—stand forth in their very chosen-ness" (ix). As Ford suggests, there is nothing demonstrably southern in Catledge's images: Catledge is not driven to record southern poverty but the poverty experienced by displaced factory workers across the nation. In the aftermath of the latest economic recession, it is far from surprising that Ford found such resonance in Catledge's work from the 1980s and early 1990s.

The work of making the poor visible is as vital today as it was when Michael Harrington wrote about the nation's blindness to poverty in the 1960s. Indeed, at the turn of the new millennium, bell hooks observed: "Even though the white poor are many, living in suburbs and rural areas, they remain invisible" (4). In terms of the US South, while David Madden notes three major periods of southern photography, the Civil War, the Great Depression, and the civil rights movement, my concern is with the two notable periods of poverty photography, the 1930s and the 1960s, that are largely responsible for generating popular conceptions of the southern poor white that continue to shape how the nation views those living on or beneath the poverty line. Focusing on poverty photography and poor whites helps to address omissions in collections such as Ellen Dugan's *Picturing the South: 1860 to the Present* (1996) that tend to offer a pictorial history of a South in which white poverty appears to end after the Great Depression. This chapter analyzes contemporary photo-narratives of southern poor whites in both rural and urban areas to consider what is at stake when looking at the southern poor white today.

Before turning directly to photo-narratives, it is useful to consider two novels published ten years apart. In Harper Lee's *To Kill a Mockingbird* (1960), despite the much lauded liberal politics of Atticus Finch, he prejudicially schools his children in how to see and think about Maycomb's poor white people. Lee not only falls into the timeworn trap of delineating between the deserving and undeserving poor (the Cunninghams and the Ewells), her lawyer-hero also promises to "show" his daughter "where and how" the Ewell family lives (34). For all of Atticus's progressivism, he has no qualms about othering the poor. His daughter uncritically accepts these lessons in class and sees the Ewells as a breed apart. By contrast, in Alice Walker's *The Third Life of Grange Copeland* (1970), when Grange similarly takes his young granddaughter to "inspect" their poor white neighbors, Ruth's response marks a shift in how to see and think about others.[2] Despite her grandfather's suspicion that the "shiftless" white family spends its time plotting how to take his farm, Ruth questions, "what I want to know, is did anybody ever try to find out if they's real people" (233). Unlike Scout, Ruth desires to go beyond what she sees in a bid to know and understand her white neighbors, asserting that as an adult she will seek out this knowledge, because she wants "to see and hear them face to face; I don't see no sense in them being looked at like buzzards in a cage" (233).

The varied attitudes of both girls expose readers to the fraught nature of observing the lives of the poor: to see as Scout sees is to objectify, to bring the weight of prejudiced assumptions to bear through the gaze, but to look as Ruth looks is to challenge the very idea of the gaze. Ultimately, Scout has inherited a visual legacy that enforces established class distinctions, yet in Walker's novel Ruth rejects any such legacy: in chiding her grandfather, and demanding dialogue with her poor white neighbors, Ruth personifies a form of countervisuality. In *The Right to Look* (2011), Nicholas Mirzoeff claims:

> It is precisely that extended sense of the real, the realistic, and realism(s) that is at stake in the conflict between visuality and countervisuality. The "realism" of countervisuality is the means by which one tries to make sense of the unreality caused by visuality's authority from the slave plantation to fascism and the war on terror that is nonetheless all too real, while at the same time proposing a real alternative. It is by no means a simple or mimetic depiction of lived experience, but one that depicts existing realities and counters them with a different realism. In short, the choice is between continuing to move on and authorizing authority or claiming that there is something to see and democraticizing democracy. (5)

While poverty does not directly form part of Mirzoeff's analysis of visuality and countervisuality, the idea of generating alternative realities is particularly relevant when considering ways of looking at the poor. The dominant gaze that has shown poor whites to be either victims in need of state intervention or shiftless and morally reprehensible degenerates, never tells the whole story, but its recirculation presents it as fact. When Scout looks at the Ewells, she is involved in merely confirming the dominant gaze and thereby "authorizing authority": the authority not simply of her father but of a society with deeply embedded class structures. Yet by 1970, and the publication of Walker's novel in the wake of the civil rights movement, Ruth's approach breaks down the racialized lines that keep poor people apart as she looks for a shared humanity and seeks to "democraticize democracy."

This chapter is concerned with the ways in which contemporary photography and photo-narratives merely reinforce existing forms of poverty visualization; or offer counternarratives, or countervisualities, that destabilize the gaze. As Susan Sontag so precisely puts it, "photographs alter and enlarge our notions of what is worth looking at and what we have a right to observe. They are a grammar and, even more importantly, an ethics of seeing" (3). The question here about who decides how and what we see of the poor relates to the broader questions throughout this book about the ethics of who talks for and who represents the poor. David Harvey proposes that "[t]he spatial image (particularly the evidence of the photograph) ... asserts an important power over history" (*Condition* 218), and the power of the visual image not merely to record but to shape history is central to my examination of the photographic representation of poor whites.

This interrogation of looking is particularly relevant in the US South, where, as Katherine Henninger explains, "photographers and photographs ... constitute a vast visual legacy: a complex series of continuities and ruptures that help to shape notions of southern identity" (8). Continuities abound, in no small part because of the profound legacy of the images taken during two major periods of poverty during the 1930s and the 1960s. These two decades catapulted the region's poor into the American imagination, turning the southern poor white into an apparently known entity. Throughout this chapter, I examine the legacy of both periods on contemporary depictions of poor whites, and as I consider both the "continuities" and "ruptures" in visual representations of the poor, I turn particularly to photo-narratives.

In his work on the spoken image, Clive Scott notes how language transforms photographs from indexes to icons, from journalistic records to documentary exploration. Although Scott acknowledges that this binary does not always hold, photo-essays, with their mixture of titles, captions, essays, and/ or conversations, form an important genre for examining the ways in which visual narratives write notions of poverty into existence. Scott claims that "[a]s we shift from the indexical to the iconic, we take advice from the title, because one function of titles is to give the image coherence, to select its principal signifying elements" (43). The interpretative, and therefore potentially distortive role of captions, titles, or other supporting words has come under intense scrutiny.[3] While Walter Benjamin asked, "Will not captions become the essential component of pictures?" (215), for Madden, "they almost always limit, distort, prove inapplicable. With a caption one can make almost anything of any photograph. Shoot a scene in Maine, give it a southern title, and the preconditioned viewer will collaborate in the deception" (38). As this chapter unfolds, I consider the complex relationships between words and images in contemporary photobooks about the South's poor whites, but before turning to those recent texts it is necessary to briefly consider the photographic projects of the 1930s and 1960s to outline the contours of this "visual legacy."

During the Great Depression, Roy E. Stryker's 1935 appointment as head of the Resettlement Administration's Historical Section (which became the Farm Security Administration [FSA] in 1937) prompted a crucial turn in the visual representation of American poverty. Unlike the thorough documentation of the poverty of immigrant groups in urban centers by photojournalists such as Jacob Riis at the end of the nineteenth century, the FSA's archival work was both government sanctioned and centered primarily on rural farming families rather than the urban poor. The nation's romantic agrarian tradition was exploded as the country was exposed to image after image of rural Americans living hand-to-mouth existences, with Stryker's army of photographers, including Dorothea Lange and Walker Evans, sent westward and southward to record the widespread desperation sweeping the nation. As discussed in chapter 1, the images they captured defined not only the period but also the nation's idea of the poor for years afterward. For Jack Hurley, "the FSA group was committed from the beginning to a policy of total truthfulness. Their pictures were often used as propaganda for the agency, but it was propaganda in the best sense—that is, the photographs focused attention on real problems and hinted at real solutions" (ix). However, Hurley's belief in the "total" truthfulness and effectiveness of FSA work does not resonate with more recent scholarship on the work of Stryker's team. Stuart Kidd saliently argues that the FSA photographs provided "highly mediated insights into the lived experiences of the underclass" that "encourage intuitive or counterfactual readings of them" ("FSA" 30).[4] Indeed, under the sway of postmodern inquiry, critical debate on the photographic form demands that any discussion of photography engage with the processes of mediation. For Walter Benn Michaels, it is clear: "[W]e all know that the realism of the photograph—its ability to show us what really happened, its ability to tell us the truth—is problematic" (*The Beauty* 12).

Critically examining the photographic projects of the 1930s certainly reveals a far from altruistic approach. As John Tagg argues, in their appeal to the "truth" of photographic "realism," the FSA and Franklin Roosevelt's administration ensured the success of "a liberal, corporatist plan to negotiate economic, political and cultural crisis through a limited programme of structural reforms, relief measures, and a cultural intervention aimed at restructuring the order of discourse, appropriating dissent, and resecuring the threatened bodies of social consent" (8). To get the nation back on solid economic footing, the "limited" aid programs, including the Works Progress Administration, brought relief to many, but as Charles Cunningham surmises, the dominance of iconic photographs of the time, including Lange's "Migrant Mother" (1936), meant that "[t]he real migrants and their real problems" were often "rendered merely symbolic (or mythological)" (286).

These contemporary readings of the FSA's objectives contribute to the debate about the role the state plays in authoring class discourse. In her work on the democratic potential of photography, particularly in the contemporary world where social and digital media render boundaries porous, Ariella Azoulay nevertheless reflects on the emergence of photography and how "the modern state contributed to the perpetuation of the social power relations of power, turning weak, disadvantaged, and marginal populations ... into utterly exposed objects of photography. These groups served as guinea pigs for the mass utilization of photography by the modern state" (*The Civil* 116). Indeed, as Sontag (among others) has noted, FSA photographers

> would take dozens of frontal pictures of one of their sharecropper subjects until satisfied that they had gotten just the right look on film—the precise expression on the subject's face that supported their own notions about poverty, light, dignity, texture, exploitation, and geometry. In deciding how a picture should look, in preferring one exposure to another, photographers are always imposing standards on their subjects. (6)

In addition to being objectified by the photographers at the time, later interviews with some of the prominent subjects of FSA photography, most notably Florence Owens Thompson (Lange's "Migrant Mother"), revealed that many of these individuals and families felt betrayed, often because they did not know how their images had been used and circulated, but also by the lack of financial recompense.[5] Azoulay reminds us that "whether during moments of happiness or disaster, the photographed persons renounce in advance—or, more accurately, have been treated as if they have renounced in advance—any legal right to their own image, entrusting it to the hands of others" (*The Civil* 99).

We might imagine that the photo-essays of the time, such as Caldwell and Bourke-White's *You Have Seen Their Faces* and Agee and Evans's *Let Us Now Praise Famous Men*, were more successful in presenting a fuller, more collaborative account of the lived experiences of their subjects. However, Caldwell saw fit to speak for his subjects, and even Agee, who agonizes at length about the difficulties of writing about and on behalf of the tenant families, not only talks for them but also struggles to overcome the class distinctions that separated him from his subjects, whereas Eudora Welty's Depression-era photography perhaps captured greater empathy for the poor in Mississippi because she was driven less by the sociopolitical agendas of the time than by personal concern for the plight of black and white sharecroppers.

Whatever the problems with the photo-essays, or wider FSA-commissioned photography, their influence on later southern poverty photography is not in question. Joseph Millichap is not alone in arguing that the photographic work of the 1930s continued to "influence future developments of southern life and art, both literary and visual" (3). Indeed, for Warren Zanes there is a southern form of "regionalism haunted by the ethnographic spirit of '30s documentary work" (10). Before turning to its impact on the second great wave of southern poverty photography in the 1960s, it is useful to consider the specific legacy of *Let Us Now Praise Famous Men*. The most obvious manifestation of that haunting legacy emerged when Agee and Evans's book was reissued in 1960, sparking a new appetite for ethnographic studies in the US South. In particular, as Scott L. Matthews notes, "a legion of other writers, photographers, and filmmakers" descended upon Hale County, Alabama, "to re-photograph people and places Agee and Evans documented" (34). However, "these rephotography and follow-up projects also presented Hale County as a kind of museum of the Depression South where a person could experience the world Agee and Evans saw in the summer of 1936" (Matthews 49). This idea of Hale County as a museum points to an inherent failure to register the ongoing poverty affecting families in the region long after the end of the Depression.

Maharidge and Williamson's Pulitzer Prize–winning *And Their Children After Them* (1989) is the most well-known of these rephotography projects.[6] Together, journalist Maharidge and photographer Williamson dedicate much of their work to documenting the lives of the nation's poor, particularly in times of economic instability. Before their Agee/Evans follow-up, Maharidge and Williamson's *Journey to Nowhere* (1985) captured stories and images that provided counternarratives and countervisualities to the dominant narratives of Reaganomics. While researching *Journey*, Maharidge read Agee and Evans's text for the first time. Driven by "curiosity" to discover "what had happened to these three families," the two men headed to Hale County to track down the descendants (*Journey* xvii). But Maharidge's language gives the reader pause: their curiosity, as discussed in chapter 1, carries traces of neocolonialist desires to seek out the foreign other. In her consideration of the book, Martha Rosler argues that it "manages to institute a new genre of victimhood—the victimization by *someone else's* camera of helpless persons, who then hold still enough for the indignation of the new writer to capture them, in words and images both, in their *current* state of decrepitude" (319). Not all the descendants live in such abject conditions, and Maharidge and Williamson's interest in the Ricketts family ultimately poses difficult questions about representation and how far this work makes a break with *Let Us Now Praise Famous Men*. Maharidge and Williamson certainly follow the layout of the urtext to the extent that the photographs precede the narrative, and readers might question whether there is anything at all new in this book given the foreword by FSA photographer Carl Mydans in which he celebrates the fact that Williamson shows "the same eye and feeling that marked the pictures of the FSA photographers" (xiii). If Williamson just offers the same as Evans, then we must suppose that Maharidge offers something different to make the book worth reading at all.

Yet, surely we must also question whether Williamson's photographs are in exactly the same vein as Evans's. Some of Williamson's photographs sit alongside those of Evans, and the first two-page spread is particularly striking in the similarity between shots: in them, we see Centerboro's main street then and now, and while the car models have certainly changed, the continuity of the C. A. Johnson & Son store implies that this part of the South has changed little over a fifty-year period, a point strengthened by images on the other side of the two-page spread. Opposite the Centerboro shots are two photos of Margaret Ricketts standing at the kitchen table, the first taken by Evans in 1936 and the second by Williamson in 1986. In Williamson's, there is a different kitchen, different furniture, and a clearly aged Margaret, but the sense of continuity is pronounced. Yet as the photographs unfold, images of change appear: on page 6, where Evans's photo of Bud Woods's home in 1936 sits above Williamson's image of the dilapidated ruins of the house; or image 59, whose caption reads: "A new mobile home being delivered, on a highway near Birmingham" (261). Notably, Williamson also takes a more inclusive approach by including images of black families and individuals. Both Old and New Souths appear in the photographs, just as Maharidge's prose pivots between past, present, and future: yet the past dominates the beginning of Maharidge's narrative just as it does the photographs, with his narrative opening with a stand-alone section entitled "Maggie Louise." Over five pages, Maharidge laments the tragic life of Maggie Louise Gudger, in whom, when she was a young girl, Agee had seen so much potential, setting the tone for a narrative in which he shows a similar fascination with Debbie, one of Maggie Louise's daughters.

Maharidge celebrates Debbie's material success and work ethic, repeatedly highlighting how her determination helped her to escape poverty and enter the middle class (146). In his eyes, Debbie's engagement with higher education fulfills the potential that Agee saw in her mother, a success Maharidge gauges on a consumerist model as he croons over Debbie's apartment with its modern appliances and "tasteful furniture" (151). Of Debbie's success, he states: "It took fifty years and a delay of a generation, but the dreams a ten-year-old shared with a poet from the North are coming to something" (149). The marker for success here is the move into the middle class, which is determined by the ability to purchase consumer items. Debbie stands as the success story of this rephotography project: she has moved beyond the confines of place and poverty, following an American narrative of self-improvement and progress that Maharidge immediately recognizes. His journey to understand those descendants who have neither left Hale County nor found a way out of poverty is more complex and forces him to contemplate the nuances of value and belonging.

Before Maharidge offers a detailed account of his meeting with the Ricketts family, he draws distinctions between types of poverty: all poverty is "tragic," he claims, but while the Gudgers' poverty "is often tragic because of the element of crushed potential," the Rickettses' poverty is "pathetic" (139). He does not use these terms lightly: Gudger poverty is tragic because Maggie Louise demonstrated an inquiring mind associated with those outside her class; her inability in the end to rise out of the class of her birth renders her story tragic and her daughter's success epic. In opposition, the pathetic Ricketts poverty emerges because neither then nor now does the family demonstrate any of the qualities needed to propel itself out of poverty and reshape the future.

In the preface, Maharidge hints at the contemporary "horrors" he and Williamson encountered during their first meeting with Margaret Ricketts and her son, Garvrin Arlo (xviii), promising to inform readers about what they "discovered" later in the book (xix). While Maharidge goes on to develop a complex picture of the lives led by Margaret Ricketts and her son, our first detailed encounter with mother and son in the present day does little to dispel any of the "horror" that Maharidge promised at the outset. Although Williamson's close-up photograph of Margaret's feet shows us the bodily wear and tear of poverty, Maharidge's later description of his first encounter with Margaret fails to arouse empathy. As she opens her front door, she is picking her nose, and Maharidge's language underscores a sense of instant repulsion, as he writes: "A right finger was thrust up her nose, pulling a hunk of whatever had dried up there, and she started hugging these visiting journalists, snot still stuck to the finger, lips sinking tight around memories of molars in smile" (167). If this image does not repulse, then Maharidge turns to Garvrin Arlo to deliver up already entrenched ideas about the inbred rural poor. To impress their visitors, this grown man runs into the house and slams "his belly down on the floor with such force that the walls of the shack shook" (168). The description of him slapping "his head with a force that knocked him backward," to which he "laughed and laughed and laughed," presents Garvrin Arlo as an archetypal poor fool, when in actual fact he is the family's main earner. These first impressions of mother and son are followed with detailed, sensory descriptions of the interior of Margaret Ricketts's home:

> The smell was a mixture. Unwashed flesh. (They bathe every few months by rubbing their bodies with a damp washcloth.) Stale urine. A blend of milk, vinegar, cheap sardines, stewed every few days on the stove, a recipe created by Garvrin

Arlo ("I'm a chef too!"). Wood smoke. Chain-saw fuel. Toxic chemicals bled from the factory clothes worn by Garvrin Arlo. It combines, rushing the nose. Unlike some odors that grow less sharp with familiarity, until easily ignored, this one stays conspicuous. Each component takes its turn welling to the forefront, depending on the part of the house in which a person stands, but each smell is present every minute you're there. (169)

Readers are confronted with each individual smell as Maharidge unearths layer after layer of dirt and grime in the Ricketts home, just as Agee listed the odors of the same poor white tenant home, specially detailing the old, worn-in smell of the Ricketts home as "hard to get used to or even hard to bear" (136).

Yet, after reading the Ricketts sections it becomes clear that at the outset Maharidge plays on the idea of first contact. If his "curiosity" about these families echoes colonialism, his initial "horror" in the Ricketts home invokes the moment of colonial first contact when initial judgments and misconceptions lay the foundation for the "othering" of people. In Maharidge's narrative, to see and smell is not to know the people. He notes that Margaret's way of life, and the fact that she was one of the easiest descendants to track down, made her the subject of many of the follow-up projects to *Let Us Now Praise Famous Men*. In those other ethno-documentary works, he writes, it is just "easier to focus on the surface truth as confirmation of a convenient stereotype," arguing that "gawking at Margaret and Garvrin Arlo exposes an ugly and voyeuristic side in the townsmen, in journalists, in readers, in this book, in society" (170). However, just as Agee struggled to move beyond his own class prejudices, so Maharidge passes judgment on how the family lives even as he tries to build a more nuanced account. In the time that Maharidge and Williamson spend with Margaret and Garvrin Arlo, they come to understand that while Garvrin Arlo earns a minimum wage, the family has enough money to live differently; indeed, during the time that the two journalists spent with the Ricketts family, Garvrin Arlo meets and marries Jeannie Kay, who has the house painted and brings "a modicum of sanitation" (177). Maharidge decides that "theirs is a queer kind of self-imposed poverty. It is the way they know best" (176). To an extent, this may be true: on Garvrin's "net income of about $13,000" they could have necessities such as indoor plumbing. At the time, his income certainly placed them above the poverty line, but it is equally not an income that allows for the type of consumer activity that would suddenly propel mother and son out of the working class.[7] In addition, Margaret does not place any value in commodities, labeling herself "rich-poor" because she has her "son" and her "Bible" (177). While Maharidge comes to respect the honesty of Margaret's and Garvrin Arlo's lives, Debbie's success is held up as the true discovery. In contrast, the descendants whom Maharidge and Williamson find, including members of the Gudger clan, who have stayed in place both geographically and in class terms fail to offer a narrative of change.

So vital is the idea of class uplift that Maharidge and Williamson promise to create "a trust fund" for the education of "the children of the descendants of the tenant families" from their book's profits (xxii). In 1990, Maharidge and Williamson "presented the first installment of royalties, $5,200, to the University of Alabama for an endowed scholarship fund" ("Campus Life"), a scholarship still running today. The Alabama Tenant-Farming Legacy Scholarship is a small scholarship available to freshman university students from Tuscaloosa, Hale, Greene, and Perry Counties in Alabama, who must be direct descendants of tenant farmers or sharecroppers.[8] The ambition to help educate young people and raise them out of poverty rings with the sentiments of the 1960s, President Lyndon Johnson's Great Society, and the second major wave of southern poverty photography.

Indeed, the majority of *Let Us Now Praise Famous Men*'s rephotography work coincided with the national recognition of persistent poverty in the southern mountains.[9] In the same year as the book's reissue in 1960, Appalachia witnessed both the formation of the Conference of Appalachian Governors, with the remit for addressing the region's high levels of abject poverty, and the visit of John F. Kennedy to West Virginia during his election campaign. This "discovery" of Appalachian poverty captured Kennedy's attention, both during the campaign and once in office. Despite Cold War tensions taking precedence for the new president, he took several steps to address poverty, and in 1963 he formed the President's Appalachian Regional Commission (PARC), which was tasked with developing a coherent set of objectives to bring economic relief and growth to the region. However, Kennedy's assassination led PARC to submit its report in 1964 to southerner Lyndon B. Johnson, who was now the president.[10] In addition to these political undertakings, the publication of Michael Harrington's *The Other America* in 1962 had also stirred the attention of the general public, so it was no surprise when President Johnson's plan to create the Great Society included what is commonly referred to as the War on Poverty. It was during this period that Appalachia was inundated with Vista workers and saw the implementation of initiatives such as Project Head Start.

However, the interest of both presidents in alleviating poverty in the southern mountains was not solely beneficent. As Sheyda Jahanbani saliently argues, "[b]y the 1950s, the idea that poverty anywhere was a source of vulnerability for the postwar order that the US sought to build had become conventional wisdom." In effect, she suggests, "poverty became a geopolitical problem for the United States" (943). With America's global democratic principles tied to capitalist models of economic success, progress, and innovation, poverty was an ugly, uncomfortable reminder that rampant inequality was a by-product of such an economy.

Appalachia in the 1960s witnessed the descent of Vista workers alongside an array of journalists, documentary filmmakers, and photographers intending to record, report, and alleviate poverty. Unemployed or poorly paid workers and their families once again captured the national imaginary as predominantly black-and-white photographs and film footage presented an Appalachia stuck in the past with people mired in cycles of poverty, perpetuating a one-dimensional view of the region and its people to which local residents responded with mixed feelings. Furthermore, little about this new period of southern poverty photography indicated a sharp break with the FSA. Both the FSA and War on Poverty photographic studies were offered up by outsiders, who, no matter how well intentioned, still saw and recorded poor people and places with the detached eye of the observer. Paula Rabinowitz argues: "The photograph, revealing the lack of material objects in the lives of the poor, affirms by contrast the abundance of its viewer; the case study, revealing the lack of coherence in the neurotic's story, affirms by contrast the health of the well-plotted life" (36). As the War on Poverty reached its peak in the late 1960s, hostilities between these outsiders and local communities culminated in the murder of Canadian journalist Hugh O'Connor by Kentuckian Hobart Ison in 1967.

In her documentary *Stranger with a Camera* (2000), Kentuckian filmmaker Elizabeth Barret examines O'Connor's death and seeks to understand what motivated Ison, not to justify his actions but to learn what precipitated them. Barret asks, "What is the difference between how people see their own place, and how others represent it?" (*Stranger* 00:05:49–55). She turns to this question throughout her documentary, in which she employs film footage, photographs, and interviews to examine the impact of media coverage on the region, particularly during the War on Poverty, as numerous television stations and documentarists descended on Appalachia to record this "other" world of deprivation. The blurred lines Barret creates through the documentary as she continually challenges ideas of representation reflect a wider shift in contemporary documentary photography. Gemma-Rose Turnbull believes that "[i]t is possible to see the development of a range of alternate approaches towards documentary photographic practice since the 1970s, including subject participation, as both a general move away from modernist photographic practice and its tendency to accept the evidential nature of the medium" (81). In that vein, *Stranger with a Camera* poses difficult questions and champions the idea of narrating from within the region rather than simply telling about the region. For Ardis Cameron, "[j]uxtaposing images with image-makers allows Barret to keep the audience focused on the contested nature of camera work and the kinds of visual skirmishes it has historically produced" ("When Strangers" 415).[11] Indeed, Barret's work forms part of a wider movement in the southern mountains to provide counternarratives and countervisualities that speak back to the ways the region was depicted during the 1960s, but also more broadly to challenge long-held, culturally established views of poor whites.

Notably, Barret has worked extensively with Appalshop, a community-based arts, media, and education center in Whitesburg, Kentucky, where she is currently director of Appalshop Archive. Appalshop, founded in 1969, was originally known as the Community Film Workshop of Appalachia, and it emerged out of the American Film Institute's New York–based Community Film Workshop Council, which was funded by grants from President Johnson's Office of Economic Opportunity (OEO). Among others, Stephen P. Hanna and Stephen Michael Charbonneau have critically examined the transition from the Community Film Workshop to the relaunched and renamed Appalshop in 1975, and the tensions that have arisen over time as this community-based organization resists the dominant mainstream views of the region but also promotes essentialized identity politics.[12] Both critics note how in its current format, Appalshop has widened its approach by engaging with global communities. Appalshop's most current mission

> is to enlist the power of education, media, theater, music, and other arts to: document, disseminate, and revitalize the lasting traditions and contemporary creativity of Appalachia; tell stories the commercial cultural industries don't tell, challenging stereotypes with Appalachian voices and visions; support communities' efforts to achieve justice and equity and solve their own problems in their own ways; celebrate cultural diversity as a positive social value; and participate in regional, national, and global dialogue toward these ends. (Appalshop)

While the debate continues about the politics or lack thereof in some of Appalshop's earlier documentaries, its move beyond region was well underway by the time photographer Wendy Ewald's *Portraits and Dreams: Photographs and Stories by Children of the Appalachians* (1985) was copublished by the organization. Ewald's photographic projects make a decided break with earlier photography: as Azoulay notes, Ewald and her contemporary Susan Meiselas "were not the first to engage in collaborations, but they were certainly decisive in foregrounding the collaborative dimension of their photographic work and making it an explicit topic" ("Photography" 188). Azoulay argues that all photography was and is collaborative, but that the key difference in recent years has been the way that collaboration is articulated and presented. Now, she suggests, collaboration and the interplay between photographer and subject are more explicit and, in many cases, more democratic. Certainly, in the case of Ewald, as she educates and trains young photographers she allows them to articulate their own world with the tools she provides, which is why, for Katherine Hyde, Ewald "provides a convincing reminder of the value of alternative epistemologies" (179).

Ewald's first Appalachian publication and another in conjunction with Appalshop, *Appalachia: A Self-Portrait* (1979), is an edited collection that includes the work of seven photographers as well as personal stories about the subjects and snippets of conversations. Her second Appalachian work, *Portraits and Dreams*, is a project that Ewald continues to work on today: in collaboration with Elizabeth Barret, Ewald plans a revisitation project to retrace the lives of the children she worked with.[13] Ewald taught photography to schoolchildren aged between six and fourteen, from three southeastern Kentucky communities (Cowan Creek, Kingdom Come Creek, and Campbells Branch), resulting in *Portraits and Dreams*, a collection of photographs taken by and of the children, alongside a series of narratives formed "from conversations ... with eight students who were eleven, twelve and thirteen" (11). The collection provides a significant insight into how the children see and interpret their own world; Ewald claims: "Their photographs speak from within their lives and record moments that suggest rhythms of everyday life" (11). As children, they have a greater ability to capture those patterns of lived experience, because the camera does not create the same distance between themselves and their subjects as it does for the teenagers and adults who undertake projects at Appalshop. In their work at Appalshop's Appalachian Media Institute (AMI), a multimedia skills and training project for local fourteen- to twenty-two-year-olds, Katie Richards-Shuster and Rebecca O'Doherty note that "critical media literacy ... provides a space where young people can be radical—question authority, challenge dominant media constructions of young people and their communities, and reimagine new possibilities for themselves," but they recognize that while such experiences help participants to develop a critical vocabulary for reading the community and its representation in the media, such a radical position can also cause tensions and divisions between participants, their families, and local communities

(81). Ewald's work with younger children sought to ensure that the children's forays into family and communal life were less intrusive.

Before considering the photography in Ewald's collection, it is worth considering the conversations with some of the children that Ewald intersperses throughout the collection. There is no order to the conversations: they often sit alongside mismatched images, in one case two conversations sit side by side, and there is often a series of images before readers encounter the next dialogue section. The haphazard layout reflects the dreams, aspirations, and often unconnected streams of thought that appear through the dialogue. Despite the power of these children's stories, in the afterword Ben Lifson problematically argues that "[d]epicting neither advertising signs nor automobiles ... this collective document is largely dateless. The moments it describes occur in emotional not historical time. The children's Letcher County has something of the remoteness of myth or of those ballads whose action occurs in a far country ruled by a nameless lord" (122). Reading the collection as ahistorical ignores the photographs that contain markers of time and place, and reduces the significance of the children's representation of their own lives. As Lifson even notes himself, the children chose to make changes to their photographic collection ahead of its 1977 exhibitions in Chicago and New York. In presenting their communities to a national audience, the children "decided that they had to photograph the mines and the land the better 'to explain' the place to outsiders" (121). Some of those additional photographs appear in the collection across a four-page spread, showing miners inside a mine as well as at the end of a shift (80–83). Lifson's ahistorical reading romanticizes the collection and overlooks the concerns that seep through the children's words and several of their photographs.

The conversations contain the worries specific to children whose parents undertake dangerous occupations. Allen Shepherd recalls how his father, a coal miner for "about eighteen years," had to stop work "because that lung of his collapsed because of coal dust," and how one of his uncles "got his skull busted. A rock fell on him and his knee was crushed. He can't work and they won't give him social security" (Ewald, *Portraits and Dreams* 23). Here, the damaged, laboring body and attendant issues of a lack of welfare provision preoccupy the everyday thoughts of this young boy. Some of the students also dwell on the wider environmental impact of the coal mining industry. Dewayne Cole laments how "they're tearing the mountains up with bulldozers—getting the coal out and making places for houses.... They've killed almost everything that's up there" (79). In a similar vein, Darlene Watts believes that "[t]he earth can feel the hurt from the way we've used it" (85). The children surely relay parts of adult conversations, exposing a deep concern in the local communities about the economic dependency on mining that devastates the working body as well as the landscape. The children carry the burden of these concerns, and for many of the young boys who envisage a future in coal mining, they see in the damaged bodies around them the future damage of their own.

Whether in terms of the destruction of the human body or of the landscape, violence runs through many these conversations, reflecting the everyday forms of destruction that shape the lives not just of the workers but also of their children. As their everyday chatter dwells on violence, their conversations stand as a rebuke against the corporations that fail to recognize the whole worker, seeing instead a unit of labor. For Janet Zandy, the voices of the working class produce "a necessary encounter with violence—not the packaged kind of tabloids and crime shows—but the violence of work that the human body endures" (12). Whether through their photographs or their conversations, the children in this collection offer key insights into the lived experience of poor families in the mountainous South.

For instance, one of the young photographers in Ewald's collection, Freddy Childers, posed for two images on his first photographic project at home. Both images reveal not only family love and affection but also the burden of responsibility and mourning. The first image is of Freddy with his disabled brother, Homer, and in the second we see Freddy holding a framed photograph of his dead brother, Everett, "who killed himself when he came back from Vietnam" (Ewald, *Portraits and Dreams* 27). In the introduction, Ewald recalls conversations with Freddy, noting that he "takes care" of his older brother and "never thought to be ashamed of Homer" (13–14). If the first image shows the young boy's tenderness toward Homer, the second reveals the family's mourning for their other son. Like the other photographs in the collection, Freddy Childers's photographs take the viewer beyond the one-dimensional ideas of life in the southern mountains propagated by so many preceding images of the region.

Freddy's images are particularly relevant because the Childers family also features prominently throughout the work of controversial Kentucky photographer Shelby Lee Adams. After a discussion of the 1960s, the emergence of Appalshop, and its championing of counternarratives and countervisualities, my focus now turns to a range of recent Appalachian photo-narratives to consider how far contemporary photographers have embraced collaborative approaches, to what extent their depictions take us beyond the debilitating stereotypes of the southern mountains, and how far nostalgia for a supposed simple existence influences today's photo-narratives. Without exception, the photographers under examination here, both southern and nonsouthern, emerge out of middle-class backgrounds, so that even when the southerners among them stress their regional credentials, this selection of photo-narratives exemplifies how class outsiders depict poverty.

Shelby Lee Adams is the one of the most controversial photographers of Appalachia and its people. Ewald introduced Adams to the Childers family in 1976, and some of his early photographs of the Childers and Caudill families appear in *Appalachia: A Self-Portrait*. Since then, he has returned repeatedly to photograph the Childers and other families. In Ewald's collection, the photography lacked augmentation; as Lifson notes, the children were shown "how to create many special effects both with the camera and in the darkroom," but they "rejected these techniques as uninteresting novelties. They were after a blunt and naked presentation of subject, a photography unembellished and direct" (117), so the photograph of Freddy and Homer lacks the stark, highly embellished quality of Adams's work in *Appalachian Portraits* (1993), *Appalachian Legacy* (1998), *Appalachian Lives* (2003), and *Salt and Truth* (2011). As Adams has faced criticism about his potentially distortive depictions of the region, he has become more and more concerned with underlining his connection with his subjects. Adams regards himself as a photographic documentarist, writing in his essay at the beginning of *Salt and Truth*: "The people look to me as a resource to help document their lives and preserve their memories" (19). In addition, he stresses in *Appalachian Portraits* that the people whose lives he records are not "typical of the area" and therefore "should not be interpreted as a general representation of all Appalachian people or their culture today" (7). Instead, he focuses on what he regards as the culture of those people who reside in the backwoods, those who in his mind are "the authentic salt-of-the-earth people, who are now being overrun by a more sugar-coated society" (*Salt* 25). As he tries to explain the honesty and realism of his work, he turns again and again to the notion of the "authentic," and while the mournful lament for a dying culture is particularly pronounced in *Salt and Truth*, it runs through each collection.

At first glance, Adams's work disturbs with what seems to be blatant stereotyping. Commenting on Adams's first work, *Appalachian Portraits*, Dwight Billings argues that it delivers "what mainstream culture expects from the region." He goes on: "[A] number of the down-and-out subjects displayed by Adams appear to be mentally challenged." He notes that, although *Appalachian Portraits* "has received praise in reviews from outside the region . . . Adams's photographs received little attention in Appalachia publications, perhaps indicating the uneasiness and confusion they generate" (Billings, Norman, and Ledford, Introduction 6). Perhaps, though, it is the "uneasiness" and "confusion" that Adams's work evokes that is worth dwelling upon. His photography provokes, but what it provokes and why is surely vital. Madden asks:

> [D]o some of those southerners who are reluctant to make a total commitment to photography hesitate to shoot the South for fear of perpetuating stereotypes and hostility? Does that help to explain a certain neutral quality in some recent photographs by southerners? Does the southerner feel as he is about to shoot the South that his photographs will be overwhelmed by the imagery of literary and folk voices, songs, stories, and by earlier photographers? (18)

Adams's work can hardly be described as neutral. Throughout his photographs, Adams delivers up a slice of southern Gothicism and grotesqueness. In a review of Jennifer Baichwal's documentary on Adams and the reception of his work, *The True Meaning of Pictures: Shelby Lee Adams' Appalachia* (2002), Dennis Harvey notes that Adams's photographs often make "these 'hollar dwellers' look grotesque and pathetic" (53). Throughout Baichwal's documentary, we hear from several detractors, including academics such as Billings and locals angered by Adams's depictions of the region. Echoing throughout their responses is Flannery O'Connor's observation that "anything that comes out of the South is going to be called grotesque by the Northern reader, unless it is grotesque, in which case it is going to be called realistic" (40). The concern is that Adams's grotesques are viewed as realistic, a fear that Baichwal plays upon near the beginning of the film as the camera looks down on, pans across, and then at ground level observes people attending an Adams exhibit at the Catherine Edelman Gallery in Chicago (00:02:00–43). Here, as we voyeuristically watch art lovers peering into Adams's work, Baichwal demands that we consider the ethics of looking. It is unnerving to see people peering with curiosity at Adams's version of Appalachia, and divorced from the words that contextualize the images in Adams's published collections, it is easy to understand the outrage that his work often elicits.

Before considering the varied narratives that populate Adams's work, it is important to consider his obvious and conscious use of the grotesque. In his essay "Making Photographs," Adams discusses his use of strobe lighting and how he currently uses "as many as five different artificial lighting sources, usually in combination with daylight," largely for aesthetic reasons (*Appalachian Lives* xxi–xxii). The artificial lighting lends a surreal quality to his photographs that is easily interpreted as another slice of southern macabre with poor whites at its center. However, Madden suggests:

> In the southern photograph, the perverse, like the surreal, looks domesticated. It is difficult to imagine the ogre Weegee prowling the South, seeking something to distort, exaggerate; the extraordinary is ordinarily available. The southern scene is, or is imagined to be, already intrinsically unreal, dreamlike, so that few photographs attempt a surreal quality, but in few distinctively southern photographs does one not feel a surreal aura. (34)

For Madden, much southern photography has a distortive, "surreal aura," so if Madden is correct, why does Adams go to such lengths to create the surreal? The sense of artifice is so pronounced in Adams's work that it cannot be taken as "realistic"; his overt turn to the grotesque may negate the idea of intrinsic grotesqueness. In her introduction to *Appalachian Lives*, Vicki Goldberg argues that Adams's use of "space and light" helps to situate "the residents of Appalachia in an artistic and indeed intellectual context that is just far enough from the norm to suggest that perhaps this is not such a simple and straightforward place" (xi).

Place is complicated in Adams's work, not only by the questions posed by the photographs but also by the narratives. His first work, *Appalachian Portraits*, was undertaken in collaboration with Lee Smith, which automatically brings the fictive into play. The combination of photographs and fiction immediately poses questions about modes of representation and narration. Smith's stories make up the first main section of the book and are, she says, "based upon interviews that Shelby Lee Adams has conducted over the years in Kentucky and upon interviews and conversations I have had with people where I grew up in southwest Virginia" (L. Smith 13). Although the similarities Smith draws between backwoods mountain people in both parts of the US South might propagate the idea of southern exceptionalism, in at least one of the stories she challenges the rumors, presumptions, and prejudices that ostracize those who do not follow societal norms. In "Mrs. Ratchett's Opinion," readers are presented with incest, an all too familiar southern stereotype, but Mrs. Ratchett condemns the treatment of a local family who have suffered violence because of rumors of incest between the father and his daughter and/or between the brother and sister. Locals believe that the girl conceived two children with either her father or her brother, but even years later, married and with more children, the girl and her family are persecuted by locals. Mrs. Ratchett believes that "[i]t's awful what folks will do to one another, do in particular to them that is any way different" (L. Smith 20). Driven by her faith not to judge others, Mrs. Ratchett rejects the official church that preaches against the family. In many ways, Smith's story asks readers to postpone judgment as they navigate Adams's work: in Mrs. Ratchett's eyes, to look at his photographs and only see stereotypes is a failure to see the humanity his photography elicits.

It is a struggle to find that humanity in Adams's work, with critics in Baichwal's film arguing that his subjects do not fully comprehend how the photographs are used and interpreted in the wider world, a point reinforced by Louise Hall, the daughter and sister of the subjects in "Melissa and Brice, Johnson's Fork, 1978," which appears in *Appalachian Portraits*. Now a successful, college-educated woman, Hall can barely contain her anger at her family's exploitation. She says, "I would like to take every one of these books and rip that picture out . . . he has disgraced our family" (00:35:00–12). Hall's rise out of poverty attests to the idea that only with education is she able to see the images as art rather than simply as photographs and thereby recognize the exploitative nature of Adams's work. So when Baichwal's film turns to interviews with some of his subjects, who talk in warm terms about their relationship with the photographer, the audience has already been led to believe that these individuals have not grasped the full import of Adams's work and their role in it. Yet, unlike Evans's subjects, Adams's subjects see their photos and the collections they end up in. In his essay "Beyond the Stereotypes of Appalachia," Adams addresses the negative responses to his work:

> Some who see my photographs suggest that I perpetuate those worst assumptions, showing people in unbecoming poses and in an unflattering light. To my mind and eye, the photographs I make are as authentically Appalachian as pictures can be. I approach my subjects with wonder and awe, and I try not to change anything essential about their appearance. To present a sanitized, idealized view of Appalachia, it seems to me, would be to indulge in stereotyping of another kind. I suspect that the viewers of these photographs are the uncomfortable ones, and not the people pictured in them. (B10)

There is no easy viewing of Adams's work, and its provocativeness will continue to divide critics. Contradictions within Adams's own narrative about how he takes his photographs only serve to feed the debate. Despite arguing that he works collaboratively with his subjects, there are also moments when he reveals the structured and predesigned nature of some of his work. In *Salt and Truth* he discusses taking pictures of children, stating that he often asks they be washed, but stresses that he allows them to "hold the pets or toys they wish to include" (20). Yet in *Appalachian Lives* he explains the process behind the photograph "Tyler and Sheba 2001" (8). At the house of Sherman, one of his primary subjects, Adams claims that while he sat and thought about images, he "figured out exactly how" he could "make a photograph on the back porch and with whom" (9). His subject for this clearly structured image is Tyler, "a little boy about five years old," whom Adams directs "to get Sheba, the Boston terrier" (9). For this photograph, both the child and the dog are specifically chosen to create "a perfect shoot" (9).

Perhaps the most successful representation of the local communities comes in *Appalachian Lives*, where Adams offers a rare opportunity for readers to hear his subjects speak. Sherman's insights are particularly enlightening: he is a self-taught car mechanic and musician, but more importantly he dwells on the healthcare provision for those without insurance. Adams then follows up with details about Sherman's daughter, Sally, who still has "shreds of glass lodged in her right cheek" after a car accident. He writes: "The doctors never removed all the glass from her face because she didn't have coverage for plastic surgery, and they told her that getting it all out was not necessary" (5). Here, necessity is entirely dependent on class and access to adequate health insurance, highlighting that the health and well-being of some is more important, more "necessary," than it is for others.

In the same collection, Adams discusses his relationship with the Childers family. In previous collections, images of this family only appear with titles or captions rather than with a narrative. In this collection, Adams champions the Childers family for caring for their disabled children rather than institutionalizing them. In Baichwal's film, which preceded the publication of *Appalachian Lives*, Billings hears Adams talking about his connection with the Childers family and his celebration of their strong family bond. Billings states:

> As I listen to that story there's some plausibility there to an interesting tension between the sanitized middle-class way of disposing [of] people and the keeping of people in your family no matter what condition they're in. That's interesting and it tells me maybe something about the motivation of the photographer but that's a story which is not in the book and that's not what the viewer's going to think about. (1:04:30–1:05:06)

Adams may already have written or planned to write a section on the Childers family in *Appalachian Lives* before watching the completed documentary, but the criticism of his work seems to compel Adams to make explicit the collaborative nature of his work and his close relationships with his subjects.

Adams's work may deliberately challenge the viewer, but that does not displace the nostalgia that is present throughout his work. In each collection, Adams writes about the unique quality of these local Kentuckian communities and how he is trying to preserve that culture before it disappears. In *Salt and Truth*, he writes:

The families who occupied this land for more than a couple hundred years are now interspersed with a new breed of Appalachian and land developers driving Hummers and Escalades, owning oddly shaped swimming pools and mansions built into the mountaintops after the coal is removed and the mountains reclaimed.... It is a more varied and diluted world now. Salt preserves wholesomeness and prevents decay, but the people from the earlier, harder formed age who bear that special look are now in decline. (25)

The grotesqueness of Adams's work, however, disturbs this nostalgic mourning for an idea of Appalachian culture. In the end, it may be the very grotesqueness of his work that actually saves it from merely stereotyping and delivering up a lament for a changing culture. The sheer artificial quality of his photographs points to truths that lie beyond the images, rendering his poor white subjects mysterious and therefore complex, rather than fully known.

The same might not be so easily said of Adams's peers. An anonymous reviewer of *Appalachian Lives* claims that Adams "employs careful, unsettling poses not unlike those of Sally Mann, but his subjects register an uncanny combination of bemusement and desire to articulate something deadly serious rather than Mann's difficult sexuality" ("*Appalachian Lives*" 67). Discussions of Mann tend to focus on her preoccupation with children and sexuality, including her decision to use her own children throughout her work. Yet Virginia-born Mann extensively captures the US South in her work, most notably in *Deep South* (2005), her series of haunting southern landscapes. In Mann's work, Suzanne Schuweiler finds an "oppressive, appalling fecundity, along with a sense of the decaying, slow death of the agrarian South" (328). Despite the sense of death and decay running through Mann's southern landscapes, Schuweiler suggests that Mann "avoids the nostalgic appeal of rural shanties so strongly associated with Walker Evans. There are no signs of sharecroppers or modernization in her South" (332). Southern poverty may not appear in Mann's South, but in a similar vein to some of the travel writers discussed in chapter 1, in the narrative sections of *Deep South* Mann romanticizes poverty. Describing a drive from Virginia to Mississippi into what Mann refers to as the "real," true South, she writes: "From the moment I passed into Mississippi, my time became ecstatic.... Once I put those first twelve hours of transitional driving behind me and the shotgun shacks began to appear alongside the road, I broke into that dimension of revelation and ecstasy that eludes historical time" (49). She might not depict the region's poor in a manner reminiscent of the FSA, and she does ponder the horrors of slavery and segregation, but Mann, like so many, finds tranquility in the idea of the sharecropper's shack: a romanticization that robs the shacks of their socioeconomic resonance and makes them simple, architectural reminders of an imagined lost, agrarian past.

Mann is not alone in producing problematic southern images and narratives. Fellow photographers Tim Barnwell and Susan Lipper are equally remiss in detailing the actualities of poverty. In addition to the images of North Carolina he produces for travel guides, Barnwell's three major publications to date, *The Face of Appalachia: Portraits from the Mountain Farm* (2003), *On Earth's Furrowed Brow: The Appalachian Farm in Photographs* (2007), and *Hands in Harmony: Traditional Crafts and Music in Appalachia* (2009), bring together photographs and oral histories in a romanticized elegy for a "simple" agrarian life. From Madison County, North Carolina, Barnwell, like Adams, grew up in a middle-class family and only came to know his subjects once he began to photograph them. The similarities do not end there: just as Adams believes that he captures a unique place and people that is dying out, so too does Barnwell. Neither set out, as did Bourke-White, Lange, and their contemporaries, to facilitate societal change, yet the slipperiness of Adams's work leaves a gap that allows for questions and inquiry. Barnwell's images, on the other hand, often close down meaning. In a review of Barnwell's first collection, *The Face of Appalachia*, David Bryant argues that it offers up images of a "timeless place" (72), which is equally true of *On Earth's Furrowed Brow*. At least the front cover of the second publication shows a tractor being used at harvesting time, but despite a few images throughout the collections that point to the late twentieth century, there is not much to distinguish between the photographs taken at the start of Barnwell's career at the end of the 1970s and those shot in the twenty-first century. The titles, including dates, are often the only clues that locate the images in time. *Hands in Harmony* is arguably the most contemporaneous of his texts, with several images clearly depicting present-day Appalachia. It is also in this collection that Barnwell provides the most extensive section of oral histories across his work, with close to a hundred pages dedicated to his conversations with his subjects. *Hands in Harmony* also comes with an audio CD of twenty-two tracks by local musical artists.

Barnwell's commitment to presenting the voices of his subjects is perhaps why George Tice, in his foreword to *The Face*, claims that Barnwell's photographs inspire viewers to listen to his subjects. Because Barnwell "approaches his subjects by getting to know them, gaining their trust before he photographs them," Tice argues, when the subjects "are ready they look directly into the camera. They strike their own pose, giving their portrait to him" (11). Following Tice, this sense of collaboration imprints each image with the individual and her or his story, yet if that is the case, one wonders why we need the supplementary oral histories at all; furthermore, Tice directs the reader to view the photos in a particular way, demanding: "Examine the photograph of Byard Ray. Could it possibly have been composed better than it is? Within its modest and fragmentary frame is a complete and perfect portrait, the very essence of the man" (11). His desire to interpret and provide meaning for the reader continues: "Look at Kate Church; she looks as worn as the mop next to her. She might be younger than she appears. If so, you know she has had a hardscrabble life, much of it spent outdoors. But she looks happy and grateful for the attention paid her" (11). Here, Tice directs the reader and imposes meaning onto particular images, thereby colonizing the subject. Access to the oral histories at least offers alternatives, with Kate Church's matter-of-factness betraying neither happiness nor sadness, and Byard Ray talking about feelings of homesickness for his childhood farm and the feeling of "the mud between my toes" (Barnwell, *The Face* 148). If readers follow Tice's reading of Ray's photograph, the fiddle represents everything we might need or care to know about the man. Despite the general sentimental tone that runs through most of Barnwell's images, some of his images resist the easy categorization placed on them by Tice. Barnwell's image of Ray shows him looking down at his fiddle with his hat covering his eyes. The covered eyes and downward glance rebuff our gaze, denying us access to any complete sense of Ray. By and large, though, the force of Barnwell's work rests more in the oral histories than his photographs. As Max Kozloff reminds us, "[t]he picture does so very much on its own but then stops suddenly short of delivering, not its particulars, but their significance. It supplies an enormous amount of what we may need—visual data—but finally denies us what we want—the import of its message" (13).

In *On Earth's Furrowed Brow*, for example, the nostalgically simple image of Mamie and Tommy Banks in their kitchen belies the force of their oral history, in which they discuss Shelton Laurel (30).[14] Mamie and Tommy Banks remember that "people used to call it Bloody Shelton Laurel, 'cause people would get killed all the time in fights, and shootings, and quarrels and such" (131). Yet, unlike the nostalgia for the past that runs through so many of the other oral histories in Barnwell's collections, Mamie and Tommy talk with pride about how things have changed, saying: "We've done a lot up here in Shelton Laurel to try to correct" its bad reputation. With government aid, the locals set up "a meals program for the old people," and by pulling their resources together they "rented a tobacco allotment." With the proceeds from the tobacco, they "bought two fire trucks" and had "money left over in the bank for other things for the community" (132). Their narrative reveals a place and people not mired in the past but working to enact positive communal change in the present. So much depends, though, on access to these oral histories that take the viewer/reader beyond a one-dimensional understanding of rural life.

Sometimes, though, even words cannot take us beyond restrictive ideas about the region's poor. Susan Lipper's photographs of Grapevine Hollow, a small community in West Virginia, cast the locals and the landscape as odd and eerie. In *Grapevine* (1994), New York photographer Lipper offers up a series of untitled images with a short section at the end devoted to her conversations with three residents: Mother, her brother Bob, and her neighbor Gene. According to Val Williams, while Lipper's work has been mistaken for documentary photography, she "saw her work very differently. For her, photography was an expression of the self, a way of manifesting the imagination through the mapping of elsewhere. The series was embedded in both a magic realism and a Carveresque sense of the absurdity of dysfunction" (56). That may well be true, but the title of the collection firmly grounds it in place, and photographs of snake-handling, gun-toting men and the Ku Klux Klan connote the US South more than any other region.

The tone of the collection is set by the front-cover image of a deer hanging from the frame of a basketball hoop, set against a background of trees, power lines, cars, and a house. Grapevine, the front cover indicates, is a place as peculiar as we are conditioned to expect. The starkness of this and many of the images in the collection is supposedly tempered by the collaborative nature of the work. Rachel Churner, for instance, is reassured by the fact that "Lipper explicitly acknowledged a 'contract' between her camera and the men before it, giving her subjects license to actively and self-consciously shape their own representations . . . and then [she] reviewed the prints with the sitters, allowing them to refine their poses" (217). That sense of reciprocity does not account for the shots without live subjects in which Lipper intensifies the horror. One image, for example, of two stuffed raccoons with bared teeth confronts the viewer and leads into a photograph of a fully costumed Ku Klux Klan member. These images, without titles or captions, are entirely left to speak for themselves, and Lipper's reference to them as a "journal" of her time in the community presents each shot as a reflection of daily life in the mountains (5). In a review of a recent exhibition of Lipper's Grapevine images at the Higher Pictures Gallery in New York (2016),[15] Loring Knoblauch notes that on their own, these images serve up a familiar Appalachia, and that only with the knowledge of the collaborative nature of the work do they take on wider meaning. To what extent gallery audiences have prior knowledge of Lipper's intentions remains in question.

Even in the published collection, Lipper only includes the conversations with Mother, Bob, and Gene at the end. Here, smaller images interrupt the dialogue, marking the first time in the collection that words and images sit together, so that, as we hear Mother, we see her. Set out in large blocks, with each speaker highlighted in bold, the conversations are deliberately made difficult to follow, presumably to reflect a sense of oral history. Williams suggests that the oral history is crucial to the collection because "these interviews are a haunting vernacular poetry, which Susan Lipper orchestrates" (56). Therein lies the problem: despite the layout pointing to the idea of oral history, Lipper directs the conversation and manipulates it to her own ends.

Work, for instance, dominates parts of the discussion between Mother and Bob, and at one point the siblings reflect on the contemporary destruction of "unions in West Virginia" and the way their parents were dragged into earlier conflicts between miners and "Baldwin thugs." They mention Blair Mountain as they remember how the thugs kicked their "mother's ass out of the car" and then forced their father to drive into the miners (Lipper 100). At the very mention of the site of the successful 1921 labor uprising, Lipper interrupts the siblings with a question about Sid Hatfield. This marks a turn in the conversation from their thoughtful consideration of labor and unions, to one of the key stereotypes of the region. While Sid Hatfield is synonymous with the Battle of Blair Mountain, Lipper's interjection provides readers with the familiarity of Appalachian "feuding families" rather than Mother's and Bob's attempt to trace the origins of the breaking up of unions throughout the 1980s and early 1990s. So while Williams argues that these interviews are key to *Grapevine*'s success, she glosses over the difficult moments during which Lipper's status as community "outsider" is pronounced.

Lipper also prompts turns to race. She asks Gene the names of Mother's dogs, something that she clearly knows, but his answer reveals why she asks this trivial question. Gene tells her "Peanut and Nigger," which leads Mother to add: "I've had three 'Niggers.' Gene gave me the first one, and I've called every one of 'em 'Nigger.' . . . Named 'em 'Nigger' 'cause they're black" (105). Rather than probing the casual employment of the N-word, Lipper simply asks at this stage, "What kind of dogs are they?," only returning to the question of race toward the end of the interviews. In her penultimate set of questions for Mother, Lipper focuses on the presence of the Ku Klux Klan in the local community. After all, and as I've mentioned, one of Lipper's images in the collection shows a hooded and robed Klansman confronting the camera (71). Since Mother has traveled more widely than many of her neighbors, travels she undertook as a young woman to escape her violent father, Lipper asks, "What do you think about the people around here not liking black people?" (107). Mother discusses both her own friendly relationships with black people and examples of local racism, but all the while the reader remembers

Mother's own casual use of the N-word. When Lipper specifically probes about the presence of the Klan, Mother states:

> I've never seen a Ku Klux Klan but one time. We lived on Big Coal River and there was a man named Walter Dilbeck stayed with us and he whipped his woman, May was her name.... They was a staying with us—and I was just a little girl. And the Klan marched in on our yard and they told him after he whipped her, "We don't want after dark to catch you here." And honey he packed his clothes and he got out from under there. Yeah. They come to the house and then they laid a big wad of switches on the porch. (108)

Lipper retorts, "So you've seen a whole lot of Klan people then?," to which Mother responds, "Yeah. I've seen quite a few of them" (108). Lipper's question implies a distrust of Mother's claim to have only seen the Klan once. However, when Lipper claims that Mother must have "seen a whole lot," there is no clarification as to whether Mother's response refers to seeing several Klansmen in that one instance, or whether she has seen them repeatedly throughout her life. Of course, Lipper needs it to be the latter, because in her journal the Klan is an everyday part of life in Grapevine, West Virginia. We might think turns to the Klan make Lipper's work more "honest" than that of Adams or Barnwell, more representative of the complexities of the region, yet in its current formation the Klan is no more representative of southern racism than it is of racism in any other part of the United States.

It may be in her later collaboration with writer Frederick Barthelme, *Trip* (2000), that Lipper comes closer to depicting a South that is far from unique. The images in *Trip* are only loosely located in place and are offered more generally as a trip around anywhere, USA, that just happens to begin: "On the highway outside Lake Charles, Louisiana." However, in an overview of the collection at the end of the book entitled "Photographs by Susan Lipper," Matthew Drutt suggests that "the pictures bear the unmistakable imprint of the American South." They are decidedly southern, he writes, because "[w]here else would one find a wall of photographs memorializing forty years of home grown beauty queens . . . a bathroom stall sporting a still from the Southern epic *Gone with the Wind*; or, perhaps most telling, a wall of devotional votive prayers inscribed on Post-it notes and stuck on a fake wood panel wall beneath dime-store images depicting the life of Jesus?" Interestingly, what Drutt highlights as distinctively southern features are anything but, and he overlooks actual southern reference points, including the image of a bag of Evangeline Maid flour sitting next to a set of keys on a dresser.[16] But, given the focus in the collection on transience, motels, and cafes, all the photograph indicates is that the flour, produced in Lafayette, Louisiana, was probably bought somewhere in the Southeast, but where it now sits is far from certain. Many of the images could have been taken in motel rooms across the nation, undercutting regional distinctiveness.

Thus far, the photo-narratives discussed are all produced by middle-class observers peering into the lives of the poor. Henninger usefully notes:

> The public visual legacy of poor white representation in the United States is thus one of double-erasure: a middle-class subjectivity asserts a right of access to poor white bodies and renders them visible only to the extent that they support a middle-class national imaginary as (1) the demonized or comically corrupt "other" against which the purer nation is formed or (2) the purer, tragic "other" against which any true notion of Americanness can be measured. (145)

I turn now to consider the images of poverty presented by those from poor backgrounds and to writers who use family photography in their work. Rabinowitz states: "We need to rethink how subaltern groups create counterpublic cultures and how their alternatives effect the dominant public spaces organizing the political and cultural life of a nation" (77–78). In considering the use of photography by poor white memoirists, I question the degree to which these writers produce alternatives, or countervisualities, to the dominant narratives about the poor. As Marianne Hirsch questions: "[C]an photographs, the very cultural objects that support dominant ideologies, also be used to resist and contest these ideologies?" ("Familial" xiv).[17]

Several recent poor white memoirists have brought photography and narrative together to provide their own personal accounts of hardship and survival. In her autobiographical essay "Appalachian Images: A Personal History" (1999), Denise Giardina writes about Appalachian stereotypes and her engagement with family photographs:

> I examine old photographs of these kin, looking for signs of encroaching barbarism....
>
> The images are soft and faded.... My grandmother Flora looks eleven or twelve years old.... No one is smiling, nor are they scowling. They are intent, dignified, aware of their own presence and the record they are making.
>
> I search the photograph for clues. It seems my great-grandmother was an accomplished seamstress.... My grandmother was a dainty and stylish child. My

great-grandfather was comfortable holding his three-year-old daughter—who is reaching for something off camera—on his knee. It seems mountain people in 1900 knew what a camera was. It seems mountain people looked normal. (163)

Scouring family photo albums reveals another narrative about life in the mountains, just as the family snapshots that appear in memoirs offer a broader interpretation of poverty across the US South. Family photographs, of course, are markedly different from photography intended for public exhibition. Deborah Chambers notes: "Despite being in continuous dialogue with public discourses of space, albums remain intended for private consumption among the exclusive group of extended and nuclear family and friends and never for the public domain, for publication" (103). While they might not be set for galleries in New York or Chicago, family photographs are always shaped by external drivers. Chambers continues, "The narratives of albums are tied to cultural myths of collective memory expressed by documenting fulfilment in marriage and parenthood, the innocence and potential of childhood and the realization of familial aspirations through material success" (113). The display of photographs within the home attests to the idea of familial and collective memory: the photographs stand as memory triggers for family members but also help to tell a story about the family to visitors to the home. In short, family photographs are not neutral documents, and as with all photographs there is a continual "struggle for control of image, narrative, and memory" (Hirsch, "Familial" xi).

Images are crucial to Dorothy Allison's project in *Two or Three Things I Know for Sure* (1996), the memoir that emerged out of her performance pieces. In both the performances and the memoir, Allison confronts us with the often distortive nature of family photographs. Throughout the memoir, readers encounter numerous family snapshots, but a two-page spread near the middle of the narrative is particularly significant. These photographs show Allison and her sister as children, but the paragraph that precedes this set of images reads:

The man raped me. It's the truth. It's a fact.

I was five, and he was eight months married to my mother. That's how I always began to talk about it—when I finally did begin to talk about it. (39)

The photographs then interrupt the narrative, abruptly moving readers away from the "facts" to the seemingly contented images of childhood. As Timothy Dow Adams observes, Allison "selected photographs that seem to be the most benign, the most 'normal,' and the least indicative of poverty for the two-page spread ... that most directly reveals the deepest horror of her past" (92). In *Two or Three Things I Know for Sure*, the combination of life-writing and photography serves to remind readers that no one photograph or set of photographs defines an individual or a class. So while Adams is troubled by the happy, confident photographs of women in the narrative, especially those of Allison's mother, Ruth Gibson Allison, together the narrative and the images shout out that poverty is desperation and hope, is ugly and beautiful, and is always complex.

Photographs and memoir work in a similar manner in Barbara Robinette Moss's first memoir, *Change Me into Zeus's Daughter* (1999). The book only contains four photographs, including the front-cover image of Moss's mother on the porch with her children. Selecting this image for the front cover directly engages with and challenges FSA and War on Poverty images. Didier Aubert argues that in documentary photography the "doorstep portrait" is "tacitly understood as a willing presentation of the self in a space located exactly on the line between public and private, a border which documentary usually makes its mission to cross, while nevertheless preserving the subjects' agency and dignity" (16). Moss relegates the documentarist, claiming authority to narrate her own story and to take readers across the threshold.

The careful choice and dispersal of photographs through the narrative helps to support the account Moss provides of her mother, a talented, educated woman broken down and beaten by her violent, alcoholic husband. The first three photographs, including the front-page porch photograph, position Moss's father at the center of the mother's transformation. After the porch photograph showing Dorris Robinette Moss swamped by her seven children, who take up most of the lower-left side of the frame, the next image of her shows Dorris before her marriage when she was involved in the buddy system of the Women's Marine Corps. The single, independent, smartly uniformed Dorris Robinette looks directly into the camera with an open smile. In between the two contrasting images of Dorris sits a blurred photograph of Moss's father, sitting casually smoking a cigarette. Moss's choice of photograph positions her violent, abusive father as an isolated, indistinct figure, removed from his family. He may be indistinct in the photo, but the narrative underscores his insidious presence in the lives of his wife and children, so the position of his image between the two shots of Dorris emphasizes his pivotal role in her transformation.

That transformation is made manifest by the position of the Marine Corps photograph in a chapter entitled "Shed No Beam upon My Weak Heart," a line taken from Stephen Crane's poem "Places among the Stars" (1905). In this chapter, Moss details a visit to her mother by a college friend, Betty, who descends unannounced to find a heavily pregnant Dorris and a home in disarray. Significantly, Betty brings photographs, and her visit exposes the children to a new way of thinking about and seeing their mother. They already knew about their mother's education and excellent recitation skills, but the photographs illuminate alternative epistemologies. I quote at length:

> I reached out and lifted a photograph from Mother's lap. She was singing, holding an open songbook. The photograph was black and white, but had been hand-painted. Bright red-orange shaped Mother's full mouth and her perfect curls were tinted a deep burgundy-brown. Teardrop diamonds dangled from her ears. She wore a robe, black ankle-strap heels with a V-cut toe and the watch hidden in her jewelry box. Her fingernails and toenails matched her red lips. I stared at the photograph, astonished. My mouth fell open like the one in the picture. I could tell it was Mother, but not the one I knew. I had never seen lipstick on her lips nor her lashes tinted dark, and had never seen her wear jewelry at all. It was as if this photograph had been taken of a movie star who looked like my mother: uniform curls, dark spidery lashes, perfect white teeth and dimples.... Mother took the photographs away from me and put them back on her lap underneath a photograph of her and Dad. (114–15)

The combination of photography and memoir allows Moss to chart her mother's journey, revealing that she is not just the mother we see on the front cover, nor is she any longer the woman in Betty's photograph. Confronted by the images of herself before marriage, Dorris actively represses that previous self, hiding those images "under a photograph of her and Dad" (115). Moss's recreation of this scene in the memoir plays on the notion that photographs may tell stories, but those stories are often incomplete. Family photographs capture people in the moment, freezing them in time, so Betty's photographs on their own cannot tell Dorris's story. Only in combination with later photographs and Moss's narrative can readers access a fuller account of the woman's story.

Similarly, in Rick Bragg's memoir series, images are the reader's gateway into his world. The first editions of all Bragg's memoirs contain photographs: family members adorn *All Over but the Shoutin'* (1997), *Ava's Man* (2001), and *The Prince of Frogtown* (2008); an old photograph of factory workers features on *The Most They Ever Had* (2009); and his culinary memoir *The Best Cook in the World: Tales from My Momma's Table* (2018) also shows a black-and-white photograph of his mother as a young girl alongside other women in the family. Although privileging the image at the outset, each of Bragg's texts works to reveal the limitations of photography. For instance, Bragg's second text, *Ava's Man*, contains two photographs of his maternal grandfather,

Charlie Bundrum, the subject of the memoir. The front cover shows a studio photograph of Charlie, dressed in his "Sunday-go-to-meetin' clothes," while the second image, which sits opposite the title page inside the book, shows Charlie displaying his fishing skills as he holds a sizeable catfish. Bragg kindly informed me that he selected the studio shot for the front cover because it clearly shows Charlie's face, but he also explained that he is "happier" with the fishing shot.[18] Bragg distinguishes between these two shots, placing greater worth on the family snapshot. Of the studio image, he writes:

> The face staring out from under a misshapen straw slouch hat looks tense and hard-edged, as if it can't wait for this foolishness to be over, and the eyes bore into you, challenge you. It is a studio photo, taken on Noble Street in Anniston, Alabama, in front of a painted-on palm.
> A poor man, posing.
> "That ain't Daddy," my aunt Jo said. (*Ava's Man* 10)

The second image, he says, is "more honest" and is

> the one I have on my living room wall. He is wearing ragged overalls, faded to gray, the legs specked with what seems to be fish blood, and he is prison-camp thin. In one big hand, strong fingers hooked through its gills, is a catfish three feet long, its head as broad as a bull calf.
> A poor man, winning. (*Ava's Man* 10)

Interestingly, the front-cover image is cut off above the hands, so the hands that Bragg invests with layers of meaning throughout the narrative are not immediately discernable. As I have argued elsewhere, Bragg renders Charlie's hands as symbols of poor white labor that provide a rebuke against notions of idleness (Robertson, "Memorializing" 459–74). Only in the second image, a family snapshot, do we see the strength of Charlie's hands as he lifts the large fish with his fingers. As Hirsch contends, "Family photographs trigger in their viewers an inclusive, affiliative look that embraces images of vastly different cultural origins" ("Familial" xvii). We can all recognize Charlie's delight in catching the big fish, so while Bragg reaffirms class distinctions by labeling Charlie as a "poor man" and draws attention to class markers such as the "ragged overalls," of all the photographs Bragg might have chosen, this one also transcends class by showing a man "winning." As a result, placing family photography into the public domain can be a political act, something that seems less and less obvious in a digital world that features several platforms saturated with inane photographs.

Of all poor white memoirs, the most overtly political photography appears in Janisse Ray's work. In *Wild Card Quilt* (2003), Ray's photographs adorn both the front and back cover of the book as well as numerous pages inside. Given Ray's role as an environmentalist, we expect to see the image of a pine flatwood forest being logged (240), but one image is striking for different reasons. At the end of the chapter "Keeping the School Open," Ray includes a photograph of Altamaha Elementary School. The image shows the school in the background, and in the foreground a banner tied between two trees reads, "Vote No to Save Our School." The caption states, "My mother attended rural Altamaha School" (62). Both the chapter and its photograph underpin Ray's personal commitment to rural communities but also to the sense of activism among locals. Ray charts throughout the chapter the sense of activism and the commitment of those campaigning to keep the school open and who "fight," "strategize," and demand a referendum by swiftly collecting "twenty-five hundred signatures" (54). In addition to this activism, Ray reveals that the town precincts voted to close the school, and only once results came in "from the outlying precincts" did it become clear that the vote was won and the school would remain open (61). This contradicts all those stereotypes of enlightened towns and cities versus backward-thinking, regressive rural areas.

Ray champions localism in *Wild Card Quilt*, and the chapter entitled "Local Economics" is particularly revealing. While Svetlana Boym warns of the "global epidemic of nostalgia" and the "affective yearning for a community with a collective memory" (xiv), Ray's localism contains little trace of nostalgia. Ray puts forward arguments for "co-sufficiency," cooperative farming, and economic reciprocity that suggest a localism for life, not just for Christmas (104). Her call for people to "become involved in local economics" may be idealistic, but at least she poses it as a viable alternative grounded in economics rather than an empty nostalgia for a lost or disappearing way of life that cannot move beyond its own longing (109). At the end of the chapter, Ray includes a photograph of a key Wayne County, Georgia, landmark, the disused building once used as a general store before becoming the home of "Fancy Honey: The Altamaha Apiaries." Ray's caption reads: "Tupelo honey is one of our regional products" (110). The building may be disused, but the caption refers to the vibrancy of local production, and unlike the photographs of deindustrialization and ruins that signify death that one sees elsewhere, the positioning of this image and its attendant caption signify a way forward rather than back.

Here, then, is a crucial difference between those photo-narratives that merely present a longing for some lost past without any future orientation, and the employment of photography to critique the status quo and put forward ideas for positive change. Walter Benn Michaels suggests: "Maybe what's needed is an art that's less interested in the abuses of the system than in the system itself" (*The Beauty* 41). In conclusion, the work of Maharidge and Williamson, in both *Journey to Nowhere* and *Someplace Like America*, tries to locate the causes of poverty. *Someplace Like America* specifically covers the years immediately after the 2008 recession and is not specifically southern in focus: unlike their Agee/Evans rephotography project, throughout the rest of their work Maharidge and Williamson are interested in the common experience of poverty across the United States. They venture south in this work, but never to reveal distinctiveness: only to reveal commonalities.

Each of the six parts of *Someplace Like America* opens with statements by various politicians, economists, and organizations, as well as with key dates in America's economic and labor history since the late 1970s. The subsequent narrative and photograph sections take us behind the sound bites, dates, and statistics to flesh out the actual lived experience of poor, working-class Americans. See part 3, section 9, "Hunger in the Homes," for example, in which Maharidge discusses their journalistic project on child poverty that was "published before the 2000 presidential election." He notes:

> America had never been richer—on paper. But the reality was that 13.5 million American children were living in poverty, according to the Children's Defense Fund. That was one out of every five kids. And 74 percent of their parents worked—they didn't take welfare. Many held two or three jobs, but the wages weren't enough to bring their children out of poverty or protect them from hunger. (89)

Williamson's shots of parents and children in long lines for healthcare provision and food banks visually underscore Maharidge's point that poverty is rife across the nation for working-class people of all races and ethnicities.

At the outset of *Someplace Like America*, Maharidge outlines the methodological questions that have underpinned their study of America's underclass since the 1980s:

> Do we want to tolerate hunger and desperation, with a large and growing portion of our population living in Third World conditions? Or do we want to care for one another? Do we want to reserve life chances for a very few who are wealthy, or do we desire to be a nation of opportunity, offering a level playing field for everyone? (4)

Despite the clear attempts throughout the work to link poverty directly to American politics and economics, Maharidge, just like several of the travel writers discussed in chapter 1, aligns abject "hunger and desperation" with developing countries rather than with the US economy. Nevertheless, he and Williamson are impassioned in their bid to bring American poverty to the foreground. For Andrew Martin, though, while Maharidge offers

> examples of ordinary Americans who have hit rock bottom and managed to make a new life for themselves, the people he documents tend to gravitate toward individual-level solutions to a structural problem; living within one's means and avoiding the trap of possessions. As movement scholars have so ably documented in case after case (Civil Rights, the women's movement), it is often only through collective action that the forces of inequality are successfully challenged. (305)

In his review of *Someplace Like America*, Martin clearly overlooks part 6, entitled "Rebuilding Ourselves, Then Taking America on a Journey to Somewhere New." In section 25, "A Woman of the Soil in Kansas City," Maharidge details his encounter with Sherri Harvel and her "new business Root Deep Urban farm." If readers of Ray's *Wild Card Quilt* think that her brand of cooperative farming is specific to rural locations, Maharidge shows otherwise. Readers of *Someplace Like America* may fear that Maharidge has slipped into idealism at the end of the book as he wonders, "could some of us find a way to live through hard times by growing our own food, not only surviving but finding some peace amid economic chaos?" But his account of Sherri's business and the Kansas City Center for Urban Agriculture shows that this alternative has an economic foundation (191). Oddly, the stories of hope toward the end of the book are not supported by Williamson's photographs. The introduction to this final part is preceded by an image of "[t]hirty-five hundred people waiting as long as fourteen hours to seek health care from the Remote Area Medical Volunteer Corps, an organization that once served only the desperately ill poor in Third World Nations but now operates in the United States. Wise, Virginia, 2008." Perhaps the lack of photographs detailing the community organizations covered in the final part reflects that, however powerful, these movements have yet to overturn the deeply entrenched poverty that Maharidge and Williamson encountered again and again.

Maharidge strikes positive notes throughout his narrative, perhaps none more so than in an account of their collaborative work with Bruce Springsteen, whose song "Youngstown" was drawn from their depiction of the town in *Journey to Nowhere*. Maharidge writes:

> [S]omeone might listen to "Youngstown" and be inspired, raising the collective consciousness. That's what Bruce was talking about. . . . You do "art" and then let

it go into the river. If you are doing it for the right reason and are very, very lucky, the work gets picked up downstream. It becomes a continuation of a story that must be told, a voice speaking over decades and centuries. (85)

So, while the FSA and War on Poverty images still play a key role in shaping the nation's ideas of poverty, perhaps works by Maharidge and Williamson, and others, will contribute to a reshaping of how we see and think about the poor.[19] In many ways, the FSA and War on Poverty case studies authorized authority, to return to Mirzoeff's argument, and have become shorthand for visually reading the southern poor white. In contrast, several contemporary photo-narratives, including memoirs, show us that there is more to see if democracy is to be truly democratized; the next chapter makes a more concerted turn to poor white life-writing to explore in greater detail how those with firsthand experiences of poverty expose capitalism's inherent inequalities.

CHAPTER THREE

"What I Am Here for Is to Claim My Life":
Life-Writing and Reclaiming the Poor White Self

> It is rich people, usually, who live on in biographies,
> in the pages of the social register.
> —Rick Bragg, *The Most They Ever Had*

It is well established that since the 1970s writers emerging out of southern poor white backgrounds have used life-writing to offer their own insights into economic deprivation and its impact on individuals, families, and communities.[1] As Karen Keeley recognizes, in the past, "[a]uthoring one's own story" was "a liberty not allowed to those people whom society has declared unfit; that is, the people who have been deemed unfit both to breed and narrate" (31), but in recent years, James Watkins notes, "we hear the autobiographical voices" of those "from poor and working class backgrounds affirming their regionally specific class identity" ("Contemporary Autobiography" 451).[2] Despite the regionalism that runs to varying degrees throughout this body of poor white life-writing, these texts more importantly transcend region as they debunk constructed notions of the southern community, provide a searing critique of socioeconomic policies that detrimentally shape the lives of the nation's poor, and in some cases offer alternative models based on communitarianism.

Since this body of work transcends southernness, it constitutes not a subgenre of southern autobiography but of life-writing in its broadest sense, and these works are forms of life-writing rather than autobiography, because the latter is commonly "too abstract, too masculine and Western" (Huddart 3).[3] I term this body of work "poor white life-writing," unlike David A. Davis, who labels these texts "white trash autobiographies." While writers such as Dorothy Allison embrace the term "trash" and seek to refashion it through their writing, labeling this subgenre "white trash" restricts the subversive quality of much of this writing.[4] Even where these writers celebrate aspects of the so-called trashy elements of their lives, their texts reveal the distortive, debilitating, and derogative nature of the term.

This examination of contemporary poor white life-writing begins with the postcolonial concept of writing back, but these turns to postcolonial theory do not overlook the central irony that today's poor whites are the descendants of those who moved to the South in the waves of colonization that displaced numerous Native American tribes during the eighteenth and nineteenth centuries. Indeed, many of these writers openly acknowledge the role their ancestors played in Indian removal and also, perversely, in the foundation of a southern society to which they themselves never fully belonged. Although Janisse Ray, in *Ecology of a Cracker Childhood* (1999), takes pride in the fact that her family's Georgia roots go back "a hundred and eighty years," she refuses to gloss either the violent defeat of Creek Indians in 1818 or the environmental damage wreaked upon the landscape by white colonial settlers (84). Similarly, Rick Bragg traces his ancestral lineage back to "the first white settlers" in the Deep South (*Ava's Man* 32), but in *The Prince of Frogtown* (2008) he asks readers to look "deeper" to "see the ghosts of a people who were here before," before he goes on to detail the Creek War of 1813–1814, Andrew Jackson's barbarity, and the "genocide of a nation" (42, 44). However brief their allusions to the Native peoples who were forcibly removed to make way for their settler ancestors, Bragg and Ray at least avoid entirely depending on a "myth of a native South that is white rather than red" (Benson 167). So it is, of course, the subordinate class position of these writers, and their attempts to write themselves and their people into the nation's consciousness in new and empowering ways, that enable aspects of postcolonial theory to provide a useful insight into the act of writing back.

Leigh Gilmore explains: "Every autobiography is the fragment of a theory. It is also an assembly of theories of the self and self-representation; of personal identity and one's relation to a family, a region, a nation; and of citizenship and a politics of representativeness (and exclusion)" (12). As marginalized groups talk back to and challenge the mainstream, aspects of the postcolonial come to the fore. Bill Ashcroft, Gareth Griffiths, and Helen Tiffin discuss how the process of writing back does not simply involve "reversing the hierarchical order" but instead requires an interrogation of "the philosophical assumptions on which that order was based" (32). Here, of course, it is not the empire writing back to the center, but those marginalized along class lines writing back about impoverishment to a center that promotes a grand narrative of wealth and prosperity. In her work on the postmodern and postcolonial, Sidonie Smith forwards the notion that "the wresting of an individual narrative can be seen as a necessary point of departure for liberatory practices," providing an insight into the political nature of poor white life-writing. In particular, Smith argues, "[a]ssembling an experiential history can function as counter-memory, a means to re-narrativize the past and to break the silences of official history" (39). Certainly, in Catherine Gallagher and Stephen Greenblatt's terms, these autobiographical works share a "counter-historical impulse" (67). In their study of new historicism, Gallagher and Greenblatt describe counterhistories as texts and anecdotes that "make apparent the slippages, cracks, fault lines, and surprising absences in the monumental structures that dominated a more traditional historicism" (17).

To trace the beginnings of poor white life-writing that destabilizes history, critics commonly turn to Harry Crews's *A Childhood: The Biography of a Place* (1978), which is widely regarded as the seminal text of this subgenre; Watkins recommends that Crews be "credited with writing the quintessential redneck autobiography" ("The Use of *I*" 28). Crews's text certainly laid a foundation for subsequent writers from poor white backgrounds to articulate and make sense of their experiences through the autobiographical form. Crews's work emerged out of the civil rights movement, as previously marginalized people and groups reclaimed the power of self-representation, and he explicitly champions the power of "I" to "get me to the place where I needed to go" (25). Significantly, this challenge to authorized history comes in the ability of the autobiographical "I" to work on behalf of either a familial and/or communal "We"; indeed, Henry Louis Gates Jr. surmises that autobiographical works by minority writers have the capacity to "tell a new collective history" (111).

In Bragg's first memoir, *All Over but the Shoutin'*, he attempts to transcend the authorial "I" when he momentarily turns the narrative over to his extended family and asks readers to "[l]isten to them" as they narrate the family history (30).[5] Similarly, in Allison's semiautobiographical novel *Bastard Out of Carolina* (1993), her protagonist, Ruth Anne "Bone" Boatwright, asks readers to "watch" her mother, Anney: "Watch her in the diner, laughing, pouring coffee, palming tips, and frying eggs. . . . Watch her eyes and how they sink into her face, the lines that grow out from that tight stubborn mouth, the easy banter that rises from the deepest place inside her" (14). These invitations to listen and look do not objectify but rather attempt to break down the common misperceptions of poor lives. One of Allison's central objectives, she states, is to make her readers "care." In an interview with Michael LeMahieu, Allison discusses her fascination with "background people," the people "who are not in the front of pictures, and what I do is bring them to the front of the picture. What I do is try to make an emotional connection for readers with people that they don't ordinarily have an emotional connection to" (658).

As well as encouraging readers to see their lives in new ways, most of these poor white writers had to overcome their own complex relationships to home in all of its manifestations. In Ray's *Ecology of a Cracker Childhood*, she remembers going to college and how she tried to shed her past. Having returned home to reembrace that past, she reflects: "It has taken me a decade to whip the shame, to mispronounce words and shun grammar when mispronunciation and misspeaking are part of my dialect, to own the bad blood. What I come from has made me who I am" (33). Subsequently, as she depicts both her return home and her desire to reclaim the heritage she shunned, Ray occasionally slips into a localized vernacular; similar slips into regional dialects appear in a number of poor white autobiographies, with Bragg, for example, recounting how, after learning something about race relations, he and his brother stopped throwing stones at black children who lived near them: "at least, we didn't throw no more rocks" (*All Over* 66). For Wayne Flynt, Bragg's colloquialisms are disquieting, because while "[t]his is the language and cadence of an Appalachian storyteller . . . it is sometimes grinding when the author of the memoir is a Pulitzer Prize–winning correspondent for America's most esteemed newspaper [the *New York Times*]" (323). Flynt's observation overlooks the dual perspective of poor white writers, who, although now educated and far removed from their impoverished childhoods, never completely lose the cadences of home. As Allison points out, "[y]ou lose your accent, but you never lose the rhythms, the paces of your language" (LeMahieu 668). These vernacular slips offer more than local color; they assert the authors' insider status and their connections to the places and people they write about. Yet the texts offer more than an insight into poor white communities: they often serve to reenvisage ideas of community as they interrogate ideas of belonging and the constructed, or as Scott Romine puts it, the "fantastical nature" of community or a "social group" (*The Narrative Forms* 1).

In the US South, ancestry has long been used as a means of authenticating a regionally specific, white communal identity. In *The Mind of the South* (1941), W. J. Cash considered the increased fascination with ancestry in the period between the Civil War and Reconstruction, asserting that while a fascination with ancestry was typical among the planter class, who sought to establish aristocratic lineages whose roots could be found in the Old World, such appeals were not restricted to this class. He continues:

> [T]he common whites came in this period to participate in the legend even more fully than they had done in the past. If they did not actually drift into thinking of their forefathers as having been aristocrats—and they sometimes did—their

identification of themselves with the master class was so close that the practical result was very much the same; that their pride did attach itself to the notion of the South's aristocratic heritage nearly as militantly as did that of any scion of the plantation. (125)

In a similar vein, James C. Cobb argues that contemporary southerners, both "blacks and whites alike," share "the urge to affirm their southernness" (148). For Cobb, this "urge" has been intensified in the wake of sociopolitical upheaval and the individualism championed by neoliberalism. In reaction to globalization, Cobb contends that black and white southerners come together to exist "under a common cultural canopy," to establish a "common attachment" to a meaningful idea of region and belonging (148). While Cobb is fully aware of the racial tensions that continue to prevent any easy route to a unified South, his argument depends on the idea of a cohesive, white South, one where even the "once-despised redneck" has become integral to the region in its fight against the "homogenizing pressures permeating American mass society" (206). Although the concepts of "redneck" or "white trash," as Matt Wray and Annalee Newitz explain, are now "increasingly popular and relevant ... in mainstream US culture," the idea that poor whites have now been welcomed into the bosom of the southern community implies both the dissipation of prejudices toward that group and that poor whites desired entry into an already established idea of community (Introduction 7).

Indeed, many believe that the Civil War remains the central unifier of the southern white community. In her afterword to Suzanne Jones and Sharon Monteith's *South to a New Place* (2002), Diane Roberts argues that "the Civil War is the still-obsessed-over central moment in the white southern psyche" (365). Of course, the US South has a wide range of organizations all designed to help preserve a particular brand of "southern heritage." From the long-established United Daughters of the Confederacy and Sons of Confederate Veterans to recent associations such as the Southern Heritage Preservation Group and the white supremacist group League of the South, certain southerners unite to maintain the region's Confederate past. The visual reminders of that past, from Confederate flags to Civil War statues and monuments, have come under intense scrutiny since the latter decades of the twentieth century, most recently erupting in violent, deadly clashes in Charlottesville, Virginia, in 2017 as statues were removed from public places.[6] This is not simply a white versus black issue, and southern whites are not, and never have been, united together around the Civil War and its memorialization, even though Tony Horwitz, during his Civil War quest through the South in *Confederates in the Attic*, points to the ways in which Confederate nostalgia erodes some of the region's class tensions. In particular, he describes a tavern in Charleston, South Carolina, where "a curious mix of well-dressed professionals and roughneck laborers" prop up the bar "endlessly debating the Civil War" (57).

Turn instead to Bragg's second memoir, *Ava's Man*, in which he problematizes the notion that all poor whites participate in this southern obsession with the "Lost Cause." Bragg acknowledges that "[s]ome historians say the time that defines us, as a people, was the Civil War, and I guess that is true for those Southerners who hold tight to yellowed daguerreotypes of defiant colonels, distant ancestors who glare at the camera like it was a cannon, leaning on their swords" (94). Yet, he writes:

> [Y]ou seldom hear people of the foothills talk much about the Civil War, contrary to the belief that all of us down here are sitting around waiting for the South to Rise Again, gazing at our etchings of Robert E. Lee and sipping whiskey from the silver cups our great-aunt hid in the corncrib when she saw the Yankees comin'.
>
> But you hear them talk a lot about the Depression.... They cannot tell you who commanded much of anything at Little Round Top or Missionary Ridge, but they know the names of all the knothead mules that dragged their daddies cussing and sweating across ground so poor that grass would not grow. (95)

As Bragg mocks the notion that the Civil War looms large in every white southerner's imagination, he insists instead on the significance of the Depression for poor whites, revealing that grand narratives of an aristocratic South bear little relation to the lived experiences of poor whites. As Allison surmises, "I was born trash in a land where the people all believe themselves natural aristocrats. Ask any white Southerner. They'll take you back two generations, say, 'Yeah, we had a plantation.' The hell we did" (*Two or Three Things* 32). Writers such as Bragg and Allison, as Matthew Guinn explains, have begun to "defy the traditional approaches to history, place, and community" (xi), so to read these works is to read about southern whites who, like Bragg's mother, undertook "backbreaking work" picking cotton (*All Over* 24), or like Allison's mother "worked forty years as a waitress" (*Two or Three Things* 25). For poor white writers, their attempts to express their identities depend less on a sense of passively resurrecting an older sense of community but rather on destabilizing and reenvisaging the preexisting community, and even when we find ancestral searches in poor white life-writing, they usually undermine preconceived notions of the region.

In part, Bragg and other poor white writers create fissures in the southern narrative by refusing to sanitize ancestry. Their memoirs often focus on those regarded as "the bad poor," those, as Allison explains, who do not fit into the national myth of the "good poor" (*Trash* vii). Opposed to the sentimentalized notion of the honorable yeoman farmer espoused so heartedly by the Agrarians in their *I'll Take My Stand* (Twelve Southerners, 1930), Bragg, Allison, and others write unflinchingly about their families and communities, depicting all manner of violence, domestic, sexual, and psychological abuse, drug dependency, adultery, mental health problems, and unlawful activities, to list just some of the harsh realities found across this body of writing that aligns it with the Grit Lit and Rough South categories to be discussed in chapter 4. Ray expressly states that she has worked hard "to own the bad blood" (*Ecology* 33), and for Allison, writing is "a process of making peace with the violence of my childhood, in owning up to it and finding a way to talk about it that did not make me more ashamed of myself or those I loved" (*Trash* viii). While they refuse to overlook issues of "bad blood," of family members whose stories are often marred by death, abuse, and violence, these writers do not accept easy classifications of "good" and "bad."

Certainly, in Jeanette Walls's account of her eccentric parents who inflicted abject poverty on their children, she presents them as flawed human beings with a dignity that many of their actions belie. In *The Glass Castle* (2005), Walls recounts her childhood in stark detail, which allows readers to understand why, years later in Manhattan, she did not stop the taxi she was riding in when she passed her homeless mother "rooting through a Dumpster" (3). Unlike the parents of most of these poor white writers, Walls's parents chose poverty: her mother inherited family land worth at least a million dollars but refused to sell because, she claims, "[m]y father taught me you never sell land" (323). Walls only discovers this hidden and untapped wealth as an adult and only reveals this knowledge to readers toward the end of the book to underscore the senselessness of her horrific childhood.

At the start of chapter 2, Walls confronts readers with the image of her three-year-old self going up flames as she prepared hot dogs without adult supervision. Despite her pain, she remembers the serenity of the hospital that was so far removed from her chaotic home life. She recalls, "You never had to worry about running out of stuff like food or ice or even chewing gum. I would have been happy staying in that hospital forever" (13). The terrible burns she suffers at the age of three are just the beginning of the neglect that she and her siblings endure, particularly after the family moves to the father's hometown of Welch, West Virginia. Despite her father's tall tales of the titular glass castle that he plans to build for the family, the house they purchase is the stuff of nightmares; its horrors are not fully captured in Destin Daniel Cretton's 2017 movie adaptation of Walls's memoir. In the text, the house does not have indoor plumbing and they cannot afford electricity (180), but that is far from unusual in many of these memoirs. However, their living conditions are particularly extreme: from the beginning, the kitchen (one of just three rooms in the house) is off limits because of faulty wiring and a never-repaired, leaking roof; they resort to eating "cat food" (205), and Walls witnesses her mother eating maggot-infested ham (205); Walls herself eats leftover food from the school trash cans while their mother hides chocolate from her children to feed her own self-diagnosed sugar addition (207–8); the house is so cold that in desperation to heat the house Walls's sister Lori uses kerosene to light a fire, which explodes, and Lori's badly charred legs go untreated (214). The ceiling in the children's bedroom leaks and goes unrepaired, even when Walls's brother Brian has to "spread a tarp over himself to keep the dripping water off" (222). These are just some of the terrible conditions and events that occur throughout their childhood; perhaps one of the worst, but equally predictable, arises when their father steals the money the children are saving to make their escape from the family home (272–75).

The idiosyncrasies and eccentricities of Rex and Rose Mary Walls condemn their children to a life of abject deprivation, but Walls refuses to condemn her parents, even naming the book after her father's whimsical dreams. In a *Los Angeles Times* article about Cretton's film, Walls observes that the producers, "instead of resorting to stereotypes of wacky squatters and crazy alcoholics ... captured the complexities of people like my mother and father who, for all their faults and demons, were also creative and intelligent with pride and dreams" (Walls, "Jeanette Walls Was Warned"). To that extent, the film mirrors the book, in which Rex and Rose Walls are more than just neglectful parents. For them, poverty is merely a consequence of living an unfettered life: Walls reflects that once her parents move to New York and find a squatter community on the Lower East Side, they finally locate "people like themselves, people who lived unruly lives battling authority and who liked it that way" (316). To that end, Walls's narrative shares its compassionate approach to family members who on the surface fit constructed notions of the "bad poor" with the other autobiographies and memoirs that compose this body of poor white life-writing. As these writers acknowledge the "bad blood," Katherine Henninger argues, they open up the southern canon to "the queered of southern culture" and undertake "the first step in constructing a truly accommodating 'home' and nation" (147). This requires not simply being accepted into an already existing sense of community but changing the very foundation of that community. These writers do not seek acceptance into an exclusionary southern white community but acceptance into part of a national and sometimes global community to which neither class nor race prevent entry.

There is a fine balance, of course, between depicting the nuanced lives of the poor and romanticizing poverty. The project of reclaiming the past in poor white life-writing carries with it attendant problems of nostalgic distortion. As David Harvey explains, under late capitalism and in a world increasingly shaped by generic commodification,

> historical tradition is reorganized as a museum culture, not necessarily of high modernist art, but of local history, of local production, of how things once upon a time were made, sold, consumed, and integrated into a long-lost and often romanticized daily life (one from which all trace of oppressive social relations may be expunged). (*Condition* 303)

The past is commonly seen through a sepia lens, and in the US South even those who experienced abject levels of poverty in the past often struggle to overcome regionally specific forms of nostalgia; for instance, throughout his writing Bragg struggles to avoid the pitfalls of authenticity, and his contribution to the region's most successful magazine, *Southern Living*, brings questions of nostalgia and authenticity to the foreground. As Tracy Lauder notes, since its inception in 1966, *Southern Living* has "prescribed and perpetuated its own unique vision of Southern culture": a vision both decidedly white and focused on affluent southerners (35). Lauder is among many who note the exclusions and distortions that shape the magazine's constructed vision of the South, something that the publication itself has never denied.[7] In their commemorative, *Life at Southern Living: A Sort of Memoir* (2000), John Logue and Gary McCalla reflect on an early "White Paper" from 1968 in which they stipulated that *Southern Living* "stories will not deal with civic problems, socio-economic issues, or politics" (141). Although more racially diverse today, *Southern Living* largely remains a magazine by white, wealthy people for white, wealthy people, and if its dominant whiteness is slowly being expunged, its class politics remain. In his discussion of Josephine Humphreys's *Rich in Love* (1987), Romine examines what it means to be considered "eligible for *Southern Living*": what, he asks "does such eligibility entail?" (*The Real South* 216). Poor southerners certainly do not form *Southern Living*'s target demographic, as Bragg felt compelled to point out to the editor in his piece, "The Impossible Turkey" (2011), in which he challenges the magazine's glossy depictions of perfectly prepared and presented food, claiming that its "immaculate" Thanksgiving turkey "hurt my mama's feelings" (*My Southern Journey* 90–91). The magazine not only does not cater to the region's poor, it actually depoliticizes poverty as it renders it "homely" or "traditional" in its quest for "authentic" southern foodways.[8] Bragg's celebration of the past and regionally distinctive foodways makes this once poor white more than eligible for the region's most successful magazine.

In his "Southern Journal" section for *Southern Living*, despite his constant, self-conscious attempts to "write of this South in a way beyond clichés," Bragg appears to argue for a distinctive, unique South, particularly in terms of cuisine (*My Southern Journey* 13). Bragg's entries, in line with *Southern Living*'s mantra, promote the idea that there is a "real," "unique" South that can be literally consumed, since it is possible, Bragg suggests, "to taste the past" (*My Southern Journey* 100). Even though Bragg celebrates the everyday working people of the US South as opposed to the wealthy people who adorn the pages of *Southern Living*, he appears to be invested in the idea of a "uniquely authentic" South. For Bragg, those turns to an "authentic" past often appear when he contemplates modernity. In the face of a South that has, in Bragg's terms, "become so homogenized, so bland," he idealizes localism and tradition (*Ava's Man* 18). Fred Davis critiques uncritical laments for the past, arguing that "so carried away can the nostalgic mood make one that he or she obliterates from memory the unmistakable pain and tragedy associated with what has been singled out for adoration" (38). As I have argued elsewhere (Robertson, "Memorializing"), Bragg creates his own illusory sense of the past in *Ava's Man* when he thinks about his grandfather, Charlie Bundrum, claiming that "[t]he realities of this new, true South are not as romantic as in Charlie's time, as bleak and painful as that time was for people of his class" (249). Here, while Bragg acknowledges the difficulties experienced by poor whites during the Depression, his appeal to that time as "romantic" risks dehistoricizing the past in the terms laid out by Harvey.

While Bragg's most blatant and sepia-tinged love for the South appears in his *Southern Living* articles, where in article after article he descends into foodways frivolity by bemoaning the decline of unique eateries and celebrating forms of "authentic" cuisine, and in his food memoir *The Best Cook in the World*, strains of foodways nostalgia also run throughout his earlier memoir series, notably in a section on tomatoes and gardening in *All Over but the Shoutin'*. In this section, Bragg pivots back and forth between nostalgia and the need for caution about romantic conceptions of the past. He notes: "To this day I dream not of beautiful women and wealth and power as often as I dream of sausage gravy over biscuits with a sliced tomato on the side, and a small lake of grits—not that bland, pale, watery restaurant stuff I would not serve on death row, but grits cooked with butter and plenty of salt and black pepper" (46). However, Bragg's notion of "authentic foodways" is at least tempered by his reflection that "Momma kept a garden, which sounds romantic to people who have never held a hoe" (46). Although seemingly avoiding the nostalgia trap, Bragg goes on, "[s]ometimes, even though I know it is my own foolish romanticism, I think about having a garden again, to see if I retain any of the skills of my people, or if I have just become too citified to do anything real" (46). For all his caution about romanticizing the past, he cannot seem to shake the sense that hoeing the garden or having tools to build and fix is somehow more "real," and more "authentic," than an urban life and middle-class occupation.

In a similar vein to Bragg, Ray might be seen to idealize the past as she laments the fact that "agrarian communities are diminished." Even though she acknowledges that "[f]arming communities ... are not without dysfunction, ostracism, and strife," those issues do not outweigh the fact that, for her, in these communities "the human spirit seems to thrive" (*Wild Card* xii). Nostalgia runs throughout Ray's writing as she explores her journey back to reclaim her southern past. In *Wild Card Quilt*, she focuses on her return to Georgia to live and work on family land. Once the space of many of her fondest childhood memories of time spent with her maternal grandmother, Beulah, Ray tries to bring the now "neglected" house and farm back to life so that she can enter "a history that stretched backward not simply to the limits of my memory but to the farthest point of my family's memory" (3). Yet Ray ultimately promotes localism over regionalism, and communitarianism over community; and surely Bragg is too well traveled to really believe in the "authenticity" he expatiates. For all her wistful neo-agrarian notions of returning to a simpler, more honest way of life, environmentalist Ray does not sugarcoat the ecological destruction wrought by settlers and their descendants. She might proudly reclaim her "people," but she readily acknowledges that their "legacy is ruination" (*Ecology* 87), while Bragg's nods to foodways and traditional practices often point to the inauthenticity of the "authentic." Take, for example, his account of the homemade cold remedy he was given as a child. He recalls the warming sensation of the "toddy," the hot, sweetened, and alcohol-laced drink thought to bring relief from cold and flu symptoms. He says: "They called it, oddly, a 'toddy.' Their homemade remedies ... varied a little depending on which grandparents were mixing the concoctions" (*My Southern Journey* 30). Any well-traveled, educated individual such as Bragg surely knows, or could easily find out at the click of a mouse, that the cold remedy is not unique to southern poor white culture: while the origins of the toddy are debated, with India and Ireland prime culprits, the drink did not emerge out of the US South. Although Bragg offers the toddy up as another example of the unique folkways of Appalachia, there is enough to suggest that he knows better. After all, this isn't southern folksy; at best it's global folksy. Indeed, in *The Best Cook in the World*, Bragg tempers his pleas for southern foodways' authenticity by acknowledging that many of his mother's recipes "come from across an ocean, from the French countryside ... from the Irish, English, Scots, Germans, even the Nordic people. Others came from those already here, from the Creek, Choctaw, and Cherokee" (15). When Fred Davis claims to find it "surprising" that southern poor white "stories have found a mainstream audience" (191), we might usefully look at those moments in poor white autobiographies that resonate globally and talk across race and class boundaries. Even when Bragg's memories of the "real" taste of homegrown fruit and vegetables, or an "authentic" toddy, might ring with the distortive tones of nostalgia, they are always tempered by the wider narrative of his family's struggle to eke out a living. In the work of poor white autobiographers, food references play a political function as they, in Jolene Hubbs's terms, "forge fresh ways to bear witness to hunger" (8). The need to see and recognize hunger is clearly important, because Romine suggests that in a world where "the pleasures of consumption predominate ... accounts of hunger and lack" are typically "lost to history" ("God and the MoonPie" 60). These memoirs are not just personal stories but testimonies that enter wider politicized debates about poverty and welfare, thereby transcending southernness and rudimentary concerns with authenticity.

One of the most obvious ways poor white life-writing offers an alternative history comes in its challenge to ideas of post–World War II affluence. The idea that in the postwar years everyone shared in the nation's wealth belies the truth of persistent poverty for many of those at the bottom of the economic ladder. In the US South, Hubbs explains, "Depression-era images of rail-thin, rickets-suffering southerners had given way to a postwar picture of unprecedented prosperity and plenty" (12), yet as Noam Chomsky notes, the widening gap between rich and poor countries since the 1960s is also reflected "within the rich societies as well" (112). In both the United States and the United Kingdom, the pioneers of neoliberalism, "the business press exults in 'spectacular' and 'stunning' profit growth, applauding the extraordinary concentration of wealth among the top few percent of the population, while for the majority, conditions continues to stagnate or decline" (Chomsky 112). Even the "discovery" of Appalachian poverty in the 1960s was not enough to remind Americans that poverty is as synonymous with capitalism as wealth: because Appalachian poverty was so localized, it was read as an exception to the nation's economic progress. The dominant narrative, or what Kathleen Stewart terms the "chant of certainty," defined the postwar United States as a place "of capitalism and modernization, of individualism, materialism, education, reason, democracy." As a result, Stewart continues, "the cultural productions that constitute an 'America' of sorts are frozen into essentialized 'objects' with fixed identities; a prefab landscape of abstract 'values' puts an end to the story of 'America' before it begins" (3). Several of these poor white writers open gaps in that story as they reflect on childhoods in the latter decades of the twentieth century.

In *All Over but the Shoutin'*, Bragg observes that despite witnessing his father's violent, drunken rages and his mother's suffering, he largely enjoyed his childhood, "because my momma's kin were kind to us, and helped to make it so. In those years, the early 1960s, there was barely enough for their own families, yet they shared their lives with us" (45). In this account of the postwar years, affluence plays no part in the lives of Bragg's maternal extended family. More forcefully, Barbara Robinette Moss opens her first autobiography, *Change Me into Zeus's Daughter* (2000), with a scene of abject hunger as she recollects a moment in 1962 when she and her siblings watched, in ravenous horror, as their mother washed, prepared, and ate the only food left: "poisoned corn and beans." Only once it is clear that the contaminated meal has not killed their mother do the children devour the rest (19). Hubbs defines this focus on hunger in the work of both Moss and Allison as a form of "famineways," an oppositional play on the increasingly popular wave of southern "foodways" studies. Yet Hubbs is primarily preoccupied with how famineways operate within literary parameters, only briefly considering the counternarrative at play as these writers depict "an unrecognized hunger" (13).

Moss's concern with food and hunger is deeply politicized across both her memoirs as she reflects on the welfare system in both the 1960s and the 1980s. In *Fierce* (2004), Moss details her adult life and journey toward fulfilling her childhood dream of becoming an artist from the early 1970s through the late 1990s. In conjunction with *Change Me into Zeus's Daughter*, Moss provides a searing critique of the nation's attitude to both the poor and welfare provision, and like many of the other poor white writers who engage with welfare, she offers an important contribution to the welfare debate. In his work on the erosion of welfare since the 1970s, particularly President Bill Clinton's repeal of Aid to Families with Dependent Children (AFDC) in 1996, Robert Asen notes that in the various committees convened to debate AFDC and other welfare provisions, "[e]xperts affiliated with universities, private foundations, advocacy groups, and think tanks were over represented . . . and recipients were severely underrepresented" (229). These memoirs may not play any direct role in shaping policy, but they play in a role in refashioning their readers' understanding of welfare. The direct experiences in these memoirs of receiving, or in some cases not receiving, welfare help to construct another view of poverty.

In *Fierce*, Moss remembers the financial challenges she repeatedly faced as a young, single, working mother and recounts the various ways she made money as she worked through college in Florida and then on to a graduate degree in Iowa. Readers of her earlier work will remember that her family never applied for welfare and rarely accepted charity. Her father, in particular, "was too proud to accept any government help, even when he was out of work, and he had a low opinion of those who did" (*Change Me* 192). Such antipathy toward welfare and charity is far from uncommon among the poor and is often associated with pride. Listing some of the commonalities between Bragg's *All Over but the Shoutin'* and Moss's *Change Me into Zeus's Daughter*, Flynt notes that both texts "chronicle family resentment against welfare and charity" (318). Although these writers point to feelings of pride and resentment in relation to welfare, shame is the prevailing emotion.

In *Change Me*, Moss recalls a time when her brother Stewart and her father accepted food stamps in payment for a car, but rather than spending the food stamps themselves, they asked the original recipient, Ralph, to complete the transaction to spare their embarrassment; however, compared with their usually restricted purchasing power, Moss remembers being overwhelmed by the wealth of food purchased, which made her question "how Ralph got the food stamps, exactly *where* he went to apply for them and if there was any chance to get them for us" (198). Here and in *Fierce*, while Moss levels blame at her father for not applying for welfare, she also blames a society that shames and belittles those in need.

In *Fierce*, Moss explains that despite trying to provide for herself and her son without depending on the state, when "Jason came down with mononucleosis," she had no choice but to turn to welfare. Quickly learning that during visits to the Department of Social Services she must act poor, Moss "walked like a field hand" and put on her "thickest Southern accent" (96). Despite the reality of her hardship, Moss had to perform poverty to fit the stereotype of the welfare recipient. Yet whatever resentment Moss felt, she still champions the welfare state:

> As embarrassing as government assistance was for me, it was truly a blessing. Overnight, we had enough food. And we had medical care.... I don't know how we would have survived without this program. It still scares me to think about it. As a mother, I'm supposed to protect my child; and when I did not have the

resources to do that, our government provided assistance. With all the criticism Social Services has received through the years, it's hard to think of them as heroic. But every day they help mothers feed and protect their children. (97)

Reflecting on this period of her life in the late 1980s from the vantage point of 2004, Moss writes with the knowledge that this lifeline for individuals and families has been continually eroded, thereby politicizing her personal, highly emotional case. Her emphasis on motherhood is particularly loaded given the demonization of welfare mothers in the Ronald Reagan period.[9] As Alice O'Connor summarizes, "amidst the conservative backlash of the 1980s, 'single motherhood' and 'dependency' were increasingly ideological terms. Intentionally or not, they tapped into powerful and resurgent political opposition, to welfare, to poor people's reproductive freedom, and to the long-standing feminist objective of providing women with the means to gain independence from men" (254). As Moss tries to stand alone, distancing herself from previously abusive relationships, her single income is not enough to cope with the extra demands of medical costs, leaving her with only two choices: "drop out of school or apply for government assistance" (*Fierce* 95). In short, she applies for welfare because she is a good mother, not a bad one as antiwelfare rhetoric would label her.

Welfare provision commonly appears throughout this body of poor white life-writing. In Bragg's *All Over but the Shoutin'*, he remembers that despite his mother's best efforts to financially support her children, she had no choice but to apply for government aid and to accept charity, writing, "I know it killed her deep inside to go begging, but it would have destroyed her to watch her three sons do without" (41). While for Margaret Bragg the well-being of her children comes before her own pride, in *The Glass Castle*, Walls's eccentric parents shy away from work but also flatly and resolutely refuse to accept any form of charity. As Walls depicts her parents' choice to inflict abject poverty on their children and critiques their decision to refuse charity, she builds a case for the importance of welfare. Reflecting on their neighbors in Welch, West Virginia, who receive welfare, she notes: "[I]t wasn't so bad. I know Mom was opposed to welfare, but those kids got food stamps and clothing allowances. The state bought them coal and paid for their school lunches" (227). Of course, many refuse welfare because of the stigma it carries. Bragg notes that only when he grew up and was educated in class and societal divisions did he realize: "I was supposed to be ashamed that when a teacher called roll for lunch money, my name was not called. It was stamped 'FREE.' Welfare lunches" (*All Over* 42). Once educated into shared and accepted societal knowledge, shame enshrouds welfare, so feelings of shame arise out of societal attitudes to welfare as much as they do from internal sources of pride.

Societal attitudes are at the center of Moss's consideration of welfare. When she gratefully acknowledges the welfare she was awarded, she thanks "our government," sending out a communal call in a period of increasing individuation and pushing for the reimagining of a national community (*Fierce* 97). She does so by exposing the prejudices of the local community in Iowa where she lived during the period she received welfare. If having to demonstrably perform poverty was not bad enough, in this section of *Fierce* Moss also details the treatment she faced from neighbors in a community where she and her son were the only family to receive food stamps and where the postman "made certain everyone knew about it" (97). Moss was lambasted by the postman for "[s]camming off society" (98) and found an anonymous note under her door stating: "*Food stamps come out of the taxpayer's pocket! Why should I have to raise your child?*" and "*Your trash can must be off the street before sundown*" (italics in original). Moss's presence in the middle-class neighborhood is deeply unsettling for her neighbors, who are normally reassured by the segregation of neighborhoods along class lines (99). The community's response to its poor neighbor reflects the increasing hostility toward the disenfranchised throughout the 1980s. As Asen observes, in this period "the non-needy were assigned ultimate responsibility for the country's economic woes. Reagan invoked them as the sole example of government waste. Even the truly needy did not escape suspicion, for Reagan singled out the poor as a group to be examined for waste and fraud" (85–86).

Emboldened by this antipoverty rhetoric, Moss's neighbors take it upon themselves to admonish and undertake the role of arbiters of middle-class normality. O'Connor notes how poverty research is utilized "as a form of cultural affirmation: a powerful reassurance that poverty occurs outside or in spite of core American values and practices, whether those are defined in terms of capitalist markets, political democracy, self-reliance, and/or a two-parent, white, middle-class family ideal" (15). Moss's neighbors find her guilty of dependency and breaking with familial norms: her limited purchasing power also comes under scrutiny when she fails to meet the cultural norms of the community. Moss explains: "[T]hey chopped my backyard picnic table into kindling because they thought it was 'an eyesore.' They painted white the old wooden rocking chair on my front porch—also, apparently, 'an eyesore.' And my bucket-size gargoyle planter simply disappeared" (93). Moss's neighbors, schooled in exclusionary middle-class values, respond with horror, repulsion, and assertive action to eliminate these apparent transgressions. Their response mirrors the neoliberal turn in the 1980s and "the fantasy of abundance," which, as Jodi Dean argues, promoted "the idea that anyone and everyone can participate, contribute, express themselves" but which only served to prevent "us from recognizing the underlying inequalities inextricable from complex networks" (28).

However, Moss's rejoinder to the blindness and hostility she experiences brings communitarian values into focus. In response to the "bin" affair, Moss paints her trash can "yellow" with "blue stripes" and adorns it with three biblical quotations: "*Do Unto Others as You Would Have Them Do Unto You; Thou Shalt Love Thy Neighbor as Thyself; Judge Not That Ye Be Not Judged*" (99–100). Moss's overtly religious response does not belie the wider communitarian politics at play. Her messages of shared respect clearly resonate with her neighbors, since she receives no further threating messages and her "trash can sculpture" sits in the "front yard for over a year" (100). Moss worked to bring about what Asen refers to as shifts "in processes of collective imagining," which, he says,

> must go beyond debunking disabling images to craft and circulate affirming images of the poor. Debate participants may envision affirmative images by highlighting community as an alternative to the market model of political institutions and human relationships that framed retrenchment-era debates. Within this alternative framework, welfare policy debate may proceed as an effort to bring about the minimum conditions necessary for all members to participate fully in community life. (226)

These varied autobiographies reveal the different shades and dimensions of poverty and often point to communitarian models as they call for a more empathetic approach to welfare.

Although Ray's childhood was not as impoverished as that of many of the other writers under consideration in this chapter (she remembers: "We were poor but solvent and surrounded by people much poorer"), in *Ecology* she gives a detailed portrait of both her own family's struggles and the challenges faced by their poorer neighbors (161). She remembers "John and Helen Hyatt," who "lived without electricity or indoor plumbing" and "had no choice" but to drink the water from their "shallow well" that "teemed with mosquitoes" (163). In a world saturated with choice, where companies repeatedly diversify ranges to generate a capitalist-driven notion of freedom, this story is a timely reminder that while shelves laden with choice promote the wealth of capital, for many people there is simply no choice. Even when Ray's memories of the abundance of her grandmother Beulah's kitchen, and her insertion of recipes and methods for "Buttermilk Pie" and "biscuit pudding" (182), might bring southern foodways into play, such notions are dispelled with the image of a child from one poor family eating raw chicken, or the hungry, displaced men traveling the roads (162). The contrast between eating for sustenance and consuming for pleasure is marked in Ray's text, perhaps nowhere more so than when she discusses her father's mental illness. Franklin Ray suffered periods of mental illness throughout Ray's childhood, and during these periods her mother "stepped into the role of head-of-household without a stumble" (200). Yet despite her mother's strength, those periods brought the family closer to brink of abject poverty. In one particularly difficult year, her father "tried Social Security" (200). Here, Ray makes no mention of feelings of shame or embarrassment about their need for welfare at a moment when her father "wasn't able to support a family" (200). Instead, shame rests with the government, since "[t]he Social Security people looked at their books and said, 'Yes, our records show you've paid in, you're eligible,' but they wouldn't give him back a cent" (200). The family's poverty and the failure of the state to provide support is underscored by the mental health advice given to Franklin, who is told that he and his family should "eat a nutritious diet that includes a wide variety of foods" because, the doctor informs him, "[s]ome research blames the high rate of mental illness in Georgia on poor diets" (201). Whether the research was accurate or not, even at the best of times Franklin and Lee Ray kept just above the level of abject poverty by shopping within a strict budget. Ray tries to put a positive spin on her father's deals ("five dollars for an entire buggy-load of dented cans") and describes the mystery and excitement of "miscellany," but the fact remains that the unlabeled cans "occupied a special stupefying corner of the pantry to be opened when Mama was willing to serve whatever she encountered" (25). Choice and necessity compete, but in a culture that privileges choice it is hardly surprising that necessity goes underacknowledged.

In relation to US debates on universal healthcare, Slavoj Žižek writes at length about "the ideology of choice" (33) and how, without any provision for those without financial means, "[t]he Republicans who claim that universal healthcare deprives individuals of their freedom of choice are effectively promoting a freedom of choice *without actual freedom of choice*" (25). Ray's work, like that of many writers emerging out of poor backgrounds, problematizes the notion of choice and champions the value of the welfare system for the needy. When we see individuals too ashamed to apply for welfare, these writers focus on the flaws of individuals but also point to societal imperfections that make the need for government aid so shameful and debasing. The lifewriting discussed thus far provides a useful interjection into welfare debates and challenges the tenets of neoliberalism. However, a more recent, and bestselling, poor white autobiography takes a radically different stance.

In 2016, alongside the success of Donald Trump's election campaign, J. D. Vance's *Hillbilly Elegy* hit the bookshelves. As the latest in a line of poor white autobiographers, Vance hopes to shed light on the lives of poor, working-class Americans in the nation's Rust Belt. Although Vance was born and brought up in Ohio, the title embraces his southern roots and the times he spent visiting Kentucky as a child. Moreover, the title is a eulogy for his maternal grandparents, who helped to raise Vance and his sister in the absence of their drug-addicted mother. Unlike the other autobiographies in this subgenre, Vance is preoccupied with statistics and scholarly studies of poverty, employing various studies and reports to underpin his observations, all of which are fully referenced in the notes section. Vance might be forgiven for this overly formal approach, given the questions surrounding the veracity of the autobiographical form, but his turn to "factual" studies serves to authorize his account. While the other writers considered in this chapter fulfill Michael Harrington's call in 1962 for "an American Dickens to record the smell and texture and quality" of poverty, Vance's more seemingly academic approach sees him draw on facts and figures that, for Harrington, are not enough to break down societal blindness toward the nation's poor (24).

Yet, Vance turns to studies and statistics to reassure the reader that he is well read in terms of "social policy and the working poor," and he does demonstrate knowledge of the relationship between high rates of unemployment in industrial towns and cities, and the rapid decline in manufacturing since the 1980s, particularly since President Clinton signed NAFTA in 1994 (144). However, Vance refuses to attach any responsibility to the government, emphatically arguing that poor, displaced workers must take personal responsibility for their own lives: the problem, he reiterates, is with the individual, not with the state. In this message, Vance articulates what O'Connor suggests is a "contemporary neoliberal drift in poverty research" that emphasizes "individual rather than social, morality" (10). In short, Vance echoes neoliberal, conservative beliefs that society should not bear any responsibility for alleviating poverty, arguing instead that the poor must, and can, help themselves.

This is most clearly iterated through Vance's preoccupation with the "American Dream." While many of the autobiographical works examined in this chapter rebuke any idealized notion of an American Dream, Vance is a flag-waving patriot who repeatedly endorses this national myth. He attributes his unshakable belief in the myth to Mawmaw and Papaw Vance, who, like many Appalachians, moved north for a better life in the nation's industrial heartland, settling in Middletown, Ohio.¹⁰ To these grandparents Vance credits his conviction that individual "hard work" guarantees success, asserting:

> Not all of the white working class struggles. I knew even as a child that there were two separate sets of mores and social pressures. My grandparents embodied one type: old-fashioned, quietly faithful, self-reliant, hardworking. My mother and, increasingly, the entire neighborhood embodied another: consumerist, isolated, angry, distrustful. (148)

Here, Vance retreats to a safely established binary tradition that categorizes poor white behaviors. His insistence on a good poor/bad poor dichotomy undermines the work of autobiographers such as Allison who trouble the divide between the deserving and underserving poor. Allison freely admits that in societal terms, she and her family were "the bad poor": those people Vance so despises, "the men who drank and couldn't keep a job; women, invariably pregnant before marriage" (*Trash* vii). Like many other poor white writers, Allison subverts this division in her fiction and life-writing through characters whose humanity offers a more nuanced and complex picture of poverty than the good poor/bad poor binary generates.

As a self-proclaimed Republican, Vance capitalizes on his grandparents' Appalachian heritage in a work that draws on and appeals to conservative thinking about the nation's poor. Vance can barely restrain his contempt for those "food stamp recipients" in Jackson, Kentucky, "who show little interest in honest work" (21). Recounting his part-time job in a grocery store while he completed high school, Vance fancied himself "an amateur sociologist," a role he continues throughout the book as he passes judgment on the nation's poor. As he thinks back to his time as a cashier, he realizes that he began to understand "a little more about America's class divide" as he distinguished between the wealthy customers with "good credit" and the people who "gamed the welfare system" (138–39). Again, Vance cannot hide his disgust at those receiving government aid, writing: "[T]hey'd regularly go through the checkout line speaking on their cell phones. I could never understand why our lives felt like a struggle while those living off of government largesse enjoyed trinkets that I only dreamed about" (139). As I outlined in the introduction to this book, for Alice O'Connor, "a more culturally aware poverty knowledge would demand a more accurate but also a more humanistic and less distancing language that respects how poor people think of themselves—as citizens, workers, parents, and neighbors rather than as benighted, deviant, or somehow deficient 'other' Americans," but venture capitalist Vance rails against the "welfare cheats" and "non-needy" recipients of food stamps, echoing much of the antiwelfare sentiment that has become an indelible part of American conservative thinking (293). Indeed, Asen notes how "[r]etrenchment-era debates forwarded a set of demeaning representations of poor people as delinquents," images that "gradually undermined social welfare provision" (21–22). Surely not every poor customer Vance served was scamming the system, but those are the only customers he considers because they fit his welfare narrative. In this section, he describes his feelings of outrage when he perused his monthly paycheck: "I'd ... notice the line where federal and state income taxes were deducted from my wages. At least as often, our drug-addict neighbor would buy T-bone steaks, which I was too poor to buy for myself but was forced by Uncle Sam to buy for someone else" (139). As the young Vance saw it, and there is little evidence to suggest that the adult Vance thinks any differently, the poor should live hand to mouth, and, if they must get welfare at all, they should spend their money in ways deemed appropriate by taxpayers.

He is convinced that welfare disables rather than enables, and in rhetoric straight out of the Reagan administration playbook, Vance lays much of the blame at the hands of welfare mothers. When he describes the problems of working-class culture, he turns first to dysfunctional women before using a more inclusive "we" to detail the flaws of the poor. His use of bad mothers to demonstrate the community's ills may be easily dismissed as a product of his own fraught relationship with his drug-addicted mother, but his general attitude toward welfare politicizes any example he provides. The problem, as Vance sees it, is that "Ronald Reagan is long dead" and the nation has "no George S. Patton figure in the modern army" (188). Vance's longing for Reagan glibly elides the inherent inequalities of Reaganomics, and his nostalgia for strong military leaders takes readers to Vance's own military service.

What the poor truly need, Vance implies, is a good war to reignite national pride. Having attributed the divisions in society to the loss of political figures such as Reagan and military figures such as Patton, he compares the current failure of the "American Dream" to the strength of the national spirit during the two world wars. He writes: "To understand the significance of this cultural detachment, you must appreciate that much of my family's, my neighborhood's and my community's identity derives from our love of country": a love of country demonstrated by military service, especially during times of war. He claims that Mawmaw "had two gods: Jesus Christ and the United States of America. I was no different, and neither was anyone I knew" (189). Vance proposes military service as a solution for addressing poverty and apathy among the poor; at times, *Hillbilly Elegy* reads like a Marine Corps recruiting brochure. Vance writes: "[W]henever people ask me what I'd most like to change about the white working class, I say, 'The feeling that our choices don't matter.' The Marine Corps excised that feeling like a surgeon does a tumor" (177). Vance credits his time in the military with giving him agency and helping him rise out of the working class. Claiming to have joined the marines because he "wasn't ready for adulthood," upon leaving the Marine Corps he states: "I knew exactly what I wanted out of my life and how to get there" (177). When he details changes in his Mawmaw's healthcare insurance, he offers no critique of the system but instead champions his own ability to financially help his grandmother, stating: "When AK Steel—which provided health care for Mawmaw as Papa's widow—announced that they were increasing her premiums, Mawmaw simply couldn't afford them. She barely survived as it was, and she needed three hundred dollars extra per month.... I immediately volunteered to cover the costs" (166). He overlooks the issue of healthcare provision and individuals unable to meet shortfalls in insurance payments, because his primary concern is to demonstrate that joining the military afforded him choice and economic freedom.

Yet Vance can afford to champion patriotism, military service, and war as the answers to rid the nation of poverty because he led a particularly charmed military life: as "a public affairs marine," he never served on the front line during his tour in Iraq and earned a commendation medal for organizing a successful public relations event (176). Unscathed physically during his service, Vance's time in the military only serves to strengthen his nationalistic pride. Relating an encounter with a poor Iraqi boy, Vance states, "I began to appreciate how lucky I was: born in the greatest country on earth" (173). Such jingoism and blind faith in the military ignores the fact that poor people of all races have long been put on the front lines to fight wars, and, if lucky enough to survive, many return home carrying the physical and/or mental scars of conflict.

Indeed, Bragg and Moss connect the violent, abusive nature of their respective fathers to the traumas they encountered while serving their country.[11] They do not offer solely their fathers' military service as an excuse for their behavior, nor do they present it as the only contributing factor to the men's damaged psyches, but their references to combat trauma further nuances their depictions of these violent men. Bragg turns throughout the trilogy to his father's military service in the Korean War and of a memory that plagued Charles Bragg until his death: a memory of drowning a Korean soldier in a frozen river. In *All Over but the Shoutin'*, he reflects that "in that narrow space of time, his life shifted, tumbled off balance" (21), and as Bragg's memoirs show, Charles Bragg never regained his balance. In *The Most They Ever Had*, Bragg also reflects on World War II, and, unlike Vance, who looks to that time for signs of true patriotism, Bragg details the damaged men who returned from war as well as the "[e]mpty caskets" that "were carried through the streets" (89). In *Fierce*, Moss draws attention to her father's World War II service. She tallies the "ocean of loss" her father, Stewart Karl Moss, encountered, which includes his mother's death when he was a child, and claims that he tried to escape a fractured childhood by seeking refuge in the military. However, she reflects that "if he'd had a chance for survival, World War II took it away. I don't know everything that happened to him, but I know that he was shot and bayoneted and sent to a MASH unit.... God knows what else happened to him over there. (He wouldn't say)" (82–83). Military service for these men failed to help them work their way out of poverty, and their wartime experiences appear to have exacerbated their feelings of anger and their propensity to drown out life at the bottom of a bottle. Vance's neoliberal, nationalistic outlook glosses over such nuances, but his ideas of how to "make America great again" carried cultural capital during Trump's ascendancy to the White House.

In his review of *Hillbilly Elegy*, Hari Kunzru observes that the "book contains many stories of lurid 'white trash' abjection" and that Vance is "comfortable with explanations of white pathology that rely on psychology and 'culture', but not on structural economic inequality." Despite the fact that Vance lauds his "academic" credentials as he takes on the role of "authentic" poor white guru, many of his observations lack either any consideration of socioeconomic policies, or the empathy found in other poor white autobiographies that often provides a more insightful critique of policy than any statistic could. For instance, in the interview with LeMahieu, Allison states: "Everything that I know, or believe I know, about the criminal nature of capitalism and the hatefulness of class and race prejudice, the enormous sorrow of contempt that dominates how we think about the poor in this culture, all of that is where I begin" (659). Exposing the structures of inequality is central to this poor white autobiographical impulse, and if Vance prefers to find fault with the individual rather than the state and champion the idea of an "American Dream," other writers in this subgenre expose the inherent inequities of capitalism.

Bragg directly tackles socioeconomic structures, political decision making, and inequality in *The Most They Ever Had*, his elegy to the Jacksonville Union Yarn Mill workers who were displaced when the mill closed in 2001. Bragg's interest in the history of the mill workers and their present-day plight emerges out of his concern for his brother Sam, one of the mill workers left to find alternative employment in an economy that no longer requires significant numbers of manual laborers, but instead skilled white-collar workers for service-based or IT careers. Perversely, the hard-won improvements to working conditions, alongside the ratification of NAFTA, ensured that an economic "regime of accumulation" sought out cheaper labor outside the United States (Harvey, *Spaces of Global* 29). For Bragg, the desire for greater and greater profits means that "human dignity, in a global economy, is just one more cost to cut" (24). While Bragg focuses on the specifics of one factory in Jacksonville, Alabama, he situates it within a national crisis, acknowledging that the people he writes about were just many of the "[h]undreds of thousands of workers" across the nation who "were left with nothing, with no health insurance, with just scraps of pensions or no pensions at all" (28). What Bragg describes is the by-product of neoliberal, capitalist enterprise. For Harvey:

> The fundamental mission of the neo-liberal state is to create a "good business climate" and therefore to optimize conditions for capital accumulation no matter what the consequences for employment or social well-being. This contrasts with the social democratic state that is committed to full employment and the optimization of the well-being of all of its citizens subject to the condition of maintaining adequate and stable rates of capital accumulation. (*Spaces of Global* 25)

With no measures in place for meaningful alternative employment for all the displaced workers, inequality widens and more people end up on or below the poverty line. Successive governments on both sides of the political divide have ignored or struggled to tackle the problem as "[t]owns withered" across the nation and "[h]undreds of thousands went without work and health insurance, with house and car payments and grocery bills unmet" (*The Most* 29). In Vance's book, he too easily argues that people must take control of their own lives and shows little compassion for those who want to work but simply cannot find meaningful employment. He offers plenty of examples of shiftless people, but unlike Bragg and other poor white writers, he does not dwell on the displaced workers who "wanted a tool to pound out a living" in a world where those in power have changed the rules of the game (*The Most* 29). For many workers, job security is a thing of the past, and with decreasing wages and increases in the cost of living, poverty is not an exception in some communities; it is the rule.

Several poor white memoirists not only draw attention to the structures of inequality but also offer alternative solutions—the type of communitarian solutions that Asen believes will help to overcome negative, entrenched ideas about the poor (226). Perhaps no poor white memoirist dwells more on alternatives than Ray, who combines memoir, ecocriticism, and poetry as she reflects not only on family, home, and region but also on the environmental costs of excessive capitalism. At a time when alternatives seem out of sight, Ray argues for both a different economic system and an alternative approach to understanding wealth and prosperity. She worries that we are encouraged to put faith "in our capitalist economic system" even as its limitations and failures become all too apparent (*Wild Card* 109). Localism is her answer to the problems caused by "global industrialization," which might appear to be just another form of neo-agrarianism, especially since she promotes a predominantly agricultural model. However, her localism is not regionalism, so when she promotes local production and nonmonetary exchange, she is not promoting the idea of a unique US South but instead a model that might reduce the environmental impact of global economics and bring about a sense of shared responsibility that neoliberalism has dissolved (*Wild Card* 109). While she admits that her system "seems to be most suited to poverty, especially in rural areas," some of its fundamental principles might also help to tackle impoverishment in urban communities.[12] Admittedly, when Ray advocates this alternative lifestyle in *Wild Card Quilt*, she benefits from living on family land, and even though she must turn the dilapidated land into a functioning farm, she does not bear the weight of rent or mortgage payments that many poor people face.

Having long tried to live a self-sufficient life, Ray comes to understand that "co-sufficiency" and an "economic system . . . called reciprocity" lessen dependence on monetary currency (104–5). She writes: "Although reciprocity can utilize money, it is not dependent on it. Capitalism, on the other hand, the economic system in which methods of production and distribution are privately owned and operated for profit, requires money" (105). When money is used, Ray suggests, whenever possible it should be used in the community: for her, this ensures that she knows who her "money is upholding" (108). Some readers might object to the didacticism throughout Ray's memoirs, and some might find her ideas unrealistic, but at least she is willing to think, and to some extent live, beyond the parameters of capital. For Dean, it is the failure of the political Left to generate alternatives that has allowed neoliberal agendas to go unchecked. She argues:

> In part this is because we have been unable to give voice to values of collectivity, cooperation, solidarity, and equity strong enough to counter neoliberalism's free-trade fantasy. It is also because we can't imagine how we would realize, enact, bring about such a vison. Our very supposition of democracy . . . entraps us in the inequalities of communicative capitalism. (73)

Ray embraces the idea of collectivity and cooperation, and insists that these must be the foundation stones of local communities. She focuses at the micro level, on an uber-local notion of community, which for Ray is her family, friends, and neighbors in Baxley, Georgia. Unlike her rallying call in *Ecology of a Cracker Childhood* for southerners to unite to save "Dixie," in her later work Ray moves away from such regionally based identity politics to push for political action at the granular level (*Ecology* 272), granular in the sense of the uber-local; in *The Seed Underground* (2012), she focuses on the crisis of "our seed supply" and the "tragedy of corporate robbery" (xiv). Attending to the granular, she suggests, might be the most effective way to counteract the faceless regimes of accumulation that have caused widespread inequality and wrought environmental devastation.

Ray certainly offers the most politically nuanced alternatives to ideas of community of any writer discussed in this chapter. Yet to greater and lesser extents, they all engage in much larger debates about poverty, and most destabilize commonly held notions of the poor. These writers certainly write back, but their counternarratives and counterhistories are not merely routes to enter established ideas of community: they pose much broader questions about socioeconomic policies once read beyond the categories of southern, regional writing. These writers might be southern, but their depictions of poverty are not shaped by region but by global economics, which imposes levels of inequality without consideration for national boundaries or borders. To read poor white life-writing can be to hear the voices that Asen states are largely silenced in policy debates, or at the very least to be reminded about the ways in which societal constructions of poverty never really reveal the whole picture.

CHAPTER FOUR

"A Whitegirl Helped Me": Locating Poor Whites in Literature

Since around the beginning of the twenty-first century, the categories of Grit Lit and Rough South have been applied to a body of novels, stories, and poetry detailing poverty. For Robert Rea, "Grit Lit captures a landscape of harsh realities, a rowdy world where mud tires and marijuana prevail over moonlight and magnolia" (79), and self-proclaimed Grit Lit writer Tom Franklin argues that the genre is preoccupied with "the dirty South seen without romanticism or the fake nostalgia of *Gone with the Wind* fans" (Carpenter and Franklin viii).[1] Grit Lit is typically hard, raw, violent, and visceral, but Franklin's coeditor, Brian Carpenter, stresses that Grit Lit is not distinctly southern. In his introduction to *Grit Lit: A Rough South Reader* (2012), Carpenter contends: "As bluegrass is to country, and rockabilly is to rock, Rough South is to Grit Lit. Think Grit Lit with a stronger accent" (xxviii). To that end, if Grit Lit is not uniquely southern, it is predominantly southern. Rough South, on the other hand, may be gritty, but it is always southern; for Jean W. Cash, in her edited collection with Keith Perry, *Rough South, Rural South* (2016), such writers have "a clear understanding of the value of working-class southerners and their culture," which "gives rise to realistic depictions of landscape and of working-class characters who transcend dated stereotypes and, ultimately, achieve universal meaning" (xiii). In their edited collection *Hardlines: Rough South Poetry* (2016), Daniel Cross Turner and William Wright expand on Cash's idea of the "universal," with Turner arguing that Rough South poets often transcend regionalism as they depict "a region always in a process of changing, a place of transregional, even global connectivity" (7).

Across these various debates about Grit Lit and Rough South resounds a shared conviction that this writing presents a "real" or "authentic" South: Turner defines the work in his collection as "[a] poetry that keeps things real," while Carpenter and Franklin repeatedly use the word "authentic" to describe Grit Lit (1). Carpenter might acknowledge the constructed nature of the term, claiming that "the Rough South may not be the 'real' South," but his admission is tempered by the refrain that "damned if it is not as real as Tara and as true as Yoknapatawpha" (xxviii). Meanwhile, although Cash refers to Rough South literature as merely "realistic," the majority of the critical essays in her collection with Perry are concerned with issues of "authenticity." Little wonder, perhaps, since Gary Hawkins, the filmmaker credited with coining the term "Rough South," describes how he first came across it at a cocktail party where "an authentic genteel southerner" drew a clear distinction between "the genteel South" and its counterpart, the hard-scrabble South (3). Such willing submission to the idea that there are two different Souths, as if somehow the grittier South were something distinct and separate from the "genteel South," is problematic. It supposes that such a thing as the "genteel South" actually exists, and if all the dirt and grit is attached to a different, rough South, the affluent South keeps its hands clean, thereby circumventing the connection between its wealth and the low-wage jobs and unemployment of the poor.

At its best, the writing subsumed under the banners Rough South or Grit Lit serves to deconstruct such false dichotomies and at the very least to ensure that the divisions in southern, and American, communities are discussed along class lines. As David Harvey saliently observes, "[I]f it looks like class struggle and acts like class struggle then we have to name it for what it is. The mass of the population has either to resign itself to the historical and geographical trajectory defined by this overwhelming class power or respond to it in class terms" (*Spaces of Global* 65). So, when we cloak class within constructed notions of "genteel" and rough Souths, as Zillah Eisenstein explains, "genuine systems of power are submerged from view" (7). As I examine poverty and the experience of poor whites in contemporary literature about the South, I avoid employing categories such as Grit Lit or Rough South and instead focus on the ways in which literature about the contemporary US South exposes the broader socioeconomic shifts brought about by the neoliberal turn, or financial capitalism, the demands of which, Christian Marazzi argues, "reinforce social regression under the pressure of a growth model that, in order to distribute wealth, voluntarily sacrifices social cohesion and the quality of life itself" (44). The turn to neoliberalism, as Harvey explains, involved a fundamental shift in consciousness, best expressed by Margaret Thatcher, who declared: "Economics are the method . . . but the object is to change the soul" (*Spaces of Global* 17). The move away from the welfare state to a form of individualism driven by capital growth is not purely economic but social, and in this regard, Raymond Williams's idea of "structures of feeling" asks us to consider the way these socioeconomic changes "are actively lived and felt" (132). For Williams, "the emergence of a new structure of feeling is best related to the rise of a class ... at other times to contradiction, fracture, or mutation within a class ... when a formation appears to break away from its class norms, though it retains its substantial affiliation, and the tension is at once lived and articulated in radically new semantic figures" (134–35). Contemporary forms of poverty in the US South can usefully be explored through literature that is attuned to either neoliberalism's "emergent formations" or its "dominant or residual" patterns (134).

The year 1987 witnessed the publication of Toni Morrison's *Beloved* and the release of Oliver Stone's *Wall Street*, one a historical novel about the impact and legacy of slavery and the other an exposé of Reaganomics and excessive greed. In the same year, the stock market crash on October 19, 1987, commonly known as Black Monday, exposed the limitations of the neoliberal agenda, but rather than steer the global economy toward another path, several leading world powers, most notably the United States and the United Kingdom, pursued neoliberalism as never before. As Harvey states: "If the project was to restore class power to the top elites, then neo-liberalism was clearly the answer" (*Spaces of Global* 31). In effect, by the late 1980s, neoliberalism, neatly encapsulated in Gordon Gekko's infamous lines in Stone's film, "Greed, for lack of a better word, is good. Greed is right. Greed works. Greed clarifies" (01:14:50–01:15:27), was so deeply entrenched that neither the stock market crash nor the later 2008 banking crisis derailed the system, particularly given the dearth of alternatives. Interestingly, as Slavoj Žižek observes, the wake of the "2008 financial meltdown and the measures taken to counteract it" saw a "revival in the work of Ayn Rand, the fullest ideological expression of radical 'greed is good' capitalism: the sales of her *magnum opus Atlas Shrugged* exploded" (34). If Rand's embrace of capital revived the hearts of those wedded to neoliberalism, the financial shift at the end of the twentieth century also contributed to the emergence of writers driven to expose the system's underbelly and the ways in which neoliberalism intensified rather than reduced the levels of poverty already intrinsic to capitalism.

Despite the apparently unshakable belief in free-market capitalism and individualism, even during the 1980s, as Colin Hutchinson explains, "Reaganism came to represent for many an indictment of 'trickle-down' economics in the form of an increasingly insecure, cynical and pessimistic society" (23). Feelings of hopelessness are hardly surprising, for while the richest 1 percent continue to amass even greater wealth under neoliberal doctrines, for Noam Chomsky it is clear that those same doctrines "undermine education and health, increase inequality, and reduce labor's share in income" (32). Part of the success of neoliberalism depends upon breaking down resistance: bell hooks laments that "there is no organized class struggle, no daily in-your-face critique of capitalist greed that stimulates thought and action—critique, reform, and revolution" (1). The lack of any coherent class struggle is a direct result of neoliberalism, under which, as Harvey explains, "[a]ll forms of social solidarity" are "dissolved in favor of individualism" (*Spaces of Global* 17). If Stone's film critiqued the turn to neoliberalism and the individualism and greed that are its cornerstones, so Morrison's novel, whose main events occur between the 1850s and the 1870s, rebukes Reaganomics and the demonization of the poor through ideas of communitarianism that speak against the neoliberal economy and its mantra of self-interest.

Morrison wrote *Beloved*, her much discussed novel about the haunting legacies of slavery, against the backdrop of the neoliberal turn. This is a novel in which individualism serves no productive purpose and communitarianism holds sway.[2] In *Beloved*, after escaped slave Sethe kills her two-year-old daughter, the eponymous Beloved, in order to prevent her from being taken back into slavery, her dead daughter returns to haunt Sethe and her family, and only communitarianism frees them from the past. Before emerging in bodily form, Beloved's forceful, ghostly presence haunts 124, "the gray and white house on Bluestone Road" that Sethe shares with her mother-in-law, Baby Suggs, up until her death, and her three children, Howard, Bugler, and Denver, until the sons run away, leaving only Sethe and Denver to face Beloved (3). While the novel's haunting pivots around Beloved, much of it rests on Denver: the events surrounding Denver's birth form a key part of Sethe's "rememory," and when Denver recognizes that her ghostly sister is vampirically draining her mother alive, it is Denver who ventures out into the community to procure the help they need.

Denver, named after southern poor "whitegirl" Amy Denver, underscores not just the importance of community but of cross-racial, class-based cooperation.[3] Such cooperation sits at the center of Denver's knowledge about her own birth, partly drawn from Sethe's memories of an encounter that secured her journey out of slavery, and partly from Denver's reimagining of her birth. After a violent assault by the schoolteacher's nephews at the Sweet Home Plantation in Kentucky, in which they hold her down and steal her milk, the heavily pregnant Sethe escapes but goes into labor while on the run, before reaching the safety of Ohio. When asked to recall's Denver's impromptu birth, Sethe never forgets that "[a] whitegirl helped me" (8).[4] Just as slavery and infanticide return to Sethe through the process of rememory, so too does the white girl, Amy Denver, who resurfaces through memories and storytelling throughout the novel. Sethe honors Amy by naming her child Denver, and neither she nor her child ever forget the "whitegirl" who helped a runaway slave. For Andrew Dix, Brian Jarvis, and Paul Jenner, "[t]he assistance that Amy offers to Sethe" is vital "in that the cooperation of these 'two throw-away people' is figured as both the projection and the resumption of an undistorted unity, in which class and gender alliances transcend racial divides" (66–67). While the moment between Sethe and Amy is too fleeting to ever fully "transcend racial divides," its lingering presence throughout the novel maintains a sense of hope both within the novel's late-nineteenth-century setting and for a readership in a period when the shift to neoliberalism was eroding communitarianism. Since the 1970s, hooks reflects, "notions of communalism" have been "replaced with notions of self-interest," and "contemptuous attitudes toward the poor began to permeate all aspects of our culture" (44). In *Beloved*, Morrison champions communalism both in the form of the local black women who help to rescue both Sethe and Denver from Beloved's deathly grip at the novel's close and in the ways that Amy and Sethe work together to deliver Denver. Morrison's depiction of cross-racial cooperation lays the foundation for future communitarianism, which, as Cyrus Patell argues, is based on the idea of "[p]luralist communities that respect difference—both external and internal" and "foster a healthier, cosmopolitan form of communitarianism" (180).

Despite Sethe's and Amy's indoctrination into society's racism as they brandish terms such as "trash" and "nigger" against each other, the women share a connection that momentarily transcends prejudice (32). The repeated references to how Amy "helped" Sethe and their cooperative "push" and "pull" to deliver Denver show how humanity transcends the falsely imposed racial and class distinctions that seek to order and control behavior. While Sethe places great belief in Amy's "tenderhearted mouth" as an indicator of her trustworthy nature, Amy's true "magic" rests in her "good hands" that "massaged" Sethe's feet and legs back to life (78, 76, 35). It is Amy's "strong hands" that not only deliver Denver but secure safety for both the mother and child when she takes them across the river (84). The continued references to Amy's hands underscore the class connection that joins the two women: Amy's indentured servitude carries some of the same markers of dehumanization that Sethe experiences as a slave. Her body has shrunk from being "put in the root cellar" (34), and she is no stranger to "whippings" from Mr. Buddy, who has "a right evil hand" (79). Sethe and Amy, two women reduced by their owners to laboring hands, rediscover humanity in their brief encounter. In the continual references to Amy's hands and the positive adjectives they engender, Morrison shows the interconnectedness of laboring bodies and that both women are more than mere hands. In her study of hands and laboring bodies, Janet Zandy proposes "a wider imaginary for working-class texts, one that recognizes distinct cultural differences, histories, and geographies and yet sees ways of forging radical linkages across cultural boundaries based on the common need for sustainable work inseparable from an ethos of collective well-being" (150). Morrison's novel is much more than a working-class text, but its story of Amy Denver forgoes racialized identity politics as it reveals the power of class solidarity. After Sethe and Amy have labored together to deliver Denver, the class position of both women is underscored as they swaddle the newborn:

> On a riverbank in the cool of a summer evening two women struggled under a shower of silvery blue. They never expected to see each other again in this world and at the moment couldn't care less. But there on a summer night surrounded by bluefern they did something together appropriately and well. A patroller passing would have sniggered to see two throw-away people, two lawless outlaws—a slave and a barefoot whitewoman with unpinned hair—wrapping a ten-minute-old baby in the rags they wore. (84–85)

They "struggled" together, these two "throw-away people," and despite their shared knowledge that their bond cannot survive beyond this moment of repose, Morrison stresses the communal, not only in the fact that "they did something together appropriately and well," but also that Denver is swaddled in both their rags. The knowledge of her birth, and of the role that cross-racial, class-based cooperation and communitarianism played in it, gives Denver the confidence at the end of the novel to seek help to save her mother.

If for Sethe and Amy their shared experience provides just a fleeting encounter with the connections that can transcend societal norms, the story of that experience lives on long after the two women have to part ways. Amy's namesake is a "charmed child" because her birth transcended the divides that often separate society's poorest citizens. For Wendy Harding and Jacky Martin, "Denver... carries all the auspicious signs of a new relationship with the racist context"; however, Denver surely represents class as much as racial solidarity (165). Even Dorothea Drummond Mbalia, who claims that Morrison offers "collectivism" as "the first step in eradicating the national oppressions and class exploitation of black people" and contends that the collectivism centers on "Morrison's... theme of one people, one struggle, one solution," forgoes the role Amy Denver plays in the novel (88, 99). While Alex Zamalin recognizes that Morrison reaches out beyond the black community in the novel, arguing that her choice of epigraph from Romans 9:25, "I will call them my people, which were not my people; and her beloved, which was not beloved," talks to Morrison's "generosity" and her willingness to "love the white majority of which *she* was not part," he downplays the significance of Amy's class position (101). Zamalin argues that "generosity" is the novel's political message, a "generosity that depends upon resisting the American culture of property thinking *and* its demonizing, polarizing Christian moralism" (129). Yet, via Emmanuel Lévinas, Zamalin argues that "[c]onfronted with the face of a black stranger amidst the American racial holocaust of slavery, Amy Denver becomes Sethe's hostage. Sethe's hunger, vulnerability and presence create in Amy a pre-rational, emotional response; confronted by this, she can do nothing but respond" (125). His idea that Amy is driven to help Sethe by "pre-rational" thought rather than generosity deprives her of agency, implying that Amy acts rather than thinks, effectively robbing her of complex thought processes. He overlooks the fact that this poor white girl could just as easily have turned Sethe in for the reward money; in actively choosing to help Sethe, Amy puts humanity before profit. Written at a time of ever increasing poverty levels and the further denigration of the poor through figures such as the welfare queen, the moment by the river, featuring two women who are scarred in various ways and to varying degrees by capitalism, shows the devastating effects of economic oppression both then and now and the humanity that can override it. Indeed, for Linden Peach, "Amy introduces another subtext about slavery which has often been ignored which develops Morrison's concern with the capitalist origins of the slave trade. The slavery endured by poor, working-class whites involved treatment at the hands of their masters which, as Sethe discovers, was not so dissimilar to her own" (107).

Of course, at the end of the novel it is the black community that Denver turns to for help: no matter the cross-racial labor that brought her into the world, that world is still one shaped by racialized discourses. When recluse Denver leaves 124 to seek help from Lady Jones, she walks the streets with fear and caution, and when she hears "voices, male voices" behind her, she keeps "her eyes on the road in case they were whitemen; in case she was walking where they wanted to; in case they said something and she would have to answer them. Suppose they flung out at her, grabbed her, tied her" (245). In Morrison's novel, there is hope for communitarianism, but in both the novel's setting and its time of publication, that hope is dimmed by the realities of racism, societal blindness toward poverty and the working class, and the class exploitation intrinsic to neoliberalism (Eisenstein 1).

By 2005, neoliberalism was so entrenched that it apparently came as a surprise to many Americans when Hurricane Katrina revealed widespread poverty along the Gulf Coast. Issues of race dominated the debates about Katrina and its aftermath in New Orleans because African Americans make up the majority of the city's poor; as Nahem Yousaf outlines, "[r]evenants of slavery, the southern plantation complex and the idea of New Orleans as a colony within the US have infused post-Katrina stories" (554).⁵ It is vital, however, that poverty and class remain at the foreground of debates about Katrina and its aftermath not just in New Orleans but across the affected Gulf Coast area in Louisiana and Mississippi because, as Robbie Ethridge explains, "Katrina washed away the veneer of US prosperity to reveal deep poverty and entrenched class lines that the larger US public took to be vanishing if not gone" (799). Ethridge goes on to note that "[o]nce the poverty was exposed, observers . . . drew the conclusion that in the US South, poverty and wealth coincide with race. However, along the Gulf coast of Mississippi, class lines do not neatly overlay race lines" (799). Many poor communities were devastated by Katrina, and while in New Orleans those communities were disproportionately African American, across the disaster zone all poor communities were adversely affected regardless of race or ethnicity.

Communitarianism and identity politics in the wake of Katrina come to the fore in John Biguenet's play *Shotgun* (2009), the second in his *The Rising Water Trilogy*. Each play within *The Rising Water Trilogy* depicts New Orleans at various stages during and after Katrina, as Biguenet outlines in the notes section:

> *Rising Water* is set the night of August 29 and the early morning of August 30, 2005, hours after Hurricane Katrina has passed the city. *Shotgun* opens in December 2005 in New Orleans, about four months after the collapse of Federal levees and the subsequent flooding. *Mold* is set the morning of Sunday, August 27, 2006. (217)

In the two post-Katrina plays, while *Mold* exposes the challenges of rebuilding communities, *Shotgun* reveals racial divides that are far stronger than the levees ever were. In *Shotgun*, race and class intersect in all manner of complex and challenging ways to reveal how issues of race detrimentally continue to dominate over class. The play importantly depicts the hardship that also befalls working- and lower-middle-class white communities whenever any tragedy, let alone one with the enormity of Katrina, raises the vector of poverty. *Shotgun* follows the fate of father and son, Beau and Eugene Harlan, who find themselves unable to financially survive an environmental disaster on the scale of Katrina. As Beau reveals later in the play, he chose to remain in New Orleans during the hurricane, but when his house in Gentilly flooded he, along with his wife and son, had to escape out of the attic; during their escape his wife, Audrey, sustained a "wide-open gash" on her leg that eventually became infected and resulted in her death (117). Unable to return immediately to their severely damaged home, or to pay both existing mortgage payments and extortionate rent on temporary lodgings, Beau and Eugene at the start of the play are seeking cheaper accommodation. Beau, a "white carpenter in his mid-thirties," and his sixteen-year-old son find themselves in the predominantly poor, black neighborhood of Algiers, looking to rent one side of a shotgun duplex from its owner, Mattie Godchaux, who lives in the other side of the home with her father, Dexter; like Beau and Eugene, Dex has been rendered homeless in the wake of Katrina. Despite the fact that they are all, as Beau reminds them, "in the same boat," neither Dex nor Eugene can see beyond race (79). In act I, scene 1, Dex tells his daughter: "Mixing black and white, it's nothing but a jug of gasoline looking for a match" (82), and Eugene repeatedly expresses his unease about living in the neighborhood.

Dex and Eugene are equally unable to restrain their bigotry. Dex repeatedly reminds Beau that the neighborhood is "all black," asking, "You sure you wouldn't be more comfortable somewhere else?" (85). Despite the objections from the old man and the teenager, Mattie rents the house to Beau, and as the play unfolds a romantic relationship forms between black homeowner and white renter. Worried by the closeness developing between Mattie and Beau, Dex and Eugene conspire to break them apart, with Dex encouraging both Mattie's ex-boyfriend, Clarence, otherwise known as Willie, to work harder and turn around his fortunes, and Eugene to secretly bring his family home in Gentilly back to a livable state so that he and Beau can return there.

Although Katrina plunges Beau and his son into poverty, and a deep affection grows between Mattie and Beau, these commonalities are not enough to convince Dex that racism can be surmounted, as revealed during an exchange between Dex and Beau at the end of act II, scene 3:

> BEAU: You think I'd hurt your daughter?
> DEX: You think the world will give you any choice? You tell me some future where the two of you could ever be happy together.
> BEAU: Things are changing, Dex. The flood washed away what used to be. Something new could take its place.
> DEX: You really think things are ever gonna change down here? They already going back to the way they always was—and worse.
> BEAU: But look at us, you and me, black and white, living here together under one roof.
> DEX: Yeah, with a wall running between us. (130)

Dex has fully succumbed to racial separation and cannot envisage any alternative, and since the scene ends without a retort from Beau, the wall to which Dex alludes begins to form as a metaphorical block in Beau's mind as the play reaches its climax: despite Mattie's protests, he ends their relationship and returns to Gentilly with Eugene. In the end, only Mattie is strong enough to imagine a different future: the men, all of whom are broken down financially, find it easier to fall back into racialized ideas. In the end, Biguenet's characters willingly submit to the racialized status quo, indicating, in hooks's terms, that they are "duped." She asserts:

> Class matters. Race and gender can be used as screens to deflect attention away from the harsh realities class politics exposes. Clearly, just when we should all be paying attention to class, using race and gender to understand and explains its new dimensions, society, even our government, says let's talk about race and racial injustice. It is impossible to talk meaningfully about ending racism without talking about class. Let us not be duped. (7)

Environmental degradations, abuses, and disasters surely always bring class and poverty to the fore, and John Clark writes at length about "the grass-roots, cooperative effort to practice mutual aid and community self-help" in the immediate wake of Katrina (203). Yet Biguenet's play is a reminder of the all-encompassing power of race and how it distracts from issues of class and economic inequality. As Walter Benn Michaels argues, "We love thinking that the differences that divide us are not the differences between those of us who have money and those who don't but are instead the differences between those of us who are black and those who are white or Asian or Latino or whatever" (*The Trouble* 6).

Issues of race, identity politics, and regionalism proliferate in Colson Whitehead's *John Henry Days* (2001). For William Ramsey, commenting in his work on Morrison and Whitehead, "[b]oth writers have employed resistant readings to dislodge unitary (and implicitly white) master discourse" (771).[6] In *Beloved* and *John Henry Days*, both writers "dislodge" numerous aspects of the US hegemonic "master narrative," including the racialized stereotypes that serve to keep people apart. When Whitehead's J. Sutter ventures to West Virginia to cover the John Henry Days Festival, he finds himself on a journey of reeducation. In this complex novel, which Derek C. Maus describes as "a historiographic metamyth that depicts the appropriation, alteration, dilution, and possible rejuvenation of the John Henry legend over the course of two centuries," Sutter finds himself reevaluating the initial prejudices he holds about the US South (38). In the first chapter, focalized through Sutter, readers learn that before departing, he "possesses the standard amount of black Yankee scorn for the South" alongside "a healthy stock of white trash jokes," and at the airport in Charleston, West Virginia, he quickly surmises that he'd "arrived at a different America" (14). Yet the bracketed observation that "([n]one of this is true, of course, but perception is all; to and from each his own dark continent)" (14–15) undercuts Sutter's judgments and draws stark attention to the distortive power of misperception. Indeed, Sutter's prejudices are quickly undercut, often through humor; for instance, on their way to the opening-night celebrations of the John Henry festival in Hinton, West Virginia, the cab that Sutter and his fellow "junketeers" find themselves in is hailed down by another vehicle, and while Sutter immediately believes this is "the red pickup" of his nightmares—after all, "[s]o much depends upon a red pickup truck, filled with crackers"—the other car actually turns out to be another cab, carrying their friend, One Eye, who is desperately trying to catch up with the group after arriving late (50). No matter that Sutter is a member of the urban black middle class, exemplified by his turn to William Carlos Williams; the legacy of slavery still haunts him and his ideas about the contemporary South and its people.[7] As a black man in West Virginia, Sutter does not have to reach far into his mind to see "the ropes, the guns, the fire," and the lasting, repeated message that "[t]he South will kill you" (50).

Whitehead exposes the odious nature of misperceptions and stereotyping when Sutter and his friends mock the locals during the festival's opening-night dinner. They joke about moonshine, Sutter regards the locals as "hicks" and "crackers," and they confuse and embarrass a local journalist, Broderick Honnicut, with references to a "chicken rustling ring" (68). When Sutter chokes on a piece of prime rib, he thinks that "these people" certainly "know how to watch a nigger die" (78–79). Yet Sutter's life is threatened not by menacing "hillbillies" but by both his own insatiable hunger as he chokes on a chunk of meat he hungrily devours, and by an incident days later at the fair during which a jaded, middle-class out-of-towner and "denizen of middle management," Alphonse Miggs, attempts to commit a massacre, which results in both his own death and that of innocent bystanders at the hands of a police officer (283). Whitehead leaves open the possibility that Sutter himself was one of the victims, but, dead or alive at the end, Sutter transforms from regarding the locals as "crackers" to the realization that this is not the South he imagined. At the fair, Sutter acknowledges that it is not "the Aryan Nation recruitment rally he thought it would be" (313). As he becomes increasingly aware of his "New York prejudices," he begins to see that cable TV "allows every teenager, no matter how country, to catwalk into the latest styles," and there is little sense of mourning here for a lost local culture (313).

Any notion of local distinctiveness has long given way to the onslaught of capital, which is perhaps why John Inscoe regards *John Henry Days* as neither distinctly southern nor Appalachian, despite its West Virginia setting. For him,

> place seems to matter very little to Whitehead once he has grounded his protagonist in Talcott after moving him along the winding and ever more ominous back roads of West Virginia in his opening pages. Appalachian residents appear as marginal characters, and locals appear to be of far less interest than the variety of outsiders who find themselves thrown together in this remote mountain town with little regard for or sense of relevancy to the region. ("Race and Remembrance" 92)

Rather than rendering the region and its people irrelevant, Whitehead's novel reveals that ideas of regional distinctiveness and stereotypes do not hold up under scrutiny. Lucien, of publicity house Lucien Joyce Associates with whom Sutter finds occasional work, "has never done a town before" and finds himself contemplating

> which came first, the stamp or the festival. Is the stamp a merchandising tie-in for festival, or the festival a press conference for a stamp? Looking around today, he's still confounded. There are canned preserves and men walking around in old conductor uniforms. Is this really homey or is it constructed in some way. Is their sincerity actually the hapless grasping after something they believed their fathers possessed. There's a safe deposit box containing their heritage, but they don't possess the right documentation. Lucien suspects he is falling for a deception that beguiles the con artist and the mark in equal measure. (295)

Questions of authenticity, "sincerity," and simulation confound Lucien, the master of event construction, and as Romine reminds us "[t]he South is full of fakes," some more convincing than others (*The Real South* 2). For Lucien, the scene he confronts is not southern but "small town," not distinctly Appalachian but anyplace USA. Whitehead questions whether any sense of distinctness exists in a world that is not only becoming smaller because of technological changes but also more standardized, so rather than offering up an Appalachia marked out by difference, a reading that has only ever served to limit ideas of Appalachia and its people, Whitehead draws on the commonalities between the region and the rest of the nation. When Sutter earlier contemplated the facade of the Hinton hotel where they ate on the opening night, he sees instantly that this "rustic hotel" is just "some factory concoction," created to represent some loosely constructed idea of the past with its "colonial flourishes abut[ting] antebellum wood columns" and "modern double-pane windows" that "nestle in artificially weathered frames of molting paint" (56). Neither the place nor its people fulfill the outsiders' expectations of a region that stands outside of modernity and progress, so rather than ignoring place, Whitehead challenges constructed and deeply ingrained notions of the region.

While Whitehead debunks misperceptions about the mountainous South predominantly through his "outsider" characters, Barbara Kingsolver's novel *Flight Behavior* (2012) is focalized through central protagonist Dellarobia Turnbow, whose discovery of displaced monarch butterflies on her father-in-law's land in the fictionalized town of Feathertown, Tennessee, brings outsiders to the small community in the form of scientists, eco-warriors, and eco-travelers, resulting in a series of intellectual, class, and cultural encounters that expose many of the economic and environmental challenges of the early twenty-first century. Dellarobia is a frustrated wife and mother who lost both parents by the age of seventeen, when she was trapped into marriage by an unplanned pregnancy and denied the opportunity to go to college. Having once been on the brink of leaving Feathertown, Dellarobia's intellectual curiosity, exemplified by her expulsion from the Bible study class at the local church for asking too many challenging questions, facilitates the bridging role she plays throughout the novel between the local community, the scientists, and the environmentalists.

In particular, Dellarobia knows how outsiders view rural Tennessee and its people, something she reflects on throughout the novel, most notably in her ruminations on Billy Ray Hatch, a man whom she and her husband, Cub, see one evening being mocked on a comedy show, someone who was "[n]ot an actor" but "a real man" (187). While the comedians mock the man, Dellarobia and Cub recognize someone who could easily be one of their neighbors, or even "kin" (187). Dellarobia notes that "[a]fter each reply the interviewer nodded in a stagy way, creasing his eyebrows in fake fascination. So the whole world could see Billy Ray Hatch made into a monkey" (187). The discrepancy between "the real man" and the media's re-creation distresses Dellarobia, and her thoughts often turn to Hatch throughout the rest of the novel. Indeed, Dellarobia herself is the victim of such condescending, constructed notions of the rural poor when many of the eco-travelers who descend on the family's property to see the monarchs treat her "as if she were a hired hand"; "[i]f they conversed with her at all, their syllables would sometimes broaden as if she might need help with English" (271). These feelings of inferiority are exacerbated by Leighton Atkins, a retiree who travels to out-of-the-way places where he hopes to spread his environmental word and sign people up to his pledge; he tells Dellarobia that his mission is to get "[y]ou people ... on board" (315). His ridiculous assumptions that poor people pollute on a greater scale that the rest of society, and his unabashed distinction between himself and these people, leads Dellarobia to a frank discussion with Dr. Ovid Byron, a scientist who, with a small research team, is investigating why the monarchs have chosen Tennessee over their historical winter home in Mexico and the implications of the switch for the survival of the species.

After her encounter with Atkins, Dellarobia openly explains her concerns about environmentalism and class. Having told Ovid that she thinks people are split into teams, namely climate change deniers and believers, he asks: "What, you're saying this is some kind of contest between the peasant class and the gentry?" (322). She explains, "The environment gets assigned to the other team. Worries like that are not for people like us. So says my husband" (322). Despite the fact that Ovid has given her a job and eventually helps her secure a partially funded college scholarship, she tells him frankly: "[T]rust me, if you'd first run into me as your waitress down at the diner, you would not have included me in the conversation about your roosting populations and your overwintering zones. People shut out the other side" (323). Ovid cannot dispute her words, and later in the novel, over dinner with his wife, Juliet, and Dellarobia and her family, he informs Juliet about "the theory of the territorial divide. With some confusion Dellarobia understood that this was *her* theory, he was attributing it to her, though the terms he used were unfamiliar" (395). While Ovid problematically presumes to name and define Dellarobia's ideas, Kingsolver uses this discussion to expose the inherent challenges in recognizing poverty as well as class.

Until Ovid provides Dellarobia with a job that is relatively well paid for the area, she and Cub struggle financially. Although they live on his parents' farm, Dellarobia and Cub often find it difficult to meet the mortgage payments on their house, and the farm itself does not provide financial solvency, with Cub often having to work other jobs to help to support his family. Their son, Preston, receives free school meals, and they have to shop in discount and charity stores to try to keep ahead of their bills. Ovid fails to recognize their poverty, only becoming aware of it when he and his team start to use more advanced equipment and the power goes off. When Dellarobia calls the power company, she learns that "the problem was her bill. They'd been so stretched after Christmas, so many bills coming in at once, she'd assumed the power company would give them a month's grace. Having forgotten grace was already on the table since November, carved down to the bones" (242). Money and class are as crucial to this novel as the environment, and they are framed through Kingsolver's exploration of "the measure of things" (150). The novel transcends ideas of literal measurement, such as the different forms of appraisal undertaken by the scientists, as it reflects on ideas of value and worth in everyday life shaped by neoliberalism's individualistic, profit-driven motivations.

To date, critics have predominantly explored *Flight Behavior* as an ecocritical novel that shares commonalities with Kingsolver's earlier Appalachian environmental novel, *Prodigal Summer* (2000). Although Patrick D. Murphy acknowledges that the novel takes place "in the midst of the economic downturn now labeled the Great Recession," and while he pays attention to Kingsolver's turns to financial capital, he is more concerned with her environmentalism ("Pessimism" 159).[8] Much of this novel, however, can also be usefully read through an economic lens. Notably, Dellarobia, as well as Cub and mother-in-law Hester, work to prevent logging conglomerate Weyerhaeuser from clear-cutting the woods that her father-in-law, Bear, has sold to avoid foreclosure. Although Bear is a hardheaded conservative who is a fervent supporter of excessive "CEO salaries" and shows no concern for environmentalism, he is also presented as the victim of neoliberalism (303). Bear's decision to sell the land is solely driven by the 2008 financial crisis: before the crisis, with small-scale farming becoming less and less profitable, Bear sought to expand his "machine repair and metalwork" business by taking out an "equipment loan" (38). Despite his struggling farm, Bear secured the loan under the wider economics at play leading up to the crisis. In the United States, as Marazzi explains, between 1997 and 2007 "a liquidity influx from developing countries" actively encouraged high levels of indebtedness across the American economy, exemplified by the "subprime real estate bubble" (67–68). During this period, everyday Americans witnessed a reduction in "family savings ... with recourse to indebtedness" (69). In part, Marazzi argues, this resulted in overproduction and overtrading that "allowed for the creation of virtual incomes on the basis of the presupposition, later revealed as entirely unrealistic, of their future realization" (73). In Kingsolver's novel, Bear borrows "a huge sum to expand his machine shop" based on the premise of an imagined or "virtual" future market just months before the bubble burst in August 2007 (38). Suddenly, Bear has to face the drying up of contract work, even "the steady contracts making replacement parts of factories and something for the DOT" that he had regarded as "more valid that regular farm work" (38).

Bear is left with the equipment loan that "was backed up by a lien on the land," and faces the real prospect of foreclosure (38). Bear's seemingly unrelenting commitment to the logging process is, as Murphy outlines, just one example of short-term and short-sighted solutions to systemic economic problems. It also becomes an example of how people can be persuaded by the consumerist culture in which they live to make decisions that run counter to their own personal long-term interests, as well as the long-term health of their human communities, their ecoregional communities, and the biosphere. ("Pessimism" 159)

When Dellarobia first learns about Bear's intention to sell the land, she asks Cub: "If he can't make the payment, why wouldn't they just repossess his equipment?" He responds, "Depreciation, I guess. It's not enough. They needed that lien on the farm." She struggles to comprehend: "The equipment was so nearly new. She wondered if anyone totally understood how banks could make the ground shift underfoot and turn real things into empty air, just with a word" (42). The echo of Karl Marx and Friedrich Engels's observation in *The Communist Manifesto* (1848) that "[a]ll that is solid melts into air" (6) indicates that Dellarobia's interest in the machinations of financial capitalism are as vital to the novel as her gradual awareness of environmental concerns. The devaluation of Bear's equipment is part of the reordering of the economy after the crisis, when, as Marazzi explains, "in order to reestablish an operative balance between demand and supply, one very often turns to scrapping of unsold surplus or, in any case, to its devalorization. The violence of crises consists in this destruction of capital, a destruction that in biocapitalism strikes the totality of human beings" (73–74). With his market vanished, Bear's investment is, in effect, an unsold surplus: the rebalancing of demand and supply substantially depreciates his equipment, while the impending balloon payment on his loan pressures Bear to conclude that he has no alternative but to sell part of his land. His predicament weighs heavily on the whole family, but only Dellarobia questions the nature of the economy itself.

When Cub tells Dellarobia about the townspeople's plans to capitalize on the monarch phenomenon, she tries to enlighten him by explaining that "what those guys are saying about the butterflies, is that it's all centered around what they want. They need things to be a certain way, financially, so they think nature will organize itself around what suits them" (256). Dellarobia comes to realize the interconnectedness between the violence of financial capitalism and the destruction of ecosystems, and on her own journey out of a loveless marriage to a college education, she shares her knowledge with her family in a teacherly manner that has the most notable impact on Cub. From the outset, Kingsolver presents Cub as an emasculated man who is still known by his childhood nickname, who lives with his wife and children in a home on his parents' land, who struggles to eke out a living, and who succumbs to the pressures of capitalism and the messages of the right-wing media without question.[9] Early in the novel he is convinced that they have little choice but to sell the land, and even later, after a discussion with Dellarobia about climate change, Cub continues to defer to TV weatherman Johnny Midgeon's reports, which consistently debunk the idea of global warming (261). At this juncture, his response deflates Dellarobia, who sees "her life pass before her eyes, contained in the small enclosure of this logic. All knowledge measured, first and last, by one's allegiance to the teacher" (261). Yet she continues to challenge Cub to resist the limited thinking of those around them, and by the novel's close, her repeated messages about the changing weather take hold. When the local minister, Bobby, holds a family conference to prevail upon Bear to stop the logging, Dellarobia expects to have to do most of the convincing, yet when she tardily enters the room "she registered with surprise that it was Cub speaking" (400). Not only has Cub found a voice to talk back to his father, but he has also paid attention to Dellarobia's concerns. She first hears him talking about the "well water" and "mudslides," but she quickly realizes that "she had missed something significant. Cub was already up to four fingers, and Bear looked wary and mad, as if he'd been gut-punched. Certainly he would not have expected this from his son's corner" (401). Cub not only cites a list of environmental objections to the logging, but he also challenges his father about the cost of excessive greed, a reversal from his own earlier commitment to capitalism. As Murphy notes, at Christmastime, a debate between Cub and Dellarobia reveals that Cub "would be willing to wreck the world to give his children a nice holiday, because doing so depends on the accumulation of consumer goods people are encouraged to purchase" ("Pessimism" 159). Although Dellarobia can no longer remain in an unhappy marriage, she has transformed Cub's outlook by acting as an intermediary between locals and scientists. She is best placed for this role not simply because of her intellect but also because she has never fully accepted capitalism. Her background and her contemporary experiences of poverty lead her to constantly rethink measures of value and worth.

Although Dellarobia experienced a poor childhood, it was positively shaped by both her parents' artisanal skills and her own desire for self-improvement via education. Having lost both of her parents at a young age, Dellarobia idealizes her father's carpentry and her mother's needlework skills. In her work on contemporary southern writing, Melanie Benson argues:

> An increase in the possibilities for material fulfillment fails to bring real gratification to the individuals foreclosed from such goods on the basis of their class or racial immurement; and even when accessible, the world of market relations

proves tawdry and counterfeit, offering only mirrors of empty satisfaction. These vacant searchers thus appeal to old methods, looking for reflections that secure wholeness and value by opposition, a credit balanced by an authorizing debit, or an authoritative master to give the self-meaning and value. (131)

However, Dellarobia avoids fetishizing her parents' artisan skills because when she becomes nostalgic for the "hand-turned wooden toys of her childhood," she also realizes that those toys were the product of "poverty" (129). When she and Cub shop for their children's Christmas gifts in the local dollar store, her questions about worth and meaning come to the fore. While her husband keeps "saying he wanted the kids to have a 'real Christmas' . . . she felt off balance, wondering what those words could possibly mean" (163). For her, there is nothing real about the litany of cheaply made produce in the store: she runs her hands across the "pathetically thin fabric" of clothes, and her mother's admonition about "[f]amily heirlooms made by slave children in China" comes to her mind (157). Kingsolver brings together critiques of obsolescence, poverty, and neoliberalism in the thoughts that run through Dellarobia's mind in the store. At one point she reflects:

> Maybe her father was lucky to die young with his pride of craftsmanship still intact. What would he make of this world? Realistically, it probably wasn't slave children, but there had to be armies of factory workers making this slapdash stuff, underpaid people cranking out things for underpaid people to buy and use up, living their lives mostly to cancel each other out. A worldwide entrapment of bottom feeders. (159)

While Morrison, Biguenet, and Whitehead all explore possibilities for cross-racial cooperation within the United States, here Kingsolver's environmentalism and engagement with neoliberalism brings about a crucial global turn as Dellarobia recognizes levels of global poverty and "entrapment"; furthermore, although Dellarobia appreciates artisanal skills, Kingsolver avoids what Harvey terms "a politics of nostalgia for that which has been lost," which, he argues, can only "supersede the search for ways to better meet the material needs of impoverished and repressed populations" (*The New Imperialism* 177). While Dellarobia attributes greater worth to well-made goods of the past, she equally embraces the future and its possibility for change. Although Benson argues that "the simple triumph of owning 'nothing' . . . becomes in fact the only available retreat for contemporary southerners," in Kingsolver's novel Dellarobia might reject the tawdry produce on sale in the discount store, but she does not dispense with the need to engage with consumerism (131). When her son, who is fascinated by the scientists, purchases a set of encyclopedias at the Try It Again Warehouse for a dollar, they soon realize that these books from the 1950s contain outdated information about the monarchs, and since Dellarobia wants to foster her son's love of learning, she realizes that she has to engage with new forms of technology, exemplified by a tablet computer that she presents to Preston at the end of the novel. They have to share the tablet, and its "monthly payment was going to be her biggest, after rent," but she regards it as the means for allowing her children "to reach into the river of knowledge and pull out" their "own darn fish" (425). Indeed, Frederick Buell argues that Dellarobia is "one step ahead of mourning" and "achieves a new identity and mission in a damaged world" ("Global Warming" 282).[10] Certainly, when Dellarobia looks back, she sees the flaws of the past and chooses instead to look forward, drawing on the skills of her parents but also forging a new, educational path for herself and her children. Christopher Lloyd and Jessica Rapson argue that "*Flight Behaviour* implies that robust education is fundamental to comprehending climate change" (914), yet in addition to environmental awareness, education also leads to a broader understanding of the instability and destruction caused by the economy. The flood at the end of the novel that unmoors the house Dellarobia shares with Cub is caused by climate change, but the unstable, unpredictable weather also reflects the financial difficulties faced by the local community as Kingsolver merges economics and environmentalism at the novel's close.

When Dellarobia steps outside to escape the rising water and encounters an expanse of liquidity, she immediately thinks about climate change, but also, as she looks around, imagines this is "a dead world learning to speak in dissonant, unbearable sounds. The topsoil, the slim profit margins of this farm, the ground itself, rushed away from her, and when water spilled over her boots again she backed slowly into the violent current to find a better place" (431).[11] The dissonance she imagines emanating from the damaged land also mirrors the lack of communal harmony in a world where "slim profit margins" dictate human behavior. Furthermore, the sheer violence of the water here talks to more than climate change: Dellarobia connects the fragility of the ecosystem with the instability of financial markets. The end brings together the novel's dual perspective on environmentalism and the impact of market fluctuations on the lives of the poor. When Dellarobia realizes that her family home, the house she and Cub have struggled to pay for, is being unmoored by the flood, she sees that

> [o]ne corner of the house appeared to tilt . . . shifting the structure a scant but perceptible few inches on its foundation. This time she had to see. Soon the

whole thing would drift away from its anchored steps and cement-block foundation, departing as gently as an ocean liner. Then it would not be a home, but a rigid, rectangular balloon with siding and shingles and weather-stripped doors, improbably serene, floating on the buoyant command of the air sealed carefully inside. (432)

The idea of the home transforming into a balloon naturally takes the reader back to the balloon payment that loomed over the farm. Kingsolver reflects on the concerns after the 2008 financial crisis that "dangerous imbalances will persist" ("When a Flow Becomes a Flood"). Dellarobia's future might seem brighter with the prospect of a college education, but Kingsolver avoids a neat resolution that would offer uncompromised hope: the surviving monarchs might take flight, but this does not provide complete assurance of their or Dellarobia's future. She thinks how the butterflies are now "charged with resistance," ready to "gather on other fields and risk other odds," odds, she imagines "probably no better or worse than hers" (433). Phrased in financial terms of risk and odds, the future is only as stable as financial markets dictate, which is why as she watches the monarchs depart, Dellarobia stands on "ground so unreliable" that the future is decidedly uncertain (433). In a hopeful turn at the end of his argument about financial capitalism, Marazzi argues:

> The forms and objectives of the struggle "inside and against" crisis capitalism are ...local and global. The objectives of this struggle are clear: imposing, collectively and from the ground up, new rules to govern the market and the financial system, a social mobilization for starting anew investment policies in public services, education and welfare, the creation of public employment for the conversion of energy, a refusal to defiscalize high incomes, assert the right to wages, employment and social income and the construction of autonomous, self-determined spaces. (121–22)

There must indeed be alternatives, but Kingsolver's novel suggests that there is much to be done to make "the ground" safe and secure for such movements to take root. Fiction that demands a reexamination of the lives of the poor plays a part in firming up that ground because only by moving past romanticized ideas of nobility within poverty or the denigration of the poor as voraciously draining the state, might a better understanding emerge of the ways in which neoliberal, financial capital erodes the commonalities Marazzi envisages will bring about change.

Given the unrelenting commitment to neoliberalism by both the political Right and Left, it is perhaps fitting at the end of this chapter to return to the 1980s, and the first novel written by a so-called Rough South novelist, Tim McLaurin. If Morrison's *Beloved* explores slavery though the lenses of communitarianism and neoliberalism, McLaurin's *The Acorn Plan* (1988) exposes what is at stake in obligating oneself to neoliberalism's individualist agenda. The novel is just as much about the working-class community in Fayetteville, North Carolina, as it is about the fate of its central protagonist, Billy Riley, a young man whose father recently died after working himself into the ground to achieve a middle-class life. At the start of the novel, Billy seems destined to end his life in either in a bloody, drunken brawl or in prison. In a bid to change the course of Billy's life, his uncle Bubble, who has fought alcoholism his whole adult life, decides to surrender to it by consuming "all the wine in the world," hoping that his downward descent might jolt his nephew into choosing a different future (9). As the novel unfolds, Billy is left with two choices—to become a man who never leaves the mill streets of Fayetteville, getting into regular fights avowedly to save his honor and thereby fulfilling the locals' idea of him, or a man who, having served his time in the army, takes the opportunity to go to college and leave the mill streets behind forever.

Just as Bubble started to see their neighborhood as if for the first time after he quit his mill job, seeing as "a liberated man" that "the houses were rickety as cardboard, the brief spots of color from flowers planted inside discarded tires, and candy-striped, rusty swingsets, only highlighting the decay," so Billy, having avoided jail time for stabbing a soldier, begins to reevaluate the same streets (18). Despite Billy's propensity for drinking and violence, his intelligence and perceptiveness enable him, when he contemplates leaving the neighborhood behind, to be sensitive to the life he would be rejecting. As well as drinking and fighting, he knows that life in Fayetteville would involve working at the mill and becoming one of the people "on the east side, hunched over their morning coffee, trying to read some sense into the cracks on the linoleum table top, the past-due notice on the kid's hospital bill haunting their thoughts" (75). These are the working poor, and while this novel is set just prior to the onslaught of mill and factory closures around the United States, so mass unemployment does not yet plague the streets of Billy's east side, working life is still brought into question. Here, working people are crushed by bills for even the most essential things, and their lives are "measured in units of Friday afternoon till Monday morning" (159–60). Just as Kingsolver dwells at length on how we measure worth, so McLaurin draws attention to the value of the working class. Billy's choice is either to give in to "the hopelessness of the east side" or to take a chance and give himself over to a form of hope that his aunt Ruby inspires.

As Billy contemplates his future, the eponymous acorn plan comes into play. Billy is introduced to the acorn plan by his short-term girlfriend Cassie, a topless dancer who is gradually making her way to New York to pursue her dream of becoming a ballet star and whose ambition rules over all else, including her relationship with Billy. Cassie explains her individualist drive to Billy one day on a fishing trip when they discuss an oak tree. Cassie embraces the survival-of-the-fittest notion, explaining to Billy that of all the acorns that fall, only the strongest will grow into a tree, and when Billy questions the fairness of this system, she responds:

> Let's imagine that this big old oak is a family. It has a plan. Let's call it the acorn plan. Sure, there's lots of members of the family who strike out, whatever, get burned, eaten, maybe make it halfway only to get cut down. Still, this family knows that sooner or later one of them is going to fall on rich soil—maybe there is a little luck needed—but that person will grow and grow and grow. See? (113)

For Bes Stark Spangler, the acorn plan helps "Billy to recognize that regardless of the degree to which his background has shaped him, he can reject the limitations inherent in his perceived local identity; loyal to but not owned by his heritage, he can risk attending the university that has accepted his application" (43). Yet Billy sees not the logic in this plan but only its unfairness, so while it is easy to assume that it is the acorn plan in and of itself that propels Billy to choose a different future, it is actually his critical examination of the plan that strengthens his resolve to find a life away from Fayetteville's mill streets. After their conversation, Billy wants to confront the truth behind Cassie's idea. While Cassie is only interested in the acorns that thrive and grow into trees, Billy remains sensitive to those that fall and wither. When Cassie takes him to "a steak house across town" to celebrate his acceptance letter to the University of North Carolina, they are both confused about which forks to use for which course, so they decide "to stay with the same fork, reasoning that some poor person would be washing dishes long after they had gone" (121). This very thought troubles Billy, making him "feel sort of guilty" about having choices (121). When she reminds him about the acorns, he responds: "I'm not talking about no damn acorns, Cassie. I'm talking about people—good people. People who sweat and fart and cry," people like his aunt Ruby, who has "worked like a dog all her life trying to have something," and his father, who "fought in the war. Deader than hell at fifty-five" (122). Billy maintains that the acorn plan is fundamentally unfair, so even after he has decided to go to college, as he stands on a bridge at the end of the novel looking "into the bowels of the east side," he reflects on all the "[w]orking-class people, fighting people, hoping people, someday making it people" who help society to function, the "mill people," the "table waiters and short-order cooks rising to prepare breakfast for those fortunate enough to sleep late, plumbers and carpenters sipping coffee before driving across the river to continue building those split-levels" (189). In the end, the novel is about Billy's transformation, but it is also about the labor of the working class, and in ways similar to Kingsolver's Dellarobia, Billy acts as a bridge between two worlds. While Cassie relinquishes all connections to people and places in her bid for individual success, Billy refuses that approach. If McLaurin's novel is about the acorn plan, then he is more interested in the acorns on the ground than those that grow into trees, the acorns that turn back into the earth to provide the rich soil from which future trees will grow. Billy sees and acknowledges what Cassie either cannot or will not see, that the top 1 percent thrives only off the other 99: McLaurin challenges the idea of what hooks refers to as "a class-segregated society where the plight of the poor is forgotten and the greed of the rich is morally tolerated and condoned" (vii).

Perhaps this is where contemporary writing departs from many earlier fictional accounts of the southern poor white. Brian Carpenter argues that Rough South writing "is about getting beyond the caricature and introducing a little compassion and complication into the conversation" (Carpenter and Franklin xxxvi). The focus on Grit Lit and Rough South certainly draws attention to what it means for writers emerging out of poor backgrounds to depict with firsthand knowledge the abject experiences of those living on or beneath the poverty line. Yet the novels under consideration in this chapter do more than depict poverty from both inside and out; they pose alternatives, often in the form of communitarianism and/or education, as they reflect on socioeconomic shifts that propel a profit-driven ethos above all else. For Robert W. McChesney, the "necessary by-product" of neoliberalism is a "depoliticized citizenry marked by apathy and cynicism" (10). The writers of the works in this chapter seek to move beyond "apathy and cynicism" as they explore the impact of economics and champion the need for cooperation and respect within and across racial and class lines; however, none of the characters considered here become activists in any clear and directed manner. The next chapter will consider environmental literature, which examines activism within poor communities, often believed to be nonexistent or to exist only for self-centered concerns rather than broader issues such as environmentalism.

CHAPTER FIVE

"Culture Springs from the Actions of People in a Landscape": Poor Whites and Environmentalism

On April 22, 1970, the United States participated in the first worldwide Earth Day, giving rise to modern environmentalism and ensuring future legislative change. By the end of 1970, the Clean Air Act was passed and the US Environmental Protection Agency was founded, but despite ongoing policy changes, the new environmental movement faced numerous challenges as it sought to gain momentum and effect positive, lasting change. Eileen McGurty observes that "[s]oon after the 1970 Earth Day euphoria, many claimed that environmentalism had been a fad and was now on the way out. To counter this attack, environmentalists tried to demonstrate that environmentalism appealed to a broad constituency" (375). Part of that broader support, Daniel Zwerdling wrote in his 1973 essay "Poverty and Pollution," must come "from labor and poverty groups," or the environmental movement, he feared, would "drop dead from malnutrition and irrelevance" (27). For Zwerdling, it was clear: "Pollution, poverty and worker insecurity reflect three different ways that American corporations express themselves as they exploit people and resources for maximum profits," and that only by forming an alliance could environmentalists and antipoverty groups build a strong foundation for lasting change. Writing just three years after the first Earth Day celebrations, Zwerdling was pessimistic about the success of any such collaboration given the unrelenting "economic and political system which gives enormous corporations the power to control the nation's people and resources" (29). As the twenty-first century unfolds and despite the many victories for environmental groups locally, nationally, and globally, Zwerdling's solicitude remains as pressing now as it did in the 1970s.

Societal attitudes toward poverty and waste often make it difficult to see the complex connections between the poor and environmentalism. Associations of the poor with "trash," "dirt," "uncleanliness," and "litter" define the impoverished as polluters. In societal terms, as Michael Thompson suggests, "the boundary between rubbish and non-rubbish moves in response to social pressures," such as the move in developed countries in recent years to embrace recycling as a part of responsible citizenship (11). Similarly, attitudes toward poverty and the poor have fluctuated over time, but since the 1970s and the gradual erosion of welfare provision in the United States, the poor have been consistently demonized at the same time they have been used and thrown away as a cheap form of labor. As Noam Chomsky outlines, under the auspices of the neoliberal agenda, "[f]or most of the US population, incomes have stagnated or declined … along with working conditions and job security, continuing through economic recovery, an unprecedented phenomenon. Inequality has reached levels unknown for seventy years" (28). Yet free-market, profit-driven capital takes no responsibility for the welfare of workers, and those workers who seek to retain or bring back dirty energy jobs are considered unenlightened and ignorant of environmental concerns and climate change. As Richard White observes: "Environmentalists have come to associate work—particularly heavy bodily labor, blue-collar work—with environmental degradation," completely ignoring the fact that in developed communities across the globe, every form of labor, from industrial to academic, depends upon and uses energy. White states: "There are few articles or letters denouncing university professors or computer programmers or accountants or lawyers for sullying the environment, although it is my guess that a single lawyer or accountant could, on a good day, put the efforts of Paul Bunyan to shame." The animosity that arises between environmentalists and pro-coal campaigners, exemplified in pro-coal bumper stickers demanding "Save a Surface Miner, Shoot a Tree Hugger" or "Fight Air Pollution: Gag a Liberal," only serve to obscure the grassroots movements in poor communities that work for environmental safeguards. The relationship between poverty, class, and environmentalism has also been obscured as corporations have hijacked the environmental bandwagon, not just through "greenwash" campaigns but also in their realization that green awareness and "going green" were ripe new consumer markets with high-profit yields. As Jo Littler explains: "One immediately conspicuous problem with 'buying green' is the social and cultural divisions around it. 'Green' products have often come with a higher price tag attached and are therefore ripe to be critiqued as a lifestyle option for the privileged middle classes" (101). As a result, the affluent, who can afford to purchase "ethical" and "environmentally friendly" products, are regarded as more ethically minded and environmentally conscious than the poor.

This chapter considers the ways in which recent southern literature depicts the relationship between poor whites and environmentalism, and explores the increasing levels of activism in communities where poverty and environmental abuses are bound up in neoliberalism and its "unstable and evolving regime of accumulation" (Harvey, *Spaces of Global* 29).[1] For Stefania Barca, "sustainability policies aimed at social justice must be based on new and convincing forms of articulation between labor and environmental issues," and southern literature is one of the places where dialectical issues are played out in complex, nuanced ways that trouble commonly held assumptions about the relationship between the poor and the environment (4). Significantly, the US South played an important role in the emergence of the environmental justice movement.[2] Since the environmental movement in the United States has long been lambasted for being "mostly a middle and upper class battle" (Zwerdling 26), it sought ways in the 1970s to widen its reach and become more representative, and found new voice and agency in collaboration with civil rights organizations. This union was cemented during the protests in Warren County, North Carolina, in 1982, when the poor black residents of Shocco opposed plans to build a landfill next to their community specifically designated to house the contaminated soil from the illegal dumping of polychlorinated biphenyl (PCB) across fourteen counties in North Carolina by the Ward Transformers Company during the 1970s. Locals were supported in their efforts by civil rights leaders and environmentalists, and although they were unsuccessful in preventing the construction of the landfill, as McGurty explains:

> The events in Warren County are proclaimed by activists and policymakers alike as the birth of the environmental justice movement. Environmental justice activists argue that inequitable distribution of environmental degradation and systematic exclusion of the poor and people of color from environmental decision making is perpetuated by traditional environmental organizations, also known as mainstream environmentalism, and by environmental regulatory practices. (373)

In the South, where, as Jack Temple Kirby notes, "poor and working-class people have always picked the crops amid pesticides; mined the coal, iron ore, and phosphates; and lived downwind of industrial smoke and sewage" (33), the alignment of environmentalism with race and social justice provided the South's disenfranchised groups with a means to challenge environmental and public health abuses.

The emergence of the environmental justice movement in the United States, however, has not been without its critics. Joan Martinez-Alier, in *The Environmentalism of the Poor: A Study of Ecological Conflicts and Valuation* (2002), notes that this movement often sidelines ecology in its commitment to social justice. It has, he suggests, a shortsighted preoccupation with the rights of individuals and communities in the present, without "concern for the rights of other species and of future generations of humans" (11). Yet he is less concerned with this imbalance than he is with the apparent divergence between the US environmental justice movement and similar movements across the globe. For Martinez-Alier, that tension is a direct result of the union between environmentalism and the civil rights movement in America—a union, he believes, that "is a product of the American mind so obsessed with racism and anti-racism" (11). He in no way dismisses the significance or seriousness of racism but argues that identity politics obscures the issues of poverty that are central to global environmental debates and movements. At both the global and local levels, Martinez-Alier champions moving beyond the parochial limitations of NIMBY (not in my backyard) and identity politics in a bid to trace the economic networks that lead to environmental destruction and the further denigration of the world's poor (263).

Just as Martinez-Alier works to reveal the commonalities between US and global environmentalism, in *Slow Violence and the Environmentalism of the Poor* (2011), Rob Nixon also traces the connections between global ecological disasters and abuses, and the activism of individuals, communities, and movements, as he argues for "a transnational ethics of place": not NIMBYism or localism but a sense of ethical responsibility that transcends the borders of nation-states (243). The challenge, as Nixon sees it, is "to bring into imaginative focus threatened communities and ecosystems rendered invisible by the celebratory developmental rhetoric that gushes from big dam technocrats, cabinet ministers, World Bankers, and media moguls" (160). As well as engaging with the potentially democratic nature of new media forms that connect people across geographical divides and allow for different voices and counternarratives to emerge, Nixon is also interested in "the complex, often vexed figure of the environmental writer-activist," most notably "combative writers who have deployed their imaginative agility and worldly ardor to help amplify the media-marginalized causes of the environmentally dispossessed" (5). Yet Nixon takes issue with a number of American environmentalist writers and academics whose work and outlook is predominantly US-centric, and who therefore fail to engage with "a transnational ethics of place." For Nixon, unlike postcolonial theorists, "most prominent American environmental writers and critics are mononationals with a deep-rooted experiential and imaginative commitment to a particular regional locale"; he continues: "These regionally rooted national writers" carry "forward the place commitments evinced in the New England writings of Thoreau and Robert Frost and in Willa Cather's Nebraska" (327–38). Before turning to Nixon's consideration of the Global South, it worth pausing here to reflect on the idea of

American environmental and nature writers as solely "mononational" in their approach. Although Nixon does not include Janisse Ray in his consideration of American environmentalists, as a writer who emerged out of a poor white background, her work offers a useful case for examining the degree to which localism is devoid of global perspectives and concerns.

For Richard Kerridge, "[n]o perspective is valid in ecocritical terms if it allows one to immerse oneself in a single place, oblivious to the lines of economic and ecological connection that lead to other places" ("Environmental Fiction" 73–74), a concern echoed by Paul Sutter, who believes that "the challenge is to avoid a literature that becomes regionally parochial" (19). Localism, Kerridge argues, more than just preventing us from seeing global networks, might actually "be implicated in our failure to respond to the global ecological crisis" ("Environmental Fiction" 67). The question is whether to speak locally can also be to speak globally. In his work on the US South in global contexts, James Peacock proposes the concept of "grounded globalism," which recognizes "the strength of both forces, global and local" and the need to create "paths that productively and creatively unite them" (13). Peacock is not the first to posit this move from regionalism/nationalism to localism/globalism: what he terms grounded globalism is what Hugh Bartling regards as "pluralistic localism" (137). Lawrence Buell also notes that "the locale cannot shut itself off from translocal forces even if it wanted to" (88). Indeed, as Ray charts her ecological activism and commitment to a communitarian existence "off the grid, free of consumer guilt," her localized approach contains the idea of "transnational ethics" as posited by Nixon (*Pinhook* 3).

As discussed in chapter 3, Ray is a prominent American environmentalist and poet whose multigenre approach details increasing levels of environmental destruction and its impact on local communities. Her communitarian ideal certainly emerges out of ruralism, and throughout her work strains of Thoreau, Rachel Carson, and Wendell Berry are evident: indeed, some might also hear neo-agrarian strains. Just in the introduction to *The Seed Underground: A Growing Revolution to Save Food* (2012), Ray employs a Thoreau quotation as an epigraph and then moves from a critique of Wall Street economics to rural Georgia and an encounter with her neighbor, a potentially neo-agrarian move that privileges the rural over the urban. She writes: "I gather yesterday's mail from our box on Old River Road and am running back when I meet my neighbor, puttering along in his faded black truck. Not that many years ago he would have been on a horse, and suddenly I miss something I have never known" (xi). Such wistful longings for an imagined, idyllic past can easily be read as a form of neo-agrarianism (272). She also dwells on ideas of southern exceptionalism, arguing that "[c]ulture springs from the actions of a people in a landscape, and we, especially Southerners, are watching a daily erosion of unique folkways as our native ecosystems and all their inhabitants disappear" (*Ecology* 271). The damage she outlines, however, is not particular to the South, nor to the United States, and her emphasis on regional uniqueness seems radically opposed to Nixon's ideas of "transnational ethics."

Yet in much of her work, Ray's environmental concerns center on microregions and microbiodiversity,[3] such as her concern in *Ecology of a Cracker Childhood* with the destruction of longleaf pine, or in *Pinhook* (2005) with the Pinhook swamp on the border between Georgia and Florida, or simply with the "land between" the Okefenokee Swamp and Osceola National Forest (272),[4] and she hopes that her resistance to dominant economic forces and lifestyles at the local level resonates globally, as she outlines in *The Seed Underground*:

> This book is for everyone, but it is especially for young people, in hopes that, given all the bad, you start building. Not skyscrapers or oil rigs, but lives that make sense, that contribute to a lighter, more intelligent, more beautiful way of living on the earth, lives that are lived as far outside and beyond corporate control as possible. (ix)

Hope and hopefulness is the running theme throughout the book and across Ray's writing as she promotes an anti-neoliberal, communitarian approach that she perceives as the bedrock for resistance. In his study of disaster and hope, Ronald Aronson argues "that we are left today with one fundamental principle of hope: action" (293). Writing at the end of the 1980s with the threat of nuclear war still looming, Aronson's argument is no less relevant today, but while nuclear threats still abound, recent environmental catastrophes and predictions are as doom laden for humanity as any nuclear war. Aronson's notion that hope must be active, not passive, resonates with Ray's approach. He believes that "hope *is* political practice," and in a world "grown so threateningly out of control ... only an active, political mode of apprehending it can restore a sense of it as fluid, unfinished, and capable of redirection" (294). Ray also believes in collective action and the possibility of effecting change, writing: "The easiest thing to do is to give up. But so much needs to be done; every mind and body is crucial for putting new systems in place" (*The Seed Underground* ix). She fully realizes that we can cannot, nor should we want, to return to some idealized notion of the past: instead, she observes, "[w]ith some of the old knowledge intact and armed with fresh knowledge, we are looping forward to a new place. And we're coming there different" (xiv). All of the environmental destruction that Ray charts could easily lead to despair, and she might seem overly idealistic in her belief that a life off the grid is more "authentic" than any other, but if the question arises as to how her localism can be read transnationally, then it must be through her hope that, globally, humanity can take steps to halt the relentless assaults against the environment (xv). When Ray writes about the environment, even when she seems lost in the local, she is always aware of the wider global networks, of the "corporate robbery" that "is being acted out on a world stage" (xiv). Ray's work is just one example that problematizes Nixon's assertion that mainstream American environmental and nature writers often fail to engage with issues beyond local, regional, or national borders.

Throughout Nixon's argument, he also highlights the inequities between the Global North and the Global South, but as he does so he risks creating an overly simplified binary between the privileged, affluent Global North and the underprivileged, poor Global South. While the United States obviously forms part of the Global North, the inequity faced by its poor citizens seemingly has much more in common with the Global South; however, aligning US poverty with that of developing countries ignores the reality that abject poverty is not an aberration in the United States but actually an intrinsic feature of capitalism. Nixon finds it easier to sideline the commonalities between the poor across the Global South and Global North, as evidenced in his comparison between the compensation payouts after 2010 Deepwater Horizon oil spill in the Gulf of Mexico and the 1984 Bhopal disaster in India, to exemplify the stark differences between the two regions, arguing that "the US administration could leverage its power against BP, whereas the Indian government found itself in a weak bargaining position in relation to a US-based corporation" (274). The disparity is clear, with Union Carbide only agreeing to pay out $470 million years after the Bhopal disaster in comparison to the "initial $20 billion" set aside by BP (274-75); however, while the payouts drastically differ in amount, the failure of that money to always reach the worst affected shows the common experience of local populations across the Global North and the Global South. Indeed, Brian Mayer, Katrina Running, and Kelly Bergstrand argue that despite the amount of money on offer from BP, "the claims process itself emerged as a secondary trauma that led to social disruption and collective uncertainty regarding financial recovery from the spill" (369-70). More broadly, in her work on Louisiana's "cancer alley," Barbara L. Allen details the devastating environmental and social degradations that have arisen since the early twentieth century as oil and chemical corporations have expanded their production sites along the "150-mile stretch of the lower Mississippi River between New Orleans and Baton Rouge" (235). In 2006, she notes, Louisiana, among a host of other damning statistics related to environmental abuses, was "first in the nation for cancers attributable to air and water pollutants," all because the state government "has opted to promote itself to industry regardless of the cost to its citizens and their environment" (246). So, while the treatment of the poor might be relatively better in the Global North than in the South, it is still shaped by the same neoliberal dynamics that, as Harvey explains, are driven by the need "to optimize conditions for capital accumulation no matter what the consequences for employment or social well-being" (*Spaces of Global* 25).

Certainly, the levels of inequity within the United States reflect patterns of economic disenfranchisement and environmental abuses across the globe. As Jimmie Killingsworth and Jacqueline Palmer note, "in the United States ... the places where the earth suffers the greatest insults are the very places most likely to be inhabited by African Americans, Mexican Americans, Native Americans, and the working poor and dispossessed of all colours and kinds" (196–97). The binary, then, between the Global North and the Global South only takes us so far, and it certainly risks rendering the poor in the Global North and the wealthy elite in the Global South invisible.

In the United States, there are several places where environmental abuses and poverty coalesce, which is hardly surprising given Daniel Payne's assessment of "the predominant American worldview ... that sees the earth as a virtually limitless storehouse from which humankind can extract resources and where it can dispose of waste and alter the landscape with little concern for the ways in which these actions will affect the local or global environment" (2). In this context, the US South is particularly interesting not only because large areas of the region have suffered a vast array of environmental depredation, but also because the enduring stereotypes of poor "white trash" connect the southern poor with utter disregard for ecological concerns. Across southern literature, stereotypical depictions of poor "white trash" are replete with images of slovenly homes and gardens: junk-laden spaces that confirm eugenicist claims that trash breeds trash.[5] Exploring the connections between the poor and environmentalism in southern writing serves to highlight the ways in which even the most apparently localized issues and concerns form part of larger debates and movements that center on the exploitation of workers and the landscape. Serenella Iovino suggests that "[t]o talk about ecocriticism and an 'ecological' humanism means to imagine an evolved form of culture which is a culture of responsibility for both nature and society. Such a culture could make us better citizens, because it would enable us to listen to the language of otherness, fragility, weakness" (46). Reading southern literature ecocritically allows for a more nuanced understanding of the relationship between the poor and environmentalism. As Jay Watson argued in his work on Larry Brown's *Joe* (1991) and Ray's *Ecology of a Cracker Childhood*, reading the South via an environmental lens demands a full recognition of the region's complexities, which include "the economics of the Cracker landscape" (513).

Economics has typically regarded poor white bodies as disposable as the junk that supposedly litters their homes and yards, thereby occluding the forms of activism that emerge out of poor communities. This chapter explores moves to realign the poor white relationship with the environment, using ecocritical and multicultural debates that serve to make trash meaningful. Approaching southern literature from an ecocritical perspective "implies a move toward a more biocentric world-view, an extension of ethics, a broadening of humans' conception of global community to include nonhuman life forms and the physical environment" (Branch et al. xiii). The "extension of ethics" also relates to the ways that an ecocritical reading of southern literature can lead us to rethink the relationship between poverty and the environment, taking us beyond ideas of the poor as polluters or as mere victims of wider socioeconomic forces.

To unpack the relationship between the poor and environmentalism, it is necessary to explore the ideas of waste and wastefulness that proliferate around poverty: trashy people live trashy lives, or so the idea goes. Those labeled "white trash," "hillbilly," or "cracker" are perceived as demonstrating little care for themselves or, by extension, their environment. John Scanlan notes:

> A common element in perceptions of all such outsiders is that they do not take measures to sustain their lives against simply wasting away, without having achieved anything noteworthy or virtuous. And because of their inability to subject themselves to control, social morality (as well as the law) sees to it that the wasteful activities of such people are looked down upon disdainfully, and regarded as bad examples for the rest of society. (32)

This conflation of degenerate lives and waste is apparent in numerous depictions of poor white lives, such as in Cormac McCarthy's *Child of God* (1973), in which, despite the empathy created for poor white necrophiliac Lester Ballard, readers encounter familiar territory at the dumpkeeper's lair, with its "levees of junk and garbage," and "degenerate," "rotting," and "niggerized" cars that reinforce long-held ideas linking "white trash" with equally trashy environments (26). Yet, we see the revisioning of trash across a number of texts that depict the contemporary poor white experience and pose a series of different questions about the relationship between people and waste.

Waste, of course, is not an issue under the sole purview of the poor. As Scanlan observes, the monumental waste problem facing society is a result of a period of increased obsolescence; quite simply, what we encounter is "the debris of unfettered consumption" (32). Such excessive consumption is commonly associated less with the poor than with the affluent, and as Alvin Toffler reminded us, "[t]he idea of using a product once or for a brief period and then replacing it, runs counter to the grain of societies or individuals steeped in a heritage of poverty" (56). Yet even then, as he developed his idea of the "throwaway society" in 1970, Toffler was aware that the "new, fast-forming society based on transience" rather than "permanence" was likely to sweep across most classes in developed countries, even the poorest (55). "Resistance," he predicted, "is dying all over the developed world" (56). Indeed, one of today's most urgent environmental issues is the management of, and attempts to curtail, the sheer amount of waste that arises from submission to the "throwaway" model. In her work *Waste and Want* (1999), Susan Strasser argues, with a particular focus on contemporary American society, that in addition to the massive industries that have emerged to manage waste disposal, at the individual level "[d]iscarding things is taken to be a kind of freedom" (16). Freedom, here, is intrinsically bound up in capital and the misconception that consumer choice equates to freedom. In fact, much of what we purchase is "not easily reused, repaired, or returned to nature," so we make use of "landfills and garbage disposers" to make way for new and "better" products that will become equally obsolescent in time (16). Such conditioning, she implies, does not set us free but instead enslaves us to the will of the market and subjects the environment to exponential levels of waste.

Scanlan argues that once discarded, trash takes on the guise of the "uncanny," since it "becomes capable of inducing horror because of the presumed harmful effects it has on the bodies of personal and social order, indicating their fragile and transient nature" (36). Scanlan's work echoes not just Freud but also Julia Kristeva's theory of abjection and Mary Douglas's ideas about pollution and taboo. While there is a clear distinction between reusable and nonreusable waste—Kristeva uses the example of corpses as nonreusable—in both cases she argues, "refuse and corpses *show me* what I permanently thrust aside in order to live" (3). Rather than confronting the horror of waste, we systematically dispose of it, both at the individual and corporate level. Here, it is worth reflecting on the removal of dirt or waste in the terms set out by Mary Douglas. Douglas believes that "[d]irt offends against order" yet argues that "[e]liminating it is not a negative movement, but a positive effort to organise the environment" (2). Surely, in the case of dumping household or toxic waste, the only positive impact is for those with the power to organize: the affluent ensure that waste sits far beyond their own borders, with landfills, incinerators, and other refuse sites typically located near poor communities. Removing dirt or waste and situating it beside the poor is a class-based form of societal organization that aligns hidden waste with unseen poverty. The connection between materialism, the disposal of waste, and the possibilities of recycling in southern writing reconfigures ideas about poverty and worth.

It is hardly surprising that for many poor people, going through other people's trash is a last resort. In his memoir *All Over but the Shoutin'*, Rick Bragg recalls trips to the "city dump at Jacksonville" where he, his mother, and his brothers would ransack piles of rubbish to find "treasure," things that the boys would hope to play with and objects that his mother could sell: "copper wires, aluminum, Coke and Orange Crush and RC bottles, worth a penny" (42). Bragg's retrospective glance back at those times offers no environmental gloss on recycling: rather, he cannot erase the pervasive and lingering "smell" of the dump where they used to burn trash. For Bragg, "this is what hell smell likes" (*All Over* 42). Even in Ray's *Ecology of a Cracker Childhood*, it is only as an adult that she can look back on her father's junkyard business and see his labor as intrinsically worthy: as children, she and her siblings "were ashamed of the junkyard. Our daddy was a junk dealer, but when we filled out his occupation on forms from school we wrote 'salesman'" (29). Despite being taught by their parents that the rest of society was "wasteful and threw perfectly good things in the garbage," Ray recalls, "[w]e thought that meant they were better than we were" (29). Questions of worth revolve around waste and trash, but unlike Bragg, Ray positions her father's junk in the wider context of environmentalism, thereby dwelling more on the value that still resides in the objects thrown away on a daily basis.

Similarly, in Larry Brown's novel *Joe* (1991), the itinerant poor white Jones family has returned to Mississippi after time spent traveling across numerous states; Brown details how the family survives despite the actions of the father, Wade, the morally vacuous, stereotypically idle, alcoholic and devious head of the household. With no money to their name, the Jones family squats in an abandoned log house they find in the woods, scavenging to survive, until the eponymous Joe Ransom, the foreman of a logging crew who remains firmly attached to his blue-collar roots, employs and befriends Wade's son, Gary. Wade remains a constant threat in the novel, stealing Gary's money and ensuring that his family can never leave the rundown house throughout the course of the novel, but Gary's job allows them to eventually eat well after he purchases "proper pans" and Joe gives "them a little green Coleman stove."

Yet every night they sleep "under their mildewed quilts recycled from the hands of the haves," while "these have-nots lay with their ears pricked in the darkness as the drone of the mosquitoes moved toward them" (205). Brown is attuned to the plight of the "have-nots" in this novel, and although Wade is a stock poor white character, Gary and indeed his sister Fay, who plays only a small part in this novel but whose fate forms the subject of Brown's novel *Fay* (2000), become Brown's vehicles for examining humanity caught up in abject poverty. Gary, having spent so long mired in poverty, seeks to make home improvements with secondhand items, keeping "an eye out for a castoff screen door" even though they "seemed hard to come by" (205). His recycling ethos is, of course, driven by economics rather than ecology, but throughout the novel Brown exposes the wastefulness of consumer society through Gary. When the family first arrives back in Wade Jones's native Mississippi, the roadsides are strewn with refuse from passing traffic, and down the same roads Gary and Wade collect these empty, discarded cans to sell for cash.

Before Gary starts working for Joe, he and his father also work out a strategy to raid the local Dumpster; Gary roots around inside, opening up bags and dumping the contents out the door. When the guard catches them on their first scavenging mission, he chides them for making a mess, and although they are untidy as they search for items to resell, what they find draws attention to needless and excessive societal waste. Among the general waste, such as cigarette butts, they discover a mass of food waste, and the "three Diet Coke cans and fourteen Old Milwaukee cans" that Wade throws in their sack reveals the vast amount of potentially recyclable material set for landfill (46). The guard embodies society's deferral of trash and the horror, or uncanny feeling, that arises when waste returns: glancing toward the mess Gary and Wade have made, "[h]e looked at the pile of trash again as if he couldn't believe it was still there" (48). Developed society has become so proficient in handling waste and rendering it unseen that to encounter trash laid bare creates confusion. As Ben Campkin and Rosie Cox argue:

> Ideas about dirt are so pervasive that they frequently seem to dictate a benchmark of "normality."... As such, beyond the specific architectures of hygiene, notions of dirt and cleanliness can be said directly or indirectly to influence the arrangement and occupation of all interior and exterior space, informing the minutiae of human behaviour and actively influencing relations between people. (4)

In Brown's novel, the guard is so appalled by the waste and the people scavenging though it that, despite his demands that they clean it all up, when he sees Gary "pushing small piles of rubbish together, pushing them up against the wall of the Dumpster and using his hand to get it in the shovel," he puts an end to it, telling Gary and Wade to stay away in the future (49). Seeing Gary deep in trash uncannily reminds him about the source of all that waste.

To explore the reenvisioning of waste, it is also useful to turn to Dorothy Allison's *Bastard out of Carolina*, in which protagonist Ruth Anne (Bone) has vital lessons to learn about her own self-worth and the meaning of value, lessons she receives from her Aunt Raylene, who is both her niece's rescuer and the resurrector of trash. Both during the years that Bone's stepfather abuses her and as she recovers after he rapes her toward the end of the novel, Bone finds a safe haven at Raylene's home, away from not just the rest of her family but also society. At her riverside home, Raylene reeducates Bone, helping her to find self-worth and to stop seeing herself through the eyes of others. Unlike most of the Boatwright family, who struggle to stay above the poverty line or out of jail, Raylene, although not wealthy, certainly lives a more comfortable life than the rest of her family. Christopher Rieger defines Allison's novel as "an antipastoral coming-of-age tale," arguing that Raylene's home is one of the few places in the novel where readers encounter "natural imagery" and stating that "Bone's escape at the novel's end is to a farm, not away from one. Raylene's small patch of land is a hopeful new beginning in a natural setting" (*Clear-Cutting Eden* 165–66). Raylene's home may be the most natural setting in the novel, but it is certainly not an idyllic agrarian space in any traditional sense. Raylene lives downriver, where "[a]n amazing collection of things accumulated on the river bank below her house" because "[p]eople from Greenville tossed their garbage off the highway a few miles up the river" (181). This marks Raylene's home out as what Kathleen Stewart defines as "those 'trashy' pockets of life across the American cultural landscape" where "collections of used-up things [are] still in use." For Stewart, these "are the kinds of places where the matter has already been settled that this is a place apart—an 'Other America'" (41).

Allison's depiction of Raylene and her labor subvert any sense of "othering," since Raylene's approach to the trash of others offers up a model for a less wasteful, less consumer-driven society. Raylene believes in reusing and recycling, or upcycling: as well as supporting herself with food sales, she supplements her income by reenlivening society's waste. When Bone brings home hauls from the riverbank, Raylene tells her niece: "I can clean and patch those clothes up. We'll soak the dishes in bleach and give the rest of it a scrubbing. Saturday morning we'll put out blankets and sell it off the side of the road" (182). Although Raylene deals in trash, Bone remembers that her "house was scrubbed clean": the repeated references to cleaning and scrubbing reconfigure the ideas of dirt and grime associated with poverty and show how, with a little labor, societal waste is reconfigured and becomes part of a cyclical process (181). The transformation of trash is central to Raylene's schooling of Bone: when Raylene informs her niece that "[t]rash rises.... Out here where no one can mess with it, trash rises all the time," she refers metaphorically to more than the potential for breaking out of class designations. During the time she spends with her aunt, Bone reconsiders her ideas of worth that were previously bound up in materialism.

Bone's material desires are exacerbated in two key moments in chapter 7, when she recounts both the time her mother Anney forced her to go to Woolworths to return the Tootsie Rolls she and her cousin had stolen, and the time she spent in the home of her stepfather's parents. In Woolworths, despite Anney's honesty, the manager humiliates Bone and her mother, suppressing a laugh and banning Bone from the store. At that moment, a hunger forms inside Bone: as she looks around one last time at the shop's displays, "at the bright hairbrushes, ribbons, trays of panties and socks, notebooks, dolls, and balloons," she suddenly feels a "raw and terrible" hunger, a hunger comprising both consumer desire and "the lust to hurt someone back" (98). Similarly, when she visits Glen's parents' home and is confronted by their material wealth, Bone struggles to "speak around the hunger" in her throat (102). In the face of their displayed materialism, Bone questions whether she and her sister were "worthy of all that, the roses in their garden, the sunlight on those polished windows and flowered drapes, the china plates gleaming behind glass cabinets" (102). For a child who "knew to the penny what everything cost" because she kept her mother company while she toted up the weekly expenditures (65), and who has to accept the lesson that the Boatwrights "an't the people who buy things for show" (66), the displayed wealth in the Waddell home, or on the shelves in Woolworths, equate, in her mind, to worthiness. Not until Bone spends extended periods of time with Raylene does she come to understand that worthiness rests in use-value, and her full realization of where value rests comes when Bone makes her revenge trip to Woolworths.

When Bone decides to break into the local Woolworths with her cousin Grey to rewrite earlier wrongs, she sees the store through new eyes. Schooled by Raylene, Bone is instantly assaulted by the "smell of dust and cheap goods," and when she looks at "all the *things* on display," things that had once provoked such desire, all she can see is "[j]unk everywhere: shoes that went to paper in the rain, clothes that separated at the seams, stale candy, makeup that made your skin break out. What was there here that I could use?" (223–24). Melanie Benson argues that when Bone realizes the emptiness of materialism in this moment, she is left bereft, with no alternative. For Benson, "[t]here is no fulfillment here, no dizzy accumulation of goods and with it self-worth; clinging to her hook and biting her lip, she recalls to us her violent, masturbatory fantasies and the narcissistic aftermath of her beatings, looking in the mirror for blood in her mouth and seeing 'nothing'" (150). Yet Bone does not encounter feelings of "nothing," or nothingness, in this moment—instead, she begins to form a more nuanced understanding of use-value. Although she leaves the store questioning who she still wants "to hurt" and with the same feeling of something "hard and mean" at the back of her throat that she first describes back in chapter 7, as she dwells on the idea of "use," Bone thinks about "the rows of canned vegetables and fruit at Aunt Raylene's place—rows of tomatoes and okra, peaches and green beans, blackberries and plums that stretched for shelf on shelf in her cellar. That was worth something" (224). So rather than finding nothing, Bone actually locates the source of real worth in her life. In comparison to Raylene's production and accumulation of preserved food, which both provides an income stream and gives pleasure to her family, Bone now realizes that the goods at Woolworths are "tawdry and useless" (224–25). In Benson's Baudrillardian reading, all the signs and things on display never lead Bone to any signified, yet tracing Bone's journey from coveting the point of exchange in Woolworths and the Waddells' conspicuous consumption, to Raylene's labor that produces a wealth of preserved goods and puts discarded items back into circulation, suggests that the signified in this novel is bound up with use-value. Here, obsolescence, in the form of cheap consumer goods—the "shoes that went to paper in the rain"—is juxtaposed with the solidity of Raylene's cellar, as Bone suddenly understands use-value. Neil Smith suggests that the battle between capitalism and socialism is "the struggle to control what is and is not value. Under capitalism, this is a judgment made in the market. . . . Socialism is the struggle to judge necessity according not to the market and its logic but to human need, according not to exchange-value and profit but to use-value" (89). Unlike the Waddell garden with its ornamental roses, Raylene's side garden sustains, producing the crops necessary for her business selling "home-canned vegetables and fruit" (180).

Katherine Henninger argues that "Allison's work accesses the discourse of 'white trash' and revisions it, re-ordering the narrative of access and representational power to reclaim for Appalachian white female 'trash' a legitimate place in southern, and national, identities" (139). In *Bastard out of Carolina*, Raylene, more than any other character, represents the revisioning of trash through her roles as both Bone's tutor, as she helps her niece to locate self-worth in herself rather than in material objects, and the resurrector of trash, which makes her, in Vance Packard's terms, a "resisting" citizen (234). For Packard, the resisting citizen is someone who refuses to accept the terms of the capitalist economy by finding alternatives to the consumption-dumping model. Raylene's labor rebukes the excessive waste of unrestrained capitalism as she promotes a cyclical model of use and reuse. Allison's novel celebrates the refashioning of rubbish alongside the ability of the poor to reject society's definitions of them. Félix Guattari argues that we need to "reevaluate the purpose of work and of human activities according to different criteria than those of profit and yield" (57), and novels such as Allison's take readers into communities where questions of meaning and value are not only measured in terms of material wealth and the power of acquisition.

Of course, the "purpose of work" in terms of a system of "power and yield" is so indoctrinated across the developed world that for so many it is difficult to imagine any alternative, especially for those on or below the poverty line. Under this neoliberal capitalist model, as Harvey asserts, "[i]f conditions among the lower classes deteriorated, this was because they failed, usually for personal and cultural reasons, to enhance their own human capital" (*Spaces of Global* 42). Yet when the poor fight to retain environmentally destructive jobs, such as logging or mining, they are often vilified by environmentalists and in the media as backward thinking, undereducated, and unenlightened. In repeated turns to the working lives of poor whites, southern writing continues to illuminate the tensions between environmental concerns and labor.

The poor who undertake environmentally destructive jobs are typically lambasted as too ignorant to reflect on the ecological impact of their labor and too driven by their paychecks to see the bigger picture. In his study of the pastoral in southern literature, Rieger asks, as he examines Brown's *Joe*, "[s]hould we demand that the working poor refuse certain jobs because they may damage the environment?" (*Clear-Cutting Eden* 168). In the novel, Joe and his team work for timber company Weyerhaeuser, poisoning trees to make way for the growth of more profitable pine. Rieger asks of Gary's acceptance of such a job: "Does it matter that he poisons trees for a lumber company to do it? . . . Brown's gritty pastoral raises these sorts of ethical quandaries but provides no easy answers" (168). Both Rieger and Watson have written about the interconnectedness between poverty and eco-destruction in Brown's novel, both paying attention to the chapter in which Gary's realization of the wonder of the natural world is destroyed by his discovery of Joe's team "stabbing" and "slashing" the trees, actions that confuse the boy, who cannot discern any logic in them (111–12). Watson surmises that Gary's "life is so bleak and deprived, his material need to 'get by,' to assuage his family's hunger, so urgent that no amount of spiritual value or consolation can substitute for the raw economic opportunity he now senses in the forest landscape" (504). In Brown's novel, only Joe fully understands the cost of their labor, whereas the workers, the "other hands," are presented as unthinking automatons without the capacity for contemplation, who rise "in a group like a herd of cows or trained dogs in a circus act when they [see] the bossman stand up" (202). Overseeing their work, Joe is one step removed from the zombie-like workers and is conscious of both the "dying forest" and his part in killing it (203). Yet that knowledge does not set Joe on a path of resistance and activism, since he too depends on his wage. Brown's novel underlines the difficulty of developing and maintaining environmental principles when jobs are scarce.

Similarly, in Mary Hood's short story "Moths," in her collection *And Venus Is Blue* (1986), readers encounter poor white Cheney, who oversees a small logging team clearing a thousand acres of pine trees in Georgia for real estate developer Mr. Anderson. Married with a large family, Cheney works days felling the trees and at night returns to gather "sweet gums and poplars for his own woodpile" (101). While Hood's language draws attention to the violence of logging—the workers "tear the stumps," pile the "deadfall" and "burn" the stumps—Cheney is desensitized to the nature of his work, thinking only of his next paycheck (102). The story focuses on two events that occur one day toward the end of the logging process, when Cheney discovers two moths among the dead leaves, and one of two young brothers working with Cheney, Ward, is badly injured when "the hoist chain snapped" and "the whiplash laid open" his "scalp and took out his front teeth" (107–8).

Cheney is so removed from nature that when he discovers the first moth during his lunch break he assumes it is a "paper moth," put there by the boys to trick him (103). Mesmerized by its "silver-green" color, which reminds him of "dogwood leaves," Cheney clumsily tries to pick it up but injures it, leaving "green chalk on his fingers" (103–4). Cheney then picks up the second moth, which is still emerging out of its damaged pupal case, and feels instantly parental, telling it to "[s]ettle, the way he would speak to his own baby" (105). Despite his fascination with the moths, Cheney returns to work together with the boys, only for Wade to be injured by the hoist chain. While the damaged moths point to the wider ecological impact of logging, Wade's injury exposes the vulnerability of low-paid workers without recourse to medical coverage. Turned away by a dentist because he has neither the cash nor medical insurance necessary to cover treatment, Wade's head is only attended to at a local hospital because Cheney gives them Mr. Anderson's details. When Cheney looks at Ward's repaired head, where "they had sheared off the curls," he imagines that it resembles "where Rural Electric had clearcut the powerline right-of-way through deep woods" (114). The injury helps Cheney to draw a connection between the damage wrought upon the landscape and the damage inflicted upon working bodies. Although he litters at the end of the story, suggesting that he has far to travel to fully comprehend the impact of man's actions on the environment, the injury to Wade, and perhaps more particularly the moths, open Cheney up to a new way of thinking. Indeed, as he waits for Wade to be treated, Cheney seeks out a library to gather information about the moths. Already feeling out of place in the library because he doesn't "remember from school days where to look," he encounters the librarian, who assesses him in one glance, taking in his work clothes and curtly questioning: "And you want?" (113). Here, in a public library supported by Cheney's taxes, this manual laborer is made to feel alien, too "unclean" with the "rosin on his jeans" and "Ward's blood on his undershirt," so he responds, "I come in the wrong store.... Reckon I just didn't notice where I was" (113). Thwarted in his attempts to access further information about the moths but still having to take care of Wade and then return to the worksite after dark with his family to retrieve more firewood, Cheney blurts out, "I'm so goddamn tired of being poor" (118).

While Cheney does not fully know how to end his poverty, in Ann Pancake's novel *Strange as This Weather Has Been* (2007), the issue is less about overcoming poverty than it is about finding resistance within it: with the aim of achieving not material wealth but rather communal and environmental integrity. In the novel, one family becomes a microcosm of the divides in Appalachian mining communities, as husband and wife Jimmy "Make" Makepeace and Lace Turrell represent two sides of the debate on coal. Even though Jimmy Make sees the destruction of strip mining firsthand when he and their daughter, Bant, sneak onto company land, he relentlessly holds onto the hope of resecuring a coal job, a desire that breaks the family apart at the end of the novel, when, after the death of one of their sons, Corey, Jimmy Make moves with their other two sons to North Carolina to work in the mining industry. Conversely, Lace and Bant become increasingly political as the novel unfolds, taking an active role in the resistance against strip mining. Interestingly, in this multiperspective novel, which moves between first- and third-person narration and in which we hear from extended family members and people from the wider community, Pancake denies Jimmy Make a first-person section. While his conservatism and defeatism appear throughout the novel, Pancake's overt environmentalism, which often veers into didacticism, keeps her from validating his point of view. That does not mean she presents him unsympathetically: as we see Jimmy Make through the eyes of his wife and daughter, we encounter a gradually diminished figure whose sense of self-worth is so bound up in his ability to work that he cannot entertain any option other than utter commitment to the coal industry. Yet his unwillingness to join the fight against coal operators seems all the more inexplicable after he and Bant trespass onto company land on Yellowroot Mountain and he witnesses the destruction caused by strip mining. However, when Bant asks him to explain the nature of the "fill," she realizes that he does not have any answers—he might have worked for coal operators, but the possibility of such corporate negligence is beyond his imagination. Bant recalls:

> I looked at him. His belly paunching out under the untucked shirt. His brown eyes narrowed under the camouflage cap. Then I understood that he wasn't exactly bullshitting me because he was bullshitting himself first. And right there I knew for sure what I'd suspected all along—Jimmy Make couldn't tell any more about what was going than I could. (22)

Because this moment occurs early in the novel, there is little room for Jimmy Make to recover from this position of weakness in his daughter's eyes, and, lacking a first-person chapter, he disappears even before he actually leaves his wife at the novel's close.

Yet Pancake does not present all miners as pro-coal and anti-environmental, as she strives to humanize the nuanced struggles faced by workers in Appalachia's coalfields. In her later short story "Arsonists," in the collection *Me and My Daddy Listen to Bob Marley* (2015), Pancake tells the tale of two aging men, Dell and Kenny, and the history of their fight to retain their homes in the wake of damage caused by mountaintop removal (MTR) in their hometown of Tout, West Virginia. Dell recalls how the coal operator attempted to buy their homes and reflects on the suspicious cases of arson in the homes that the company procured. He recounts how, despite the community's best efforts to catch the arsonists, the culprits remained at large. Their inability to locate the source of the fires is just another defeat in the wake of the company's aggression, with most people, including Dell, eventually selling their homes because it becomes transparent that they can no longer "make a difference" (100). Only Kenny holds out, plaguing his young wife, and Dell, with his paranoia about the company and the damage its operations are causing in his home. His paranoia is not unfounded because his house, like all the others that once stood alongside it, has suffered structural damage from MTR blasts. However, what plagues Kenny and Dell is their own complicity in damaging the environment when they worked as strip miners. Kenny alludes to this guilt in an exchange between the two friends:

> "What we did, Dell," he said. "It wasn't like this here."
> Through Dell, a cold gust flashed, from his groin to the top of his chest. He wet his mouth to speak back, to agree. Then he stopped and let it go. (106)

Dell gets the chills and they render him mute: in effect, he is haunted by his labor and his complicity in what Harvey terms "[t]he escalating depletion of the global environmental commons (land, air, water) and proliferating habitat degradations"; in short, "the wholesale commodification of nature" under the auspices of free-market neoliberalism (*The New Imperialism* 148). Dell's haunting is social and, as Avery Gordon explains it, "occurs on the terrain between our ability to conclusively describe the logic of Capitalism or State terror, for example, and the various experiences of this logic, experiences that are more often than not partial, coded, symptomatic, contradictory, ambiguous" (24). In Pancake's story, Dell's haunting can be traced to his own and Kenny's labor, and toward the end of the story, Dell reflects on their shared occupation:

> And they'd been proud of what they did, they made America's electricity, they kept on the lights. The money they earned raised their kids comfortable, like they deserved, way beyond how him and Kenny'd come up, refurbished Dell's old company house to modern, built Kenny's from the foundation up. (113)

Here, Dell reassures himself about what they did, but when he visits his son in northern Virginia and is taken on a tour of his son's construction project, Dell's haunting intensifies. As his son drives his around the construction site, Dell gets "carsick for the first time in sixty years" as he sees "acre after acre of immaculate vacant homes, bulked up and bulging on undersized lots. The street deliberately unstraight, snake-tailing into dead ends that made no sense, everywhere treeless, hill-less" (109). The replacement of hills and trees with these artificially constructed communal enclaves makes Dell "carsick" for the first time since he was a child. The vomiting, associated with childhood, is the result of what Gordon terms a "profane illumination" (205). Profane illumination, she argues, "describes a mode of apprehension distinct from critique or commentary" (205). Drawing on Theodor Adorno and Walter Benjamin, Gordon makes the case that "[p]rofane illumination is a kind of conjuring that 'initiates' because it is telling us something important we had not known; because it is leading us somewhere, or elsewhere" (205). In the first instance, Dell's vomiting recalls childhood, a time when hills and trees still shaped the landscape, so in the moment at the construction site he occupies past and present, which creates a jarring sensation between the past and a present that makes "no sense." Yet the profane illumination he experiences relates to his own role in modernity and "keeping the lights on." Between childhood and the present, Dell undertook a form of labor that ruined the environment and laid the way for the nonsensical present he encounters with his son.

The next morning, when Dell is due to drive home,

> he feared he'd overslept, light as it was outside, until he understood it was the condo complex's security lights. He'd never driven in northern Virginia before dawn, and as he loaded the Metro under floodlights, there stirred in him an uneasiness mingled with awe. Then he was passing under the streetlights that canopied the suburb's four-lane main drag and although at this time of day everywhere is people-less, it is still lit as bright as an emergency room. (114)

As Dell continues driving,

> to his total surprise—the light turned to sound. The strip malls first—they burst into roar, a crowd in his head—then the box stores, Target and Home Depot and Sam's, them louder yet, squalling and hollering bald blares of light. Among them the fast-food places, Wendy's, Burger King, Taco Bell, Sonic, each shrieking light, and then the quaint and quietful places—coffee shops, boutiques—Dell heard them, too, hissing their squander of light. He was speeding now . . . when he heard, from the near distance in what used to be fields, the wailing flare of subdivisions, each one, he knew, either uninhabited or asleep. Yet each one haloed in a great conflagration of light. (114–15)

He is overwhelmed by the sound of sheer waste, a deafening white noise of modernity that tells a tale of squandered energy. The "roar" that Dell hears, with its "squalling and hollering," "shrieking" and "hissing," helps him to realize that in "keeping the lights on," he and Kenny merely helped to feed the voracious capitalist beast: in Gordon's terms, Dell has been "notified" of his "involvement" (205). Yet the story abruptly moves from this moment of profane illumination to Kenny's bathtub, where Dell helps his friend to bathe. Gordon suggests that after the recognition of involvement, "if you don't banish it, or kill it, or reduce it to something you can already manage, when it appears to you, the ghost will inaugurate the necessity of doing something about it" (205–6). Dell feels unable to do anything to resist MTR and cannot bear his own complicity in the overwhelming roar of capital, so instead of taking action, we see that he and Kenny remain haunted at the end of the story. Bathing Kenny, Dell

> looks at Kenny's back, and for a second, Dell knows the chill of Kenny's bare skin, and for that second, a tenderness spears him. Dell banks it down. He tips the cup. Water sluices over Kenny's spine. Dell dips again, lifts, and pours. Again. And again. Sloshed water dabbling his knees, an old hurt wrenching his shoulder. Until Kenny starts to come back to himself. (115)

To alleviate Kenny's chill is, by extension, to alleviate Dell's, yet as Dell tries to sluice, or effectively let out, the chill, Pancake's language points to the inability of either man to wash away his guilt. Dell obviously carries an old work-related injury, a constant reminder of his labor, but as Dell repeatedly pours water over his friend, he "banks" and "tips" the cup, both words conjuring the soil banks or tips created by strip mining. Both men remain haunted, and in the end their frailty is set against the unrelenting power of the lights in the previous paragraphs. By the story's close, the titular arsonists are never found, and even though Dell gains insight into the profound waste of energy, he is in no position to resist.

In her essay on Pancake's *Strange as This Weather Has Been* and Kingsolver's *Flight Behavior*, Heather Houser observes that while the men are broken down and alienated from nature, the "losses and damages" of poverty and environmental destruction inspire the "women to become organic intellectuals who fuse epistemologies in order to protect the environment and Appalachian lifeways" (101). Houser is less interested in ideas of women's intrinsic connection to "Mother" earth than she is in the idea of how women's work, both physically and intellectually, helps to restore the ideas of the commons, as women "turn their labors to environmentalist purposes in the realms of activism and research" (107). Yet, in *Strange as This Weather Has Been*, the commons and ideas of communitarianism are not solely driven by the women. Local activist Charlie, who helps to educate Lace about MTR, reflects on his personal journey from miner to activist. On a drive through his virtually abandoned hometown of Tout, the same fictional community as in "Arsonists," Charlie recounts his strip-mining work, telling Lace: "Country needed the coal, I needed the work, I didn't have any problem with that. And even when these big jobs first started coming in, yeah, the mountaintop mines, if I'd been younger, I probably would have tried to get on one of them. Didn't know any better yet" (306). His gradual political awakening occurred when MTR moved to Tout and the company started "trying to buy people out" (307). He recalls the ways the company divided the local community by "[b]rewing suspicion and pitting neighbors and friends and family members against each other" (307), but only when Charlie came close to selling his house did he realize that in doing so, he would also have "to sign a form that said you'd never protest a mine again and would never move back within twenty-five miles of Tout" (308). Here, the company wants to stamp out all opposition, now and in the future, so when Charlie describes looking at Tout Mountain after MTR as "seeing your horizon gone," it is not just about MTR (309): since the 1980s, when Reagan and Thatcher crushed unions as they implemented their neoliberal agenda, a decade that for Harvey witnessed "an all out assault on the powers of organized labor," many workers, particularly those in industrial and manufacturing sectors, have lost their political voice and right to protest (*Spaces of Global* 18). Denying people recourse to strike removes hope and limits horizons, which is why Charlie refuses to sell his house and thereby his right to protest.[6] Charlie's activism, while not without complication because of his previous employment, stands in sharp contrast to Jimmy Make's apathy, which Lace faces upon her return from Tout. Jimmy Make passively accepts the power of coal operators; in his work on power and resistance in Appalachia, John Gaventa notes that the type of apathy and powerlessness that Jimmy represents is bound up in ideas of "fatalism" that have "been instilled historically through repeated experiences of defeat" (254). In contrast, Charlie refuses to be beaten: he realizes his complicity in the environmental destruction of the landscape but teaches himself about regulations and laws in order to fight back.

These novels show how difficult it is for poor people to challenge environmental destruction, and even when environmental campaigns do bring about change, the tension between ecological and labor concerns is often intensified rather than resolved. Zwerdling uses the example of Joe's employer in Brown's novel, Weyerhaeuser, who, in the early 1970s, fired "350 workers at its sulphite pulp mill in Everett, Washington," citing "environmental grounds" (28). Zwerdling observes that while the job losses were likely imminent due to poor productivity at that particular mill, environmental pressures around the logging industry were used as the scapegoat for culling workers, thereby deepening suspicion and resentment among the poor toward an environmentalism sold to them as the purloiner of jobs and livelihoods. Although Zwerdling was pessimistic about the ability of the environmental movement to "realize that neither pollution not poverty nor worker insecurity is a separate problem which can be solved on its own," the emergence of environmentalism as an academic field, in conjunction with postcolonialism, has brought about new approaches that bring together ecology, poverty, and labor to imagine alternatives to an individualistic, capitalist model that, in Zwerdling's terms, "gives enormous corporations the power to control the nation's people and resources" (29).[7] Above all else, contemporary environmental debates champion interconnectivity and the need to break down the divides that separate people as well as the divides that separate people from nature and ecological concerns. For Patrick Murphy, "[h]uman diversity can be maintained only by means of cultural conservation being practiced by the marginalized and subordinated groups who defend and recover their heritages in order to generate their futures, and thereby resist being labelled as Other" ("Anotherness" 44). However, Kerridge shares Zwerdling's concern, believing that "environmentalism has difficulty in being a politics of personal liberation or social mobility," in part due to the lack of activism in poor communities (Introduction 2). Similarly, in her 2010 study of political responses to excessive consumerism in the West, Kim Humphery interviewed a number of activists resisting corporate globalization. She claims: "It was no surprise that most of those participating in this research were from middle-class socioeconomic backgrounds and possessed university level degrees. This merely reflects the still highly classed nature of active political participation in movements such as environmentalism" (87). Their contention that the poor have not yet formed any recognizable contribution to the environmental movement exacerbates ideas that antipoverty and environmental groups continue to struggle to recognize and build on their shared interests and concerns.

Yet, as Timothy Clark notes:

> All across the world groups of people have come together outside the normal frameworks of politics to protest local outrages or environmental threats.... Together with the proliferation of various non-governmental bodies, such movements now form a kind of cosmopolitan politics, its actions and concern unconfined to the boundaries of the nation state. (87)

In the US South as much as anywhere else, local groups have worked, sometimes in conjunction with regional, national, and global movements and organizations, to challenge any number of environmental degradations. As a result, there are numerous microregions within the South that I could turn to here to examine the alignment of the poor, environmentalism, and activism, but the coal fields of Appalachia have produced consistent literary efforts to explore the ramifications of the mining industry. In an essay on the apocalyptic quality of Pancake's *Strange as This Weather Has Been*, Matt Wanat suggests:

> Nowhere is the curious marriage of marginalization and economic interest clearer than at sites of resource extraction—places critical to the continuing function of the machinery of industrial institutions that are simultaneously, by apparent virtue of their importance, places where everything is deemed expendable: the earth and its resources, human and biotic communities, life in general. (163)

Indeed, the Appalachian coalfields form part of what Ann Stoler terms "zones of vulnerability," zones "that the living inhabit and to which we should attend" (200). Appalachian literature is at least one place where the emergence of grassroots environmental activism is explored, usually as local characters are pitted against outside companies and their representatives (Stoler 14). Focusing here on "zones of vulnerability" in Appalachian fiction will offer a case study of "the connective tissue that continues to bind human potentials to degraded environments, and degraded personhoods to the material refuse of imperial projects" (Stoler 193).

Since the late twentieth century, aggressive strip mining, MTR, and fracking have continued to align Appalachia not just with the rest of the US South but with other regions around the United States and the globe that are also subjected to excessive capitalist exploitation.[8] In Appalachia, so-called hillbillies have cast off the stereotype by joining together to fight against legislation that continues to put big business before the environment and local communities. Donald Davis writes: "By the early 1970s, several well-organized grassroots groups were beginning to successfully challenge environmental and social injustices in Appalachia, among them Save Our Cumberland Mountains and Kentuckians for the Commonwealth" (viii). These groups, Bryan McNeil explains, "appear to be an attempt not to maintain the old union-versus-company dynamic but to construct a new form of opposition to work within the framework of globalization" ("Global Forces" 107). Specifically, in relation to Coal River Mountain Watch (CRMW), McNeil claims: "The group educates residents about the adverse effects of the coal industry within the community and serves as a community resource center. . . . The group also represents community concerns at public hearings and meetings with industry and regulators ("Global Forces" 107).[9] In recent years, grassroots groups have also employed social media to champion their causes, with Appalachian Voices and Appalachia Rising two key examples of moves to heighten awareness of, and activism against, environmental destruction in the region.[10] Ideas of communitarianism are central to many debates about poverty and ecology, and Guattari champions such community-based local groups, arguing that they are essential in helping "to get social and political practices back on their feet, working for humanity and not simply for a permanent reequilibration of the capitalist semiotic Universe" (51).[11] The importance of encouraging activism within and across poor Appalachian communities is vital, given the ineffectiveness of elected officials to enact positive change on behalf of their constituents.[12]

As a heavily exploited region within the US South, it is little wonder that Appalachia produces fiction writers who commonly explore the relationship between people, poverty, capitalist exploitation, and environmentalism. It is more common than not to find references to the changed landscape and/or the extinction of species in fiction that does not have environmentalism at its center.[13] Yet, Appalachia also continues to produce authors who more overtly align their politics with their fiction, and their work falls more readily into Guattari's category of eco-art, which, for him, involves a "praxic opening-out" that "subsumes all existing ways of domesticating existential Territories and is concerned with intimate modes of being, the body, the environment or large contextual ensembles relating to ethnic groups, the nation, or even the general rights of humanity" (53). I turn to Guattari's notion of eco-art and Nixon's idea of "combative writers" (5) to explore the work of some leading Appalachian writer-activists.

Author, musician, and activist Silas House is one writer who works to raise awareness about MTR and its impact on local communities. In House's *Something's Rising: Appalachians Fighting Mountaintop Removal* (2009), coedited with Jason Howard, he brings together oral stories from various Appalachian writers including Denise Giardina, and activists such as Jack Spadaro and Judy Bonds, to highlight not only the way local communities are effected by MTR but also how they resist those practices. Across his fictional trilogy *Clay's Quilt* (2001), *A Parchment of Leaves* (2002), and *The Coal Tattoo* (2004), which covers the lives of his Kentuckian Sizemore family across the twentieth century, as well as throughout his music and nonfiction writing, House engages to varying degrees with forms of environmentalism. In *A Parchment of Leaves*, Saul Sizemore leaves his wife and young daughter during World War I to work for his current employer across the county line, logging Wildcat Mountain to make turpentine for the war effort. In his letters home, the normally reticent Saul reflects on his work: "We have cut down all the trees atop this big mountain. It is the ugliest thing you have ever seen in yore life" (93). Despite his sadness, Saul remains committed to his work to ensure that his family keeps above the poverty line, another example of the battle between environmental concerns and labor. Resistance only fully appears in *The Coal Tattoo*, when Saul's grandchildren, sisters Easter and Anneth Sizemore, and their cousin Sophie, take a stand when the Altamont Mining Company sends bulldozers to begin preparations for strip-mining operations on the mountain behind their home in Free Creek, Kentucky. Caught off guard and without the support of members of the local community, who are also ready to protest, the three women sit down in the path of the bulldozers and have to be forcefully removed and carried down the mountain. They succeed in garnering media attention, and the novel ends with the hope that a legal issue concerning the deeds to the land might prevent the mountain from becoming another victim: readers of House's earlier novel *Clay's Quilt*, which is set in the years after the events of *The Coal Tattoo*, know that the women's actions save the mountain. House takes inspiration for the women's resistance from the local people who challenge mining companies in similar fashion, notably the 1965 case of Ollie "Widow" Combs, which he refers to both in the novel and in the acknowledgments (302, 324).[14] For all the turns to strip mining in *The Coal Tattoo*, House's fiction revolves far more around family and love than politics and environmentalism. For Scott Suter, House's novels are "not stories about mountaintop removal specifically, but about people who have struggled and survived in the midst of coal mining and mountain culture and continue to do so" (188). Yet for novels set in coal country, the industry's impact on people as well as place is understated. Despite the fact that in *The Coal Tattoo* Saul's daughter commits suicide after her husband, Luke, and his fellow workers die in a cave-in at the Altamont mines, and Easter's baby dies in childbirth bearing a coal tattoo on his lifeless forehead, their ill-fatedness does not prevent Anneth's son, Clay, from growing up and realizing his ambition to become a coal miner.

Even in *The Coal Tattoo*, the activism of the Sizemore women is driven more by NIMBYism than any broader concern with larger environmental movements. In House's keynote address at the Appalachian Studies Association conference in March 2008, entitled "A Conscious Heart," he begins by setting aside questions of environmental destruction, taking them as given, choosing instead to focus on "the way mountaintop removal threatens our storytelling tradition, and our pride" (7). His emphasis on distinctiveness and local traditions is why Emily Satterwhite regards his fiction as part of the "local-color revival" that she traces to the publication of Garrison Keillor's *Lake Wobegon Days* (1985). Satterwhite examines readers' reviews of these local-color novels, explaining that one outraged reviewer of *Clay's Quilt* felt that House's simplified emphasis on "tradition" overlooked "issues of poverty, under or no education, unemployment, drop outs, drug abuse," and the "large amount of people on government assistance," which are in no way unique to eastern Kentucky or Appalachia (207). Satterwhite summarizes: "He felt a heartwarming tale was not enough in the face of the challenges confronted by regional residents" (207). House's fiction seems at odds with his activism: in his "A Conscious Heart" address, House demanded that Appalachians shake off apathy in a bid to become more educated and more active in resisting MTR, an activism lacking in his Sizemore trilogy, in which issues of abject poverty and environmental exploitation are glossed over in favor of his celebration of Appalachian culture, heritage, and ideas of community.

However, in his children's book coauthored with Neela Vaswani, *Same Sun Here* (2011), which details the pen-pal correspondence during the 2008 electoral race and the months after President Barack Obama's inauguration, between twelve-year-olds Meena Joshi, an Indian immigrant living with her family in New York, and River Dean Justice, a native Kentuckian living in Black Banks with his clinically depressed mother and his Mamaw, House overtly engages with MTR. As well as breaking down ideas of difference as the two children find multiple points of common ground, River's letters also draw attention to the problems of MTR. Just as their correspondence begins, a coal company starts MTR on the mountain next to his Mamaw's land. As his letters and emails unfold, readers learn about the environmental impact of MTR as he explains how the once clear creek is now "muddy" with "some kind of orange gunk in it," the same poisoned water River later challenges the governor of Kentucky to drink when the people from coal communities march on Washington to end MTR. River also details local tensions between activists (including his Mamaw) and coal supporters, and the injuries caused to River's basketball teammates when unsecured boulders from the mine roll down the hill onto the local school (107). Activism and political dissent are the defining features of River's missives, and as the two children explore what it means to protest, they situate resistance in a global context with references to Gandhi, the Tiananmen Square protests, and civil rights battles.

If House only fully engages with the impact of mining in *Same Sun Here*, writer-activist Denise Giardina, in her two coalfield novels set in the town of Annadel, West Virginia, *Storming Heaven* (1987) and *The Unquiet Earth* (1992), combines sweeping family sagas with overt environmentalism. In the less critically discussed of these two novels, *The Unquiet Earth*, Giardina brings her saga up to the 1990s, and unlike the easy resolutions found or promised at the end of House's Sizemore novels, Giardina ends this novel with a devastating flood. In the latter chapters she reveals the cause of the flood, an unstable dam inadvertently built by the American Coal Company that dumps slate into the local river. The dam holds "back the waters of Pliny Branch and sludge from the strip mine"; ex-miner Dillon Freeman regularly inspects the dam and repeatedly warns that it is likely to break, endangering the entire town below (274). When Dillon's daughter, Jackie, the newspaper editor for the local *Justice Clarion*, runs the story, she reflects how "[t]he newspaper owner called and told me he'd had some complaints, but then a *Charleston Gazette* reporter came to investigate, so the story was out. But nothing happened." Even after her activist friend Tom Kolwiecki sent her "articles and pictures to Charleston and Washington," she still heard "nothing" (277). When the International Oil Corporation takes over American Coal at the end of the 1980s, it also ignores the dam, instead bringing in "new machines that rip and tear even bigger chunks of land" (307). In the end, when the dam bursts and floods the town, Dillon loses his own life but saves that of his daughter and numerous townspeople when he raises the alarm.

Giardina ironically entitles the final chapter "New World," which begins with a *New York Times* headline, "International Oil Calls Flood 'Act of God.' Spokesman Asks for Prayers" (338). The corporate spin machine goes into full effect, distancing the coal operator from the loss of life due to its own negligent practices. At the novel's end, Jackie, having left West Virginia for a job in Pittsburgh, feels unable to ever return to her home place but still takes phone calls from family friend Hassel, who keeps her updated on the goings-on in Annadel. Alongside his unwavering hope for an additional bridge to be constructed, Hassel's local news shows how the new world differs from the old: now, with no homes in the way, the "company has built a new road" and has "coal trucks ... running in fleets from the strip mine" (339). Hassel's account not only underscores the increased productivity of the mine: here, Giardina utilizes military language—"fleets" of vehicles—to present outside coal operators as occupying forces, a theme she plays on throughout the latter stages of this novel. Of course, the militarized nature of coal operations in this novel mirrors the actual use of the military against locals at the Battle of Blair Mountain, which Giardina depicts in *Storming Heaven*. In *The Unquiet Earth*, when International Oil takes control of Mine Number Thirteen and hires a "Property Rights Defense Team" to patrol and police the borders of the property, company workers construct a cyclone fence, and a "man in a black uniform and sunglasses films" people who get close to the fence "from a new guard tower" (308). The company builds "a barracks inside the fence where the scabs sleep," and Jackie reads a brochure about the Property Rights Defense Team, which states: "Our trained personnel are equipped with M-16 rifles, grenade launchers, tear gas, and K-9 kennels. We have available, on request, an armored personnel vehicle" (308). Jackie does not believe that the company would use this armory against the locals, reminding Dillon that "[t]imes have changed," but he retorts, "How? What's the difference between them bastards over there and the Baldwin-Felts gun thugs in my daddy's day? Bucky Collis up to Felco has sent his younguns to his brother in Ohio. You know why? Somebody drove by and shot out their front window. One bullet hit two foot above his little girl's bed" (309). The difference, Jackie reminds him, is that the violence might be the same, but corporations have "gone slick" in their publicity campaigns, shielding themselves with an aseptic sheen. Giardina does not shirk from the fact that some locals also want to employ violent means as they stand up against the company, but the company's militarized security force is also not the stuff of fiction. As David Duke notes in his study of Giardina and fellow activist Don West, Giardina has firsthand experience with the organized violence of coal operators. In 1984, she witnessed the actions of Massey Energy against its striking employees as the company sought to break the power of the union by no longer accepting United Mine Workers contracts. In the battle that Massey Energy fought against its workers, Duke observes, "[v]iolence erupted on both sides," but "Massey hired a security guard company that used helicopters and armored personnel carriers" (61). Whether keeping down strikers or environmentalists, corporate violence comes under scrutiny in Giardina's two coal novels. Given the stereotypes of Appalachian violence, from feuding families to gun-toting locals protecting stills or hidden fields of illegal crops, Giardina's popular fiction helps to focus attention on the violence enacted against locals as much as by locals. While those Appalachians fighting against the environmental movement grab the headlines, writers such as Giardina reveal that many locals stand up not just for miners' rights but also for the environment.

Similarly, across Pancake's fiction violence looms large as she explores the lives of characters in small West Virginian communities who are impacted by the legacies of natural resource extraction, particularly strip mining and MTR. She is also interested in the wider issues of real estate development in Appalachia and the ways local cultures and ecology are being marketed to the affluent who wish to purchase "a green lifestyle" (Sleipness 43). At almost every level, her characters face the threat of unparalleled mining and gentrification, both of which push poverty out of sight and out of mind. Those characters who make themselves known as they protest against coal operations encounter violence unlike anything they've experienced before in their daily lives in West Virginia. In *Strange as This Weather Has Been*, Lace recalls the intimidation she faced when she got embroiled in the activist movement, remembering specifically the moment that a company goon followed her into a convenience store, waited outside the restroom, and then blocked her way and revealed his gun. She thinks: "People don't do stuff like this around here. I'd never had a gun pulled on me in my life, never seen a gun pulled on anyone, even though in this state, there are guns all over the place" (305). In Giardina's and Pancake's novels, readers are asked to rethink common misperceptions about Appalachian culture and to look in directions other than feuds for the sources of systemic violence.[15]

In Pancake's short story collection *Given Ground* (2001), the land seethes with historical and present-day exploitation. In "Ghostless," a grown son reflects on his childhood in West Virginia, his deep connection with his father whose death precipitated the son's move away from the region, and the gradual loss of family land. Both father and son share the ability to see the dead: out on the land, the narrator remembers, they encountered the ghosts of local residents as well as countless Confederate soldiers. Alongside these visitors from the past, they must contend with new visitors to their community, the "out-of-staters," the "imports," the "foreigners. From-away-from-here" who visit second homes in mountainous retreats across Appalachia (4–5). In terms of the community, the hostility toward outsiders might ring with conservativeness and isolationism, and Pancake's stories do not provide any positive spin on these "foreigners." Having lost family land over time, father and son now find themselves trespassers on that very land: land that now seems alien to these characters who struggle to locate themselves in what seems to be a radically altered environment. In "Crow Road," the narrator reflects again on the loss of family land to real estate developers and how that land "is a foreign place" now, even carrying a different name. The rebranded "Misty Mountain Estates" comprises "new houses made to look old," each "armored with a security system and warning signs" (115). For the narrator, these new homes create "an expectation of presence," but because they are unoccupied most of the time, "their emptiness" sucks "that expectation inside out" (115). Despite the proliferation of new houses, it now feels "much emptier on Joby Knob now than when it was just trees" (115). Local residents' connection to the land is now fundamentally changed, and, as Ray writes in *Pinhook* (2005), "[e]ven a thing as insubstantial as a fence or a footpath serves to partition the landscape and significantly alter the abundance and behavior of certain species," so these changes do not just impact locals but also the ecosystem (7). While Lawrence Buell argues that "[c]oncerned citizens in their home places may prove even more so in second-home communities they care about," he does not take into full consideration the environmental damage that might be caused by the construction and maintenance of those second homes (72). Indeed, Ted Gragson and Paul Bolstad note that "[t]he scant to nonexistent zoning restrictions on rural and periurban private lands lead to a notable absence in southern Appalachia of a systematic approach to sprawling development," which results in "the most commonly identified causes of change to the structure and function of biodiversity across the region" (185).

Pancake reflects on these changes through the sense of displacement and loss felt by the father and son in "Ghostless" and the narrator of "Crow Season," and links them to the broader history of colonization in the region. Although in her work she explores the spiritual connection many of her characters hold for the land their forebears settled, in "Wappatomaka," describing the 1996 flood in South Branch, West Virginia, which brings the dead floating to the surface, the narrator collects the scattered remains of the dead, contemplates "the smell of the drowned rotting things," and remembers a story her grandfather told about discovering the skeleton remains of a Native American child

(51). Out fishing, he found a "musket ball" that had "rolled out of the skull of a child clutching a bone comb" (51). The grandfather explained that he reburied the child, but his family doubt the veracity of his story, imagining it to be just another tall tale. For his granddaughter, the truth of the story is not important because it stands as a reminder about the violent history of the land, and while her people may have arrived "on this piece of ground in 1773," the musket ball evokes the people who were displaced to make way for those settlers, the people who would have called the river "Wappatomaka" (51). From the removal of Native peoples, the story brings us to the present day and the removal of mountaintops, and when the narrator thinks of her grandfather's death, she reflects on the strip mining that has reconfigured the landscape since his passing.

Of course, Pancake's fictional exposé of MTR comes to the fore in *Strange as This Weather Has Been*, in which the marriage between Lace and Jimmy Make pits activism against acceptance. When Jimmy tells Lace, "*I've worked for 'em. I know you can't fight 'em. You won't never win,*" she refuses to accept such fatalism (84). Lace chooses to join with local activists and educate herself about the environmental damage being wrought by strip mining. She reflects, "It hurt to learn, it did. It was easier to half-ignore it, pretend it wasn't that bad anyway, or if it was, couldn't do nothing about it so why get worked up, that's how a lot of people lived. But I realized to at least know part of what was going on made you feel like you had a particle of control instead of none at all" (275). Throughout the novel, Pancake turns to real-life events such as the Buffalo Creek flood of 1972, enforcing the sense that the fear and horror that run through this novel are not the stuff of fiction but of fact. She turns to a real event at the end of the novel when Lace and Bant hear news about a nearby mining disaster in Martin County, Kentucky, where "an enormous slurry impoundment had busted," and while no one was killed, "306 million gallons of poison muck killed everything in the waterways for a hundred miles" (345). The Martin County flood in October 2000 "was considered one of the South's worst environmental disasters at the time" (Lovan), and in Pancake's novel, locals said that it buried their homes in "a toxic black pudding," something Bant imagines the taste of, "gobby and bitter on your tongue": just like the black lung that killed her grandfather and thousands of other underground miners (345). For Boyd Creasman, Pancake's reference to the Martin County coal slurry spill in 2000, alongside the many other turns to actual events in the novel, grants "more credibility to the fictional narrative" (111). It is not so much about credibility; rather, these references ground the novel in a realism that makes its overall Gothicism all the more menacing.[16] In Appalachia, Jill Fraley notes, the lack of mountaintop forests is preventing the ground from soaking up water, and thus excess water rushes to the valleys to submerge homes and schools. Mining companies disclaim any relationship between the floods and their methods, but are unable to explain why certain counties are having so-called hundred year floods every spring. (369)

While the didactic nature of Pancake's novel might undermine its literary sophistication, given the real-life risks to the health and well-being of not just the environment but also local people that Pancake explores in the novel, its heavy-handed messages might just be necessary to remind readers that there are no easy solutions to the environmental crisis, but that community-led, grassroots activism is a crucial element in the movement for change. Indeed, since the publication of Pancake's novel, numerous floods caused by MTR have continued to threaten local communities and the environment.

While the Appalachian coalfields are the focus of the case study in this chapter, there are any number of alternative southern sites, both rural and urban, where poor communities bear the brunt of environmental damage and form grassroots resistance. The work of Joan Martinez-Alier, Rob Nixon, and others is vital in reminding us that class and poverty are the major determining factors in terms of social and environmental justice. When Joni Clarke remarks that "[o]nly by recognizing the connections between the oppressions of certain peoples and places can literary critics begin to develop ecological theories and practice that can work transformatively toward an ecology of justice" (16), the oppressions to which she refers must take into account class as much as race, an issue that Robert Bullard struggles to overcome in his seminal study *Dumping in Dixie* (1990), in which, despite his continued references to the fact that both class and race are key factors in environmental abuses, he argues that "poor whites along with their more affluent counterparts have more options and leveraging mechanisms (formal and informal) at their disposal than blacks of equal status" (40). Bullard offers plenty of statistical information to underpin the assertion that "toxic waste dumps, municipal landfills, garbage incinerators, and similar noxious facilities are not randomly scattered across the American landscape" but instead are located in the proximity of "minority neighborhoods (regardless of class)" (42), but the texts covered in this chapter, even those in which grassroots activism takes shape, suggest that poor whites have no greater recourse to change policies than people in poor minority communities. While Clarke calls for global, transnational connections, even within the borders of the United States there is still much to be done to connect antipoverty and environmental movements with one another, and to look less at racial differences and more at class commonalities. Within and across the boundaries of nation-states, poverty is a widely shared experience for a large part of the world's population, and those communities remain the most vulnerable to corporate greed and environmental abuses; the texts in this chapter reveal the challenges faced by the poor as they strive for job security and/or more stringent environmental policies against a neoliberal system that regards both people and land as commodities to be used up and thrown away. Naomi Klein argues that ecocritical awareness and moves to address climate change might also be means for ending the "grotesque levels of inequality within our nations and between them" (*This Changes* 7). In order for this to happen, much of the writing in this chapter asks that we "stop looking away," not just from climate change and global warming but also from poverty and the humanity of the poor.

Conclusion

At the close of 2017, New York University professor of law and United Nations special rapporteur on extreme poverty and human rights Philip Alston began drafting a formal report after visiting several locations of abject poverty across the United States. On December 15, 2017, Alston outlined some of his major findings at a press conference in Washington, DC, stating: "The US Congress is trying desperately to pass a tax bill which, if adopted, would represent the single most dramatic increase in inequality that could be imagined. At the same time, and partly in order to fund that tax reform, the administration has indicated very clearly that it plans to embark on major welfare and healthcare reform" (00.00.00–41).[1] Just days later, on December 22, 2017, Donald Trump signed into legislation the Tax Cuts and Jobs Act (TCJA). Alongside cutting corporate taxes, the TCJA also repealed "the health insurance mandate that forms the core of the Affordable Care Act, also known as Obamacare. . . . Without the individual mandate, the number of uninsured Americans would increase by 4m in 2019 and 13m in 2027, according to the Congressional Budget Office" (Shugerman). Reducing, let alone ending poverty seems ever unlikely against the backdrop of policies designed to create a favorable corporate climate that is concomitant with an utter disregard for those struggling to stay above the poverty line.

Alston also reflected upon his visits to the South when he witnessed cases of "hookworm in Alabama," and he expressed his consternation that such infections and diseases still exist in one of the richest countries in the world (00.04.07–09). These facts are too easily obscured, he notes, by the ongoing vilification of the poor, which, in combination with the moves to romanticize or dehistoricize poverty across the travel writing and photo-narratives discussed in chapters 1 and 2, renders the realities of poverty unseen. In addition, Alston noted that persistent levels of mass inequality across the United States means that "[p]oor people have no chance of having their voices heard, no chance of influencing public policy" (00.07.08–12). While literature and life-writing about poverty might not directly influence policy making, it does play a crucial role in reimagining the poor. At the end of Sylvia Jenkins Cook's *From Tobacco Road to Route 66* (1976), an analysis of literary representations of southern poor whites during the Great Depression, she claims that during that period, "[t]he paradoxical attributes" of the "poor white" represented a complex moral, aesthetic, and political challenge to writers in an age when polemical certainty might easily have become the rule. Instead, the poor white became a tool for explaining the past mistakes of the country (most vividly represented in the savage history and rapid industrialization of the South) ... and finally, he became the agency for questioning revered traditions of independence, self-sufficiency, and stoicism to see if they were any longer worth preserving. (188)

Under neoliberalism, questions arise once again about literary representations of poverty and the poor; writing about the contemporary US South often explores and challenges not merely older ideals of "independence, self-sufficiency, and stoicism" or the stereotypes that have plagued representations of poor whites since the eighteenth century, but the very tenets of financial capitalism, which include "hyper-profitability" (Marazzi 44).² As Christian Marazzi explains, after "having dismantled the Welfare State," financial capitalism then "turned consumption and private indebtedness into the motor of its *modus operandi*" (89). In turn, societal measures of freedom, value, and worth have been gauged in terms of capital and consumerism, and for Félix Guattari, "[w]hat condemns the capitalist value system is that it is characterized by general equivalence, which flattens out all other forms of value, alienating them in its hegemony" (65). This book turned to several writers whose ruminations on the contemporary US South critique these models and measures for society: in particular Toni Morrison, Dorothy Allison, Janisse Ray, Tim McLaurin, and Barbara Kingsolver, who reflect on the need to reevaluate what constitutes value and worth. That is to say, these writers suggest that poverty will never be overcome as long as it seen and measured by neoliberal standards. They want to see an end to poverty, but they more broadly hope that the measures for success are reset, and they ask not merely how society can alleviate poverty but also how society can overcome its blind commitment to economic models that do not just create poverty but actually depend on it for their success.

Writing that generates alternatives fits with the broader call among leftist critics and theorists of class and economics for thinking and seeing beyond the force of neoliberalism. David Harvey suggests: "The more neo-liberalism is recognized as a failed utopian project masking a successful project for the restoration of class power, the more it lays the basis for a resurgence of mass movements voicing egalitarian political demands and seeking economic justice, fair trade and greater economic security" (*Spaces of Global* 66). Neoliberal policies are clearly rejected by writers who place notions of communalism or communitarianism at the center of their work. Of course, community itself is often fraught with hierarchical divisions, as Scott Romine observes: "[C]ommunity is enabled by practices of avoidance, deferral, and evasion," and notions of communitarianism are certainly not without distractors (*The Narrative Forms* 3).³ Across so-called Grit Lit or Rough South fiction, community is often presented as corrupt, limiting, and dangerous, such as in Chris Offutt's *The Good Brother* (1997), in which protagonist Virgil flees the hills of Kentucky after succumbing to societal pressure to exact revenge against the man who killed his brother, only to find himself in Montana, where once again his desire for community proves costly as he unwittingly joins a fascist survivalist cult; or in Tom Franklin's *Smonk* (2006), in which community is depicted as a vile pit of incest, murder, and infanticide.

Yet certain southern poverty texts privilege ideas of solidarity and community above individualism. If for Jodi Dean a major difficulty in conceptualizing communitarianism or communalism is "the left's failure to think beyond democracy and defend a vision of equality and solidarity, its unwillingness to reinvent its modes of dreaming" (17), then literature that dwells on alternatives at least opens up debates and allows for a reconceptualization of the poor. Those narratives might not impact on policy decisions, but in a world where sales of Ayn Rand's fiction rose as neoliberalism faltered during the 2008 financial crisis, it is vital that writers such as Allison "join the conversation" (*Trash* xv). Rand virulently attacked collectivism and celebrated "[t]he sacred word: EGO" in her celebration of laissez-faire capitalism (105), an approach also taken by J. D. Vance in his best-selling memoir about poverty and "hillbillies." Adam Sorkin argues that "if literature is political, and if we turn to it to delineate the nature and causes of our suffering and to understand the limitations and constraining structures of our condition, it is also playful, fabulous, dream-laden, celebratory, and can imaginatively transform human experience in such a way that writers and readers might realize the salvation" (7). For some, Rand's and Vance's overt commitment to capitalism and market forces offers "salvation," whereas writing about poverty by Allison and others demands that readers see beyond the smoke and mirrors of capital to engage with the complexities and challenges of poverty and dwell on forms of "salvation" that exist beyond monetary measures.

At the close of his ruminations on financial capitalism, Marazzi argues:

> Taking time means giving each other the means of inventing one's own future, freeing it from the anxiety of immediate profit. It means caring for oneself and the environment in which one lives, it means growing up in a socially responsible way. To overcome this crisis without questioning the meaning of consumption, production, and investment is to reproduce the preconditions of financial

capitalism, the violence of its ups and downs, the philosophy according to which "time is everything, man is nothing." For man to be everything, we need to reclaim the time of his existence. (96)

In a region where slavery and sharecropping overtly placed profit before people, the "anxiety" Marazzi observes has long been an overt feature of southern life, making literature about the region a useful place to turn for reflections on time, money, and humanity. Harvey insists that "in money economies in general, and capitalist society in particular, the intersecting command of money, time, and space forms a substantial nexus of social power that we cannot afford to ignore," and like Marazzi, he calls for different ways of conceptualizing time (*Condition* 203). For Harvey, "[m]ovements of opposition" form one key way of reconfiguring time, since "[m]ovements of all sorts—religious, mystical, social, communitarian, humanitarian, etc.— define themselves directly in terms of an antagonism to the power of money and of rationalized conceptions of space and time over daily life" (238). These movements, he suggests, add "color and ferment" to social forces, including "artistic and other cultural practices" (238). The writers covered in the final three chapters of this book largely demand that the measure of success for individuals, regions, and nations should not be determined by wealth, thereby reflecting wider oppositional ideas and movements, but Harvey notes the difficulty such movements face in challenging capital's hegemonic domination over time and space, arguing:

> Capital . . . continues to dominate, and it does so in part through superior command over space and time, even when opposition movements gain control over a particular place for a time. The "othernesses" and "regional resistances" that postmodernist politics emphasize can flourish in a particular place. But they are all too often subject to the power of capital over the co-ordination of universal fragmented space and the march of capitalism's global historical time that lies outside of the purview of any particular one of them. (*Condition* 239)

At the very least, oppositional thought continues unabated within literature because, as Avery Gordon states, "[l]iterary fictions play an important role . . . for the simple reason that they enable other kinds of sociological information to emerge" (25).

In Ron Rash's autobiographical poem "Invocation," written to channel his grandfather as he embarks on a poetic journey to explore his working-class roots in his 1998 collection *Eureka Mill*, he asks his ancestor for guidance as he writes about

> *those lives all lived as gears*
> *in Springs' cotton mill*
> *and let me not forget*
> *your lives were more than that.* (27–30)

Like other writers in this book, Rash wants to go beyond the laboring body to find the person used and disposed of by capital, and the need to see the whole person is as pressing today as it has ever been. In particular, Stephen Pimpare suggests there is still "a general ignorance about the lives led by poor Americans, an ignorance, whether real or feigned, that shapes public discourse about poverty and welfare, and policy itself" (5). That "ignorance" will not be overcome as long as poverty is regarded as either regionally or racially specific, which is why emphasis on the plight of poor whites highlights the misconception that poverty is primarily black, and why broader issues of class and economics that operate across regions and borders are more important than southernness. For Gordon,

> [o]ur country's major institutions—the corporation, the law, the state, the media, the public—recognize narrower and narrower evidence for the harms and indignities that citizens and residents experience. The most obvious violations—the poverty, the gaping inequality of resources, the brutality of the police, the corruption of democratic politics, the hunger and homelessness, the hateful beatings and batterings—are everywhere to be seen only in the disappearing hypervisibility of their fascinating anomalousness. (206)

With the election of Donald Trump, it remains vital to seek out alternative views of poverty and to recognize the poor beyond the hypervisibility brought about by terms such as "hillbilly" and "redneck" that only serve to elide economic conditions. Ronald Aronson claims that "[t]he world has grown so threateningly out of control that only an active, *political* mode of apprehending it can restore a sense of it as fluid, unfinished, and capable of redirection" (294). That sense of the "fluid" or "unfinished" must also be applied to how we reconceptualize poverty. In compiling his report for the UN, Alston claims that he had to ask the question, "Who are the poor?," because dominant narratives of poverty continue to belie its actualities (00.05.28–30). This exploration of poor whites in recent writing about the US South has worked on the premise of "fluidity," the need to see the poor as complex and to locate poverty within socioeconomic policies and models rather than regional contexts and behaviors.

Notes

Introduction

1. See Jon Smith's essay in which he reflects on the South, poverty, and identity politics, 72–94.
2. Among other initiatives during the 1960s and Lyndon Johnson's War on Poverty was Project Head Start, which was founded in 1965 and still runs today, to provide additional educational and health support for children from low-income families.
3. Alongside Rebein, numerous scholars have noted the emergence of writers out of poor backgrounds, including Bledsoe 68–90; Guinn, particularly chapter 1; and Gray, especially chapters 6 and 7.
4. See Robertson, "Poor Whites" 631–41.
5. Whiteness studies came to fore in a number of major works including those by Dyer, Hill, Hartigan Jr. (*Racial Situations* and *Odd Tribes*), D. Smith, Wray, and Jacobson. For a critical rebuke against whiteness studies, see Lipsitz.
6. Notably, on March 27, 2018, a tenth season of *Roseanne* reappeared on screens after a twenty-one-year break (the first run ended in 1997): in the wake of Donald Trump's victory, ABC revived the comedy show about the working-class Conner family. In an interview with the *New York Times*' Patrick Healy, Rosanne Barr reflects on her own, and her character's support for Trump. ABC cancelled the show partway through its new season after Barr posted racist and Islamophobic tweets about former Barack Obama White House adviser Valerie Jarrett.
7. Bledsoe explores the contested terms for discussing poor white southerners, 68–90.
8. In her essay on the persistence of southern "white trash" stereotypes in Hollywood, Allison Graham notes how in 2004 "US Army spokespersons ... blamed the torture at Abu Ghraib on 'recycled hillbillies' and national journalists laid responsibility for George W. Bush's reelection at the trailer steps of NASCAR devotees," 161.
9. Statistics are drawn from the BBC's "US Election 2016: The Trump-Brexit Voter Revolt," 11 Nov. 2016, http://www.bbc.co.uk/news/election-us-2016-37943072. Useful 2016 election statistics can also be found in Walley 231–36.
10. For detailed analysis of NAFTA and its ramifications, see Chomsky, particularly section 4, and Harvey's *The New Imperialism*, chapter 4.

Chapter One

1. For further reflections on the influential nature of Dickey's *Deliverance*, see Jerry Williamson, especially chapter 5. The popular appeal of Dickey's backwoods tale was

underscored by an off-Broadway production of *Deliverance* in 2014. Adapted by Sean Tyler and directed by Joe Tantalo, the small stage at the Godlight Theatre Company did not have enough space for wilderness props, so, as Tantalo informed Neil Genzlinger of the *New York Times*, "the audience is creating their own sense of what the wilderness is." While audiences might have drawn on Boorman's adaptation to imagine the landscape, the play itself drew only upon Dickey's novel, thereby denying audiences what Genzlinger terms the "infectious song, 'Dueling Banjos.'" To whatever degree the play reinforced or challenged the novel and the film's forms of othering, it is clear that there remains an appetite for this tale of intrepid city men entering Georgia's heart of darkness and pitting themselves against backward, hostile locals.

2. For useful considerations of the role of nostalgia in contemporary travel writing, see Lisle, particularly chapter 5, and Kaplan, chapter 1.

3. For a broader consideration of tourism and the South's "authentic culture," see Brundage, "From Appalachian Folk" 27–48.

4. Romine also provides an insightful critique of Naipaul's *A Turn in the South* in chapter 2 of *The Real South*.

5. Winders offers useful insights into the construction of "white trash" in postbellum southern travel narratives, 45–63. Also see Isenberg's allusions to the denigrating ideas of poor whites that appeared in travelogues throughout the 1860s, including Whitelaw Reid's *After the War* (1866), in *White Trash*, 179.

6. For a detailed overview of postcolonial travel writing, see Edwards and Graulund 1–35.

7. Such competing narratives abound more broadly in the history of exploration. As Bernard Smith outlines in his study of European explorations into the Pacific region, both "classical antiquity and the traditions of Christian thought provided a stock of attitudes and preconceptions which Europeans continually brought to bear up-on their experience of the Pacific." Those beliefs centered on the dichotomy between the "nobility and ignobility of Pacific peoples" (5). While Smith argues that such categorizing gave way to "scientific method," these ideas still resonate in the competing discourses about poor southern whites; see chapter 11.

8. For a compelling discussion of how various contemporary writers depict Atlanta, see Bone, part 3.

9. For a detailed historical account of the intrinsic links between cotton and modern capitalism, see Beckert.

10. Hicks, who died in 2003, remains a popular local figure. His story has been captured by many including Isbell, Salsi, and onscreen in *Blue Ridge Mountain Music*. In addition, the website RayHicks.com both raises money for his relatives and continues to promote the Hicks family's storytelling legacy: www.rayhicks.com/index.htm.

11. See Becker for an interesting examination of the emergence of Appalachia's folk industry and the tension between the marketplace and laborers. In the epilogue, Becker draws together her study by observing that "[t]he commodification of tradition depends upon … deceptions, along with a sort of amnesia," 236. Petro is guilty of such amnesia as she idealizes the idea of the "authentic" over the contemporary, commodified realities she actually encounters on her journey.

12. In his discussion of "negative sightseeing," MacCannell writes: "The *New York Times* reports that seventy people answered an advertisement inviting tourists to spend '21 days

"in the land of the Hatfields and McCoys" for $370.00, living with some of the poorest people in Mingo County, West Virginia'" (40).

13. See Salstrom's essay on Depression-era marketing of "authentic" items, 74–87.

14. For a detailed consideration of the way tourism impacts on local lives in Appalachia, see Billings, Norman, and Ledford, Introduction 3–20.

15. See Starnes's edited collection for several interesting discussions of travel and tourism in the US South. Particularly in relation to the "hillbilly," see Blevins's essay, 42–65.

16. For a thorough overview of the "hillbilly" figure in popular culture, see Harkins.

17. Isenberg discusses the ways in which popular nineteenth-century publications depicted poor whites as "curious," exotic, foreign, and vampiric; see chapter 6.

18. For useful considerations of curiosity and its role in travel writing, see Jarvis, particularly chapter 2; Evans and Marr; and Welch 10–25.

19. Kipling's story sets out the danger of, and punishment for, miscegenation. "A man should," the story begins, "keep to his own caste, race and breed." Trejago fails to heed this code as he pursues a relationship with the young widow Bisesa. Discovery of this relationship leads to Bisesa losing her hands and Trejago being stabbed in the groin, leaving him with a limp for life. He learns from this experience that he "took too deep an interest in native life" but now knows that "he will never do the same again."

20. Hillbilly golf remains a popular Gatlinburg attraction, promising visitors a deserved break on "the world's most *unusual* miniature golf course." *Gatlinburg Attractions*, 21 Mar. 2016, www.attractions-gatlinburg.com/public/attractions/Hillbilly%20Golf.cfm. The town is also home to Cooter's Place, the *Dukes of Hazzard* museum and shop.

21. Black British writers often also reflect on the US South as they consider the black diaspora and contemporary black identity. Of note are Younge and Griffith.

22. In the introduction to their edited collection *South to a New Place*, Jones and Monteith reflect on the contradictory relationship that black writers often have with the South, 1–19. In particular they outline the permutations of Harris's southern journey in *South of Haunted Dreams* and his realization that the South is as much like home, indeed sometimes even more like home, than any other part of the United States.

23. The surrender that Harris sees in the eyes of these poor farmers can be linked with the surrender that he claims plagues black Americans in his later book *Still Life in Harlem*.

Chapter Two

1. For a useful overview of the field of deindustrialization photography, its limits, and its possibilities for rethinking class and economics, see Strangleman 23–37.

2. I also briefly consider the contrast between Scout's and Ruth's ways of seeing in "Poverty and Progress," 104–15.

3. For wider considerations of photography, captions, and popular culture, see Hariman and Lucaites, especially the introduction and chapter 2, and Kelsey and Stimson.

4. For additional reconsiderations of FSA work, see Curtis and Finnegan.

5. Ganzel discusses how he revisited many of the FSA subjects in the Great Plains, including Florence Thompson, whom he photographed with three of her daughters in 1979, 31.

6. *And Their Children After Them* won the Pulitzer Prize for General Nonfiction in 1990.

7. For poverty threshold data sets, see the US Census Bureau, www.census.gov/data/tables/time-series/demo/income-poverty/historical-poverty-thresholds.html.

8. I would like to thank the University of Alabama for providing me with information about the Alabama Tenant-Farming Legacy Scholarship, details of which can be found here: //reach.ua.edu/uploads/2/6/5/2/26525085/scholarships-101-resource-guide.pdf.

9. *Let Us Now Praise Famous Men* continues to inspire rephotography projects. For instance, Crooke details his visit to Hale County in 2013 and the changes wrought not just to old tenant homes but also in the town of Moundville, where the main thoroughfare, Market Street, is slowly dying, 367–94.

10. The report can be found at www.arc.gov/about/ARCAppalachiaAReportbythePresidentsAppalachianRegionalCommission1964.asp.

11. Cameron has also written an interesting essay on class difference, "Spaces of Encounter" 177–94.

12. For detailed discussions of how Appalshop has developed over time, see Hanna 372–413 and Charbonneau 137–45. Charbonneau in particular is interested in the way Appalshop productions typically elide issues of class, a point also at the center of Gaines's earlier work, 53–63.

13. See Ewald and Barret's fundraising page for the revisitation project, which includes a short video including Ewald's subjects looking back and reflecting on the photographs: www.hatchfund.org/project/portraits_and_dreams_a_revisitation.

14. In Ron Rash's novel *The World Made Straight*, both historical Civil War violence and the violence of the contemporary drug trade overtake the lives of his key characters, plunging them into a land not only steeped in the blood of the past but also flowing with the blood of contemporary conflicts. The Shelton Laurel massacre, in which thirteen alleged Union sympathizers were executed by Confederate soldiers in Madison County, North Carolina, in January 1963, is described in Rash's novel.

15. See: //higherpictures.com/exhibitions/susan-lipper/.

16. Taylor's work on the global circulation of *Gone With the Wind* and its numerous spin-offs provides an interesting insight into the way the text still connotes a version of the South but is certainly not tethered to the region; see chapter 2.

17. Also see Hirsch's extended examination of family photography in *Family Frames*.

18. Bragg explained his decisions about the photos in *Ava's Man* via email correspondence in July 2014. I am grateful for his time and insights.

19. Maharidge offers further insights into his views on poverty and economics in an interview with Chiglinsky, 70–74.

Chapter Three

1. For a survey of southern poor white life-writing, see Inscoe, *Writing the South*, particularly chapter 3; and Berry's *Located Lives* and edited collection *Home Ground*.

2. Atlas considers the proliferation of life-writing in the final decades of the twentieth century.

3. Among the numerous critical examinations of autobiography and life-writing, notable studies include those by Olney, Folenflik, and Smith and Watson.

4. Allison discusses her decision to embrace the term "trash" in "Introduction: Stubborn Girls," vii–xvi.

5. For a useful discussion of both Bragg and Crews, see Weldon 89–110.

6. Bidgood et al. have created a useful map detailing the monuments removed or set to be removed at the *New York Times* website, www.nytimes.com/interactive/2017/08/16/us/confederate-monuments-removed.html. Useful critical discussions of memorialization and the South include Brundage's *Where These Memories Grow* and *The Southern Past*, and Alderman 658–60.

7. Key studies of *Southern Living* include Stephen Smith, especially chapters 5 and 6; Roberts, "Living Southern" 85–98; and Elias 253–82.

8. For an early essay on foodways in the US South, see Evans 141–49.

9. For an interesting account of the demonization of poor mothers, see Adair.

10. There are several studies of the migration of Appalachian people to urban centers; the most notable includes Hartigan's *Racial Situations*, in which he focuses on Appalachian communities in Detroit. Obermiller and Philliber have written extensively about Appalachian migration.

11. For a broader consideration of southern poor whites, masculinity, and trauma, see Watkins, "Drinking Poisoned Waters" 220–33.

12. In their photo-narrative detailing the aftermath of the 2008 financial crisis, *Someplace Like America*, Maharidge and Williamson detail a number of communal food-growing organizations in urban and suburban areas in part 6, 182–99.

Chapter Four

1. Tom Franklin explores poverty across his fiction writing, which ranges from his historical novels *Hell at the Breach* and *Smonk or Widow Town*, the latter also a reworking of local color and southern humor writing, to rural southern culture in his collection of short stories *Poachers* and his novel *Crooked Letter, Crooked Letter*.

2. Patell examines turns to communitarianism across Morrison's fiction.

3. Suzanne Jones discusses the growing interest among black American writers to reexamine stereotypes about white people, xiii–xv.

4. For key readings of Amy Denver's role in the novel, see Coonradt 168–87, and Rigney, particularly chapter 3.

5. See Troy Allen 466–68 for a brief yet interesting overview of post-Katrina New Orleans.

6. Collins briefly contrasts Morrison's ghost in *Beloved* with the ghosts that haunt Whitehead's novel, 285–300.

7. For interesting discussions of Whitehead's novel and the history of African Americans, see the special edition of *African American Review*, vol. 46, nos. 2–3, Summer–Fall 2013, especially Tettenborn 271–84 and Collins 285–300.

8. Garrard provides an engaging discussion on climate change in the novel, 295–312. In an expansive essay, Frederick Buell touches on the wider socioeconomic contexts that shape environmentalism in five contemporary American novels, but although Kingsolver's novel forms part of his examination, he does not engage with the specific economics at play in *Flight Behavior*, "Global Warming" 261–94.

9. Houser considers the gender politics of Kingsolver's novel at length, 95–115.

10. Also see Frederick Buell's interesting discussions of environmentalism, literature, and popular culture in *From Apocalypse to Way of Life*, part 3.

11. I am indebted to Richard Godden in my reading of liquidity in Kingsolver's novel. Godden's influential work on literary representations of finance and liquidity is a cornerstone for any consideration of monetary matters in fiction.

Chapter Five

1. For a detailed consideration of environmentalism in the US South, see Otis Graham 50–71.

2. Recent anthologies of environmental justice writing include those by Adamson, Evans, and Stein; and Ammons and Roy.

3. In an interesting essay, Welling regards Ray's work as bioregional in nature, focusing in particular on her attempts to revitalize localism, 118–31.

4. Nelson provides a useful case study of the exploration, extraction, and marginalization of the Okefenokee Swamp, 221–34.

5. Wray provides an overview of American eugenics and poor "white trash"; see chapter 3.

6. Numerous documentaries have vividly recorded key union activity in the Appalachian coalfields and the importance of communitarianism. In particular, see Kopple's Oscar-winning documentary *Harlan County USA*, which followed the 1974 Brookside Strike in Kentucky, and Lewis's Oscar-winning *Justice in the Coalfields*, which covered the Pittston Coal Strike in Virginia, 1989–1990, as the United Mine Workers went on strike against the Pittston Coal Company after it declared its intention to terminate the medical benefits of disabled miners, pensioners, and widows.

7. DeLoughrey and Handley's edited collection contains several interesting essays on the ways postcolonialism and environmentalism intersect.

8. Appalachian scholars have extensively highlighted the role the region has long played in the development of national and global economies, including R. Lewis 59–73 and Anglin 51–56. Anglin's essay, and the others in that edition of the *Journal of Appalachian Studies*, are just some of the many studies of the Appalachian transnational dimensions of the regional economy that regularly appear in that journal.

9. Anthropologist McNeil explores the work of CRMW at length, and the group's activities form the basis for his argument about the impact of neoliberalism and the role of activism in Appalachia.

10. Billings, Norman, and Ledford, "Supporting 'Conscious Hearts,'" consider various forms of resistance against MTR, 20–27.

11. Hufford offers a detailed account of the destruction of the commons and subsequent forms of resistance that occurred in the communities around Coal River Mountain, West Virginia, which included the formation of CRMW, 157–67.

12. Among others, historian Stoll outlines the failure of Appalachia's elected officials to represent and protect the people and environment, and proposes a commons approach as a viable alternative; see chapter 7.

13. Duke provides a comprehensive survey of Appalachian coalfield literature to the end of twentieth century.

14. For a brief journalistic overview of late twentieth-century resistance to coal mining operations in Appalachia, including the 1965 case of Ollie "Widow" Combs, see https://www.kentucky.com/news/special-reports/fifty-years-of-night/article44430654.html.

15. For pertinent examinations of stereotypes and violence in Appalachia, see Jerry Williamson, particularly chapters 5 and 6; Blee and Billings 119–37; Hsiung 101–13; Andreescu 62–75; and Young 103–17.

16. In my chapter "Gothic Appalachia," 109–20, I discuss the politicized nature of the Gothic in Pancake's *Strange as This Weather Has Been*.

Conclusion

1. Alston's press conference can be accessed here: www.facebook.com/AlstonUNSR/videos/533327963714.

2. Book-length studies of poor whites in southern fiction include those by Skaggs and Cook.

3. See Etzioni for a comprehensive account of communitarianism. For useful examinations of communitarianism and its detractors, see Tam, especially chapters 1 and 9, and Bell, notably the introduction and act I.

Works Cited

Adair, Vivyan. *From Good Ma to Welfare Queen: A Genealogy of the Poor Woman in American Literature, Photography, and Culture*. Garland, 2000.
Adams, Shelby Lee. *Appalachian Legacy*. UP of Mississippi, 1998.
Adams, Shelby Lee. *Appalachian Lives*. UP of Mississippi, 2003.
Adams, Shelby Lee. *Appalachian Portraits*. UP of Mississippi, 1993.
Adams, Shelby Lee. "Beyond the Stereotypes of Appalachia." *Chronicle of Higher Education*, 9 Oct. 1998, B10–11.
Adams, Shelby Lee. *Salt and Truth*. Candela, 2011.
Adams, Timothy Dow. "Telling Stories in Dorothy Allison's *Two or Three Things I Know for Sure*." *Southern Literary Journal*, vol. 36, no. 2, Spring 2004, pp. 82–99. *Project Muse*, https://doi.org/10.1353/slj.2004.0001.
Adamson, Joni, Mei Mei Evans, and Rachel Stein, editors. *The Environmental Justice Reader: Politics, Poetics, and Pedagogy*. U of Arizona P, 2002.
Agee, James, and Walker Evans. *Let Us Now Praise Famous Men*. 1941. Penguin, 2006.
Alderman, Derek H. "New Memorial Landscapes in the American South: An Introduction." *Professional Geographer*, vol. 52, no. 4, 2000, pp. 658–60.
Allen, Barbara L. "The Making of Cancer Alley: A Historical View of Louisiana's Chemical Corridor." *Southern United States: An Environmental History*, edited by Donald E. Davis, ABC-Clio, 2006, pp. 235–47.
Allen, Troy D. "Katrina: Race, Class, and Poverty; Reflections and Analysis." *Journal of Black Studies*, vol. 37, no. 4, March 2007, pp. 466–68. *JSTOR*, http://www.jstor.org/stable/40034317.
Allison, Dorothy. *Bastard Out of Carolina*. Plume, 1993.
Allison, Dorothy. Introduction. *The Redneck Way of Knowledge*, by Blanche McCrary Boyd. 1978. Vintage, 1995.
Allison, Dorothy. "Introduction: Stubborn Girls and Mean Stories." *Trash*. Plume, 2002, pp. vii–xvi.
Allison, Dorothy. *Skin: Talking about Sex, Class, and Literature*. 1994. Pandora, 1995.
Allison, Dorothy. *Trash*. 1988. Plume, 2002.
Allison, Dorothy. *Two or Three Things I Know for Sure*. Plume, 1996.
Alston, Philip. "Press Conference, Washington, DC." 15 Dec. 2017, www.facebook.com/Alston UNSR/videos/533327963714.
Ammons, Elizabeth, and Modhumita Roy, editors. *Sharing the Earth: An International Environmental Justice Reader*. U of Georgia P, 2015.
Andreescu, Viviana. "Violent Appalachia: The Media's Role in the Creation and Perpetuation of an American Myth." *Journal of the Institute of Justice and International Studies*, no. 9, 2009, pp. 62–75.

Works Cited

Anglin, Mary. "Toward a New Politics of Outrage and Transformation: Placing Appalachia within the Global Political Economy." *Journal of Appalachian Studies*, vol. 22, no. 1, Spring 2016, pp. 51–56. *JSTOR*, www.jstor.org/stable/10.5406/jappastud.22.1.0051.

"Appalachian Lives." *Publishers Weekly*, 7 Jul. 2003, pp. 66–67. *ProQuest*, http://search.proquest.com.ezproxy.uwe.ac.uk/docview/197085320/fulltextPDF/741E9FD41704747PQ/1?accountid=14785.

Appalshop. "About Us." www.appalshop.org/about-us/.

Aronowitz, Stanley. *The Politics of Identity: Class, Culture, Social Movements*. Routledge, 1992.

Aronson, Ronald. *The Dialectics of Disaster: A Preface to Hope*. Verso, 1983.

Asen, Robert. *Visions of Poverty: Welfare Policy and Political Imagination*. Michigan State UP, 2002.

Ashcroft, Bill, Gareth Griffiths, and Helen Tiffin. *The Empire Writes Back*. 2nd ed., Routledge, 2009.

Atlas, James. "Confessing for Voyeurs: The Age of the Literary Memoir Is Now." *New York Times Magazine*, 12 May 1996, http://www.nytimes.com/1996/05/12/magazine/confessing-for-voyeurs-the-age-of-the-literary-memoir-is-now.html.

Aubert, Didier. "The Doorstep Portrait: Intrusion and Performance in Mainstream American Documentary Photography." *Visual Studies*, vol. 24, no. 1, April 2009, pp. 3–18. *Taylor and Francis Online*, dx.doi.org/10.1080/14725860902732678.

Azoulay, Ariella. *The Civil Contract of Photography*. Translated by Rela Mazali and Ruvik Danieli, Zone Books, 2008.

Azoulay, Ariella. "Photography Consists of Collaboration: Susan Meiselas, Wendy Ewald, and Arielle Azoulay." *Camera Obscura*, vol. 31, no. 1–91, 2016, pp. 186–201. *Duke UP Journals Online*, https://doi.org/10.1215/02705346-3454496.

Baichwal, Jennifer, director. *The True Meaning of Pictures: Shelby Lee Adams' Appalachia*. Mercury Films, 2002.

Barca, Stefania. "Laboring the Earth: Transnational Reflections on the Environmental History of Work." *Environmental History*, vol. 19, January 2014, pp. 3–27.

Barnwell, Tim. *The Face of Appalachia: Portraits from the Mountain Farm*. W. W. Norton, 2003.

Barnwell, Tim. *Hands in Harmony: Traditional Crafts and Music in Appalachia*. W. W. Norton, 2009.

Barnwell, Tim. *On Earth's Furrowed Brow: The Appalachian Farm in Photographs*. W. W. Norton, 2007.

Barret, Elizabeth, director. *Stranger with a Camera*. Appalshop Films, 2000.

Bartley, Numan V. *The New South, 1945–1980: The Story of the South's Modernization*. Louisiana State UP, 1995.

Bartling, Hugh. "Organizing the New South: Local Ecologies and Autonomous Strategies for Confronting Globalization." *Mississippi Quarterly*, vol. 57, no. 1, Winter 2003–2004, pp. 135–45.

Becker, Jane S. *Selling Tradition: Appalachia and the Construction of an American Folk, 1930–1940*. U of North Carolina P, 1998.

Beckert, Sven. *Empire of Cotton: A Global History*. Alfred A. Knopf, 2014.

Bell, Daniel. *Communitarianism and Its Critics*. Clarendon, 1993.

Benjamin, Walter. "A Short History of Photography." 1931. *Classic Essays on Photography*, edited by Alan Trachtenberg, Leete's Island Books, 1980, pp. 199-216.

Benson, Melanie. *Disturbing Calculations: The Economics of Identity in Postcolonial Southern Literature, 1912-2002*. U of Georgia P, 2008.

Berry, J. Bill, editor. *Home Ground: Southern Autobiography*. U of Missouri P, 1991.

Berry, J. Bill. *Located Lives: Place and Idea in Southern Autobiography*. U of Georgia P, 1990.

Bhabha, Homi K. *The Location of Culture*. 1994. Routledge, 2004.

Bidgood, Jess, et al. "Confederate Monuments Are Coming Down." *New York Times*, 28 Aug. 2017, www.nytimes.com/interactive/2017/08/16/us/confederate-monuments-removed.html.

Biguenet, John. *The Rising Water Trilogy*. Louisiana State UP, 2015.

Billings, Dwight, Gurney Norman, and Katherine Ledford, editors. *Back Talk from Appalachia: Confronting Stereotypes*. UP of Kentucky, 1999.

Billings, Dwight, Gurney Norman, and Katherine Ledford. Introduction. *Back Talk from Appalachia: Confronting Stereotypes*, edited by Billings, Norman, and Ledford, UP of Kentucky, 1999, pp. 3-20.

Billings, Dwight, Gurney Norman, and Katherine Ledford. "Supporting 'Conscious Hearts' and Oppositional Knowledge in the Struggle against Mountaintop Removal Coal Mining." *Journal of Appalachian Studies*, vol. 14, nos. 1-2, Spring-Fall 2008, pp. 20-27.

Bledsoe, Erik. "The Rise of the Southern Redneck and White Trash Writers." *Southern Cultures*, vol. 6, no. 1, Spring 2000, pp. 68-90.

Blee, Kathleen M., and Dwight B. Billings. "Where 'Bloodshed Is a Pastime': Mountain Feuds and Appalachian Stereotyping." *Back Talk from Appalachia: Confronting Stereotypes*, edited by Dwight B. Billings, Gurney Norman, and Katherine Ledford, UP of Kentucky, 1999, pp. 119-37.

Blevins, Brooks. "Hillbillies and the Holy Land: The Development of Tourism in the Arkansas Ozarks." *Southern Journeys: Tourism, History, and Culture in the Modern South*, edited by Richard D. Starnes, U of Alabama P, 2003, pp. 42-65.

Bone, Martyn. *The Postsouthern Sense of Place in Contemporary Fiction*. Louisiana State UP, 2005.

Bone, Martyn, Brian Ward, and William A. Link, editors. *Creating and Consuming the American South*. UP of Florida, 2015.

Boym, Svetlana. *The Future of Nostalgia*. Basic Books, 2001.

Bragg, Rick. *All Over but the Shoutin'*. Pantheon, 1997.

Bragg, Rick. *Ava's Man*. Alfred A. Knopf, 2001.

Bragg, Rick. *The Best Cook in the World: Tales from My Momma's Table*. Alfred A. Knopf, 2018.

Bragg, Rick. *The Most They Ever Had*. MacAdam/Cage, 2009.

Bragg, Rick. *My Southern Journey: True Stories from the Heart of the South*. Oxmoor House, 2015.

Bragg, Rick. *The Prince of Frogtown*. Alfred A. Knopf, 2008.

Branch, Michael P., et al. Introduction. *Reading the Earth: New Directions in the Study of Literature and the Environment*, edited by Branch et al., U of Idaho P, 1998, pp. xi-xviii.

Brenden, Martin C. "To Keep the Spirit of Mountain Culture Alive: Tourism and Historical Memory in the Southern Highlands." *Where These Memories Grow: History, Memory, and Southern Identity*, edited by W. Fitzhugh Brundage, U of North Carolina P, 2000, pp. 249–69.

Brinkmeyer, Robert H., Jr. "Marginalization and Mobility: Segregation and the Representation of Southern Poor Whites." *Reading Southern Poverty between the Wars, 1918–1939*, edited by Richard Godden and Martin Crawford, U of Georgia P, 2006, pp. 223–37.

Brown, Larry. *Fay*. Free Press, 2000.

Brown, Larry. *Joe*. Algonquin, 1991.

Brundage, W. Fitzhugh. "From Appalachian Folk to Southern Foodways: Why Americans Look to the South for Authentic Culture." *Creating and Consuming the American South*, edited by Martyn Bone, Brian Ward, and William A. Link, UP of Florida, 2015, pp. 27–48.

Brundage, W. Fitzhugh. *The Southern Past: A Clash of Race and Memory*. Belknap P of Harvard UP, 2005.

Brundage, W. Fitzhugh, editor. *Where These Memories Grow: History, Memory, and Southern Identity*. U of North Carolina P, 2000.

Bryant, David. "The Face of Appalachia: Portraits from the Mountain Farm." *Library Journal*, 1 Mar. 2004, p. 72.

Bryson, Bill. *The Lost Continent*. 1989. Abacus, 1997.

Bryson, Bill. *A Walk in the Woods*. 1997. Black Swan, 1998.

Buell, Frederick. *From Apocalypse to Way of Life: Environmental Crisis in the American Century*. Routledge, 2003.

Buell, Frederick. "Global Warming as Literary Narrative." *Philological Quarterly*, vol. 93, no. 3, 2014, pp. 261–94.

Buell, Lawrence. *The Future of Environmental Criticism: Environmental Crisis and Literary Imagination*. Blackwell, 2005.

Bullard, Robert D. *Dumping in Dixie: Race, Class, and Environmental Quality*. Westview, 1990.

Byrd, William. *Histories of the Dividing Line betwixt Virginia and North Carolina*. Dover, 1967.

Caesar, Terry. *Forgiving the Boundaries: Home as Abroad in American Travel Writing*. U of Georgia P, 1995.

Caldwell, Erskine. *Tobacco Road*. 1932. U of Georgia P, 1995.

Caldwell, Erskine, and Margaret Bourke-White. *You Have Seen Their Faces*. 1937. U of Georgia P, 1995.

Cameron, Ardis. "Spaces of Encounter: The Cultural Labor of Class Difference." *International Labor and Working-Class History*, no. 69, Spring 2006, pp. 177–94.

Cameron, Ardis. "When Strangers Bring Cameras: The Poetics and Politics of Othered Places." *American Quarterly*, vol. 53, no. 3, September 2002, pp. 411–35.

Campkin, Ben, and Rosie Cox. "Introduction: Materialities and Metaphors of Dirt and Cleanliness." *Dirt: New Geographies of Cleanliness and Contamination*, edited by Campkin and Cox, I. B. Tauris, 2007, pp. 1–8.

"Campus Life: Alabama; Legacy of Two Books: New Scholarship Fund." *New York Times*, 30 Dec. 1990, http://www.nytimes.com/1990/12/30/style/campus-life-alabama-legacy-of-two-books-new-scholarship-fund.html.

Carpenter, Brian, and Tom Franklin, editors. *Grit Lit: A Rough South Reader*. U of South Carolina P, 2012.

Carr, Duane. *A Question of Class: The Redneck Stereotype in Southern Fiction*. Popular Press, 1996.

Carswell, Simon. "Hipsters and Hillbillies Clash as Donald Trump Calls." *Irish Times*, 17 Sept. 2016, https://www.irishtimes.com/news/world/us/hipsters-and-hillbillies-clash-as-donald-trump-calls-1.2794276.

Cash, Jean W. "Introduction: Rough South, Rural South." *Rough South, Rural South: Region and Class in Recent Southern Literature*, edited by Jean W. Cash and Keith Perry, UP of Mississippi, 2016, pp. xi–xiv.

Cash, Jean W., and Keith Perry, editors. *Larry Brown and the Blue-Collar South*. UP of Mississippi, 2008.

Cash, Jean W., and Keith Perry, editors. *Rough South, Rural South: Region and Class in Recent Southern Literature*. UP of Mississippi, 2016.

Cash, W. J. *The Mind of the South*. 1941. Vintage, 1991.

Catledge, Oraien E. *Cabbagetown*. U of Texas P, 1985.

Catledge, Oraien E. *Oraien Catledge Photographs*, edited by Constance Lewis and Richard Ford, UP of Mississippi, 2010.

Chambers, Deborah. "Family as Place: Family Photograph Albums and the Domestication of Public and Private Space." *Picturing Place: Photography and the Geographical Imagination*, edited by Joan M. Schwartz and James R. Ryan, I. B. Tauris, 2006, pp. 96–114.

Charbonneau, Stephen Michael. "Branching Out: Young Appalachian Selves, Autoethnographic Aesthetics, and the Founding of Appalshop." *Journal of Popular Film and Television*, vol. 37, no. 3, October 2009, pp. 137–45. *Taylor and Francis Online*, dx.doi.org/10.1080/01956050903218125.

Chiglinsky, Brian. "'A Fundamental Change': An Interview with Pulitzer Prize Winner Dale Maharidge on the New American Economy." *Kennedy School Review*, vol. 14, 2014, pp. 70–74.

Chomsky, Noam. *Profit over People: Neoliberalism and Global Order*. Seven Stories, 1999.

Churner, Rachel. "Review: Susan Lipper." *Artforum International*, vol. 55, no. 6, p. 217.

Clark, John P. *The Impossible Community: Realizing Communitarian Anarchism*. Bloomsbury, 2013.

Clark, Timothy. *The Cambridge Introduction to Literature and the Environment*. Cambridge UP, 2011.

Clarke, Joni Adamson. "Toward an Ecology of Justice: Transformative Ecological Theory and Practice." *Reading the Earth: New Directions in the Study of Literature and the Environment*, edited by Michael P. Branch et al., U of Idaho P, 1998, pp. 9–17.

Cobb, James C. *Redefining Southern Culture: Mind and Identity in the Modern South*. U of Georgia P, 1999.

Collins, Peter. "The Ghosts of Economics Past: *John Henry Days* and the Production of History." *African American Review*, vol. 46, nos. 2–3, Summer–Fall 2013, pp. 285–300.

Cook, Sylvia Jenkins. *From Tobacco Road to Route 66: The Southern Poor White in Fiction*. U of North Carolina P, 1976.

Coonradt, Nicole M. "To Be Loved: Amy Denver and Human Need—Bridges to Understanding in Toni Morrison's *Beloved*." *College Literature*, vol. 32, no. 4, Fall 2005, pp. 168–87. *Project Muse*, https://doi.org/10.1353/lit.2005.0053.

Cornwell, Rupert. "A Gourmet's Guide to the Boondocks." *Independent*, 24 Jan. 1998.

Creasman, Boyd. *Writing West Virginia: Place, People, and Poverty in Contemporary Literature from the Mountain State*. U of Tennessee P, 2016.

Cretton, Destin Daniel, director. *The Glass Castle*. Gil Netter Productions, 2017.

Crews, Harry. *A Childhood: The Biography of a Place*. 1978. U of Georgia P, 1995.

Crooke, Andrew. "All Over Alabama: On the Road to Hobe's Hill." *Let Us Now Praise Famous Men at 75*, edited by Michael A. Lofaro, U of Tennessee P, 2017, pp. 367–94.

Cunningham, Charles. "'To Watch the Faces of the Poor': *Life* Magazine and the Mythology of Rural Poverty in the Great Depression." *Journal of Narrative Theory*, vol. 29, no. 3, Fall 1999, pp. 278–302.

Curtis, James. *Mind's Eye, Mind's Truth: FSA Photography Reconsidered*. Temple UP, 1989.

Davis, David A. "Abjection and White Trash Autobiography." *Storytelling, History, and the Postmodern South*, edited by Jason Phillips, Louisiana State UP, 2013, pp. 187–204.

Davis, Donald Edward. Foreword. *Mountains of Injustice: Social and Environmental Justice in Appalachia*, edited by Michele Morrone and Geoffrey L. Buckley, Ohio UP, 2011, pp. vii–ix.

Davis, Fred. *Yearning for Yesterday: A Sociology of Nostalgia*. Free Press, 1979.

Dean, Jodi. *Democracy and Other Neoliberal Fantasies: Communicative Capitalism and Left Politics*. Duke UP, 2009.

DeLoughrey, Elizabeth, and George B. Handley, editors. *Postcolonial Ecologies: Literatures of the Environment*. Oxford UP, 2011.

Dickey, James. *Deliverance*. Houghton Mifflin, 1970.

Dix, Andrew, Brian Jarvis, and Paul Jenner. *The Contemporary American Novel in Context*. Bloomsbury, 2011.

Douglas, Mary. *Purity and Danger: An Analysis of Concepts of Pollution and Taboo*. Routledge and Kegan Paul, 1966.

Drutt, Matthew. "Photographs by Susan Lipper." *Trip*, by Susan Lipper and Frederick Barthelme, Dewi Lewis, 2000.

Dugan, Ellen. *Picturing the South: 1860 to the Present*. Chronicle, 1996.

Duke, David C. *Writers and Miners: Activism and Imagery in America*. UP of Kentucky, 2002.

Dyer, Richard. *White*. Routledge, 1997.

Eagleton, Terry. "Postcolonialism and 'postcolonialism.'" *Interventions*, vol. 1, no. 1, 1998, pp. 24–26. *Taylor and Francis Online*, dx.doi.org/10.1080/13698019800510071.

Edwards, Justin D., and Rune Graulund. "Introduction: Reading Postcolonial Travel Writing." *Postcolonial Travel Writing: Critical Explorations*, edited by Edwards and Graulund, Palgrave Macmillan, 2011, pp. 1–35.

Eisenstein, Zillah. *Global Obscenities: Patriarchy, Capitalism, and the Lure of Cyberfantasy*. New York UP, 1998.

Elias, Amy J. "Postmodern Southern Vacation: Vacation Advertising, Globalization, and Southern Regionalism." *South to a New Place: Region, Literature, Culture*, edited by Suzanne W. Jones and Sharon Monteith, Louisiana State UP, 2002, pp. 253–82.

Works Cited

Ethridge, Robbie. "Bearing Witness: Assumptions, Realities, and the Otherizing of Katrina." *American Anthropologist*, vol. 108, no. 4, December 2006, pp. 799–813.

Etzioni, Amitai. *The Spirit of Community: Rights, Responsibilities, and the Communitarian Agenda*. Crown, 1993.

Evans, R. J. W., and Alexander Marr, editors. *Curiosity and Wonder from the Renaissance to the Enlightenment*. Routledge, 2006.

Evans, Robley. "'Or Else This Were a Savage Spectacle': Eating and Troping Southern Culture." *Southern Quarterly*, vol. 30, nos. 2–3, Winter–Spring 1992, pp. 141–49.

Ewald, Wendy, editor. *Appalachia: A Self-Portrait*. Gnomon, 1979.

Ewald, Wendy, editor. *Portraits and Dreams: Photographs and Stories by Children of the Appalachians*. Writers and Readers, 1985.

Faulkner, William. "Barn Burning." 1939. *William Faulkner: Collected Stories*. Vintage, 1995, pp. 3–24.

Finnegan, Cara A. *Picturing Poverty: Print Culture and FSA Photographs*. Smithsonian Institution Scholarly Press, 2003.

Fletcher, Martin. *Almost Heaven: Travels through the Backwoods of America*. 1998. Abacus, 2008.

Flynt, Wayne. "Memoir and Historical Reality: White Poverty through the Eyes of Rick Bragg and Barbara Robinette Moss." *Southern Humanities Review*, vol. 42, no. 4, 2008, pp. 305–39.

Folenflik, Robert, editor. *The Culture of Autobiography: Constructions of Self-Representation*. Stanford UP, 1993.

Ford, Richard. "Meeting the Photographer." *Oraien Catledge Photographs*, edited by Constance Lewis and Richard Ford, UP of Mississippi, 2010, pp. vii–xvii.

Fraley, Jill M. "Appalachian Stereotypes and Mountain Top Removal." *Peace Review*, vol. 19, no. 3, pp. 365–70. *Taylor and Francis Online*, doi.org/10.1080/10402650701524931.

Franklin, Tom. *Crooked Letter, Crooked Letter*. William Morrow, 2010.

Franklin, Tom. *Hell at the Breach*. Perennial, 2003.

Franklin, Tom. *Poachers*. 1999. Flamingo, 2000.

Franklin, Tom. *Smonk or Widow Town*. 2006. Harper Perennial, 2007.

Frederickson, Mary E. *Looking South: Race, Gender, and the Transformation of Labor from Reconstruction to Globalization*. UP of Florida, 2011.

Gaines, Jane M. "Appalshop Documentaries: Inventing and Preserving Appalachia." *Jump Cut*, no. 34, March 1989, pp. 53–63.

Gallagher, Catherine, and Stephen Greenblatt. *Practicing New Historicism*. U of Chicago P, 2001.

Ganzel, Bill. *Dust Bowl Descent*. U of Nebraska P, 1984.

Garrard, Greg. "Conciliation and Consilience: Climate Change in Barbara Kingsolver's *Flight Behaviour*." *Handbook of Ecocriticism and Cultural Ecology*, edited by Hubert Zapf, De Gruyter, 2016, pp. 295–312.

Gates, Henry Louis, Jr. "Lifting the Veil." *Inventing the Truth: The Art and Craft of Memoir*, edited by William Zinsser, Mariner, 1998.

Gaventa, John. *Power and Powerlessness: Quiescence and Rebellion in an Appalachian Valley*. Clarendon, 1980.

Genzlinger, Neil. "Journey of the Soul, in a Small Space." *New York Times*, 2 Oct. 2014, //mobile.nytimes.com/2014/10/05/theater/onstage-deliverance-hews-to-the-novel-not-the-film.html.

Giardina, Denise. "Appalachian Images: A Personal History." *Back Talk from Appalachia: Confronting Stereotypes*, edited by Dwight Billings, Gurney Norman, and Katherine Ledford, UP of Kentucky, 1999, 161–73.

Giardina, Denise. *Storming Heaven*. Ivy Books, 1987.

Giardina, Denise. *The Unquiet Earth*. Ivy Books, 1992.

Gilmore, Leigh. *The Limits of Autobiography: Trauma and Testimony*. Cornell UP, 2001.

Goad, Jim. *The Redneck Manifesto*. Simon and Schuster, 1997.

Godden, Richard. "Fictions of Fictitious Capital: American Psycho and the Poetics of Deregulation." *Textual Practice*, vol. 25, no. 5, 2011, pp. 853–66.

Godden, Richard, and Martin Crawford, editors. *Reading Southern Poverty between the Wars, 1918–1939*. U of Georgia P, 2006.

Goldberg, Vicki. "Appalachia in Another Light." *Appalachian Lives*, by Shelby Lee Adams, UP of Mississippi, 2003, pp. ix–xvi.

Goldstein, Alyosha. *Poverty in Common: The Politics of Community Action during the American Century*. Duke UP, 2012.

Gordon, Avery F. *Ghostly Matters: Haunting and the Sociological Imagination*. U of Minnesota P, 1997.

Gragson, Ted L., and Paul V. Bolstad. "Land Use Legacies and the Future of Southern Appalachia." *Society and Natural Resources*, vol. 19, no. 2, 2006, pp. 175–90. *Taylor and Francis Online*, //doi.org/10.1080/08941920500394857.

Graham, Allison. "Red Necks, White Sheets, and Blue States: The Persistence of Regionalism in the Politics of Hollywood." *The Myth of Southern Exceptionalism*, edited by Matthew D. Lassiter and Joseph Crespino, Oxford UP, 2010, pp. 143–64.

Graham, Otis L. "Again the Backward Region? Environmental History in and of the American South." *Southern Cultures*, Summer 2000, pp. 50–71.

Gray, Richard. *Southern Aberrations: Writers of the American South and the Problems of Regionalism*. Louisiana State UP, 2000.

Gray, Richard, and Owen Robinson. *A Companion to the Literature and Culture of the American South*. Blackwell, 2004.

Greeson, Jennifer Rae. *Our South: Geographic Fantasy and the Rise of National Literature*. Harvard UP, 2010.

Griffith, Roger. *My American Odyssey: From the Windrush to the White House*. SilverWood, 2015.

Guattari, Félix. *The Three Ecologies*. 1989. Translated by Ian Pindar and Paul Sutton, Athlone, 2000.

Guinn, Matthew. *After Southern Modernism: Fiction of the Contemporary South*. UP of Mississippi, 2000.

Gusterson, Hugh. "From Brexit to Trump: Anthropology and the Rise of Nationalist Populism." *American Ethnologist*, vol. 44, no. 2, May 2017, pp. 209–14. *AnthroSource*, //doi-org.ezproxy.uwe.ac.uk/10.1111/amet.12469.

Hanna, Stephen P. "Three Decades of Appalshop Films: Representational Strategies and Regional Politics." *Appalachian Journal*, vol. 25, no. 4, Summer 1998, pp. 372–413. *JSTOR*, www.jstor.org/stable/40933913?seq=1#page_scan_tab_contents.

Harding, Wendy, and Jacky Martin. *A World of Difference: An Inter-Cultural Study of Toni Morrison's Novels*. Greenwood, 1994.

Hariman, Robert, and John Louis Lucaites. *No Caption Needed: Iconic Photographs, Public Culture, and Liberal Democracy*. U of Chicago P, 2007.

Harkins, Anthony. *Hillbilly: A Cultural History of an American Icon*. Oxford UP, 2004.

Harrington, Michael. *The Other America: Poverty in the United States*. 1962. Penguin, 1969.

Harris, Eddy L. *Mississippi Solo: A Memoir*. 1988. Henry Holt, 1998.

Harris, Eddy L. *South of Haunted Dreams: A Ride through Slavery's Old Back Yard*. 1993. Penguin, 1995.

Harris, Eddy L. *Still Life in Harlem*. Henry Holt, 1996.

Hartigan Jr., John. *Odd Tribes: Toward a Cultural Analysis of White People*. Duke UP, 2005.

Hartigan Jr., John. *Racial Situations: Class Predicaments of Whiteness in Detroit*. Princeton UP, 1999.

Harvey, David. *The Condition of Postmodernity*. 1990. Blackwell, 1997.

Harvey, David. *The Enigma of Capital: And the Crises of Capitalism*. Profile, 2010.

Harvey, David. *The New Imperialism*. Oxford UP, 2003.

Harvey, David. *Spaces of Global Capitalism: Towards a Theory of Uneven Geographical Development*. Verso, 2006.

Harvey, David. *Spaces of Hope*. U of Edinburgh P, 2000.

Harvey, Dennis. "The True Meaning of Pictures: Shelby Lee Adams' Appalachia." *Variety*, 24 Feb.–2 Mar. 2003, p. 53.

Haug, W. F. *Critique of Commodity Aesthetics: Appearance, Sexuality and Advertising in Capitalist Society*. Polity, 1986.

Hawkins, Gary. "'Rough South': Beginnings." *Rough South, Rural South: Region and Class in Recent Southern Literature*, edited by Jean W. Cash and Keith Perry, UP of Mississippi, 2016, pp. 3–8.

Healy, Patrick. "Roseanne Conner Has Become a Trump Supporter, Just Like Her Creator." *New York Times*, 27 Mar. 2018, https://www.nytimes.com/2018/03/27/arts/television/roseanne-barr-trump.html.

Henninger, Katherine. *Ordering the Facade: Photography and Contemporary Southern Women's Writing*. U of North Carolina P, 2007.

Herzog, Mary Jean Ronan. "Including Appalachian Stereotypes in Multicultural Education: An Analysis of Bill Bryson's *A Walk in the Woods*." *Journal of Appalachian Studies*, vol. 5, no. 1, Spring 1999, 123–28.

Hill, Mike, editor. *Whiteness: A Critical Reader*. New York UP, 1997.

Hirsch, Marianne. "Familial Looking: Introduction." *The Familial Gaze*, edited by Hirsch, UP of New England, 1999, pp. xi–xxv.

Hirsch, Marianne. *Family Frames: Photography, Narrative, and Postmemory*. Harvard UP, 1997.

Hobson, Fred. *But Now I See: The White Southern Racial Conversion Narrative*. Louisiana State UP, 1999.

Hobson, Fred. Introduction. *South to the Future: An American Region in the Twenty-First Century*, edited by Hobson, U of Georgia P, 2002, pp. 1–12.

Holland, Patrick, and Graham Huggan. *Tourists with Typewriters: Critical Reflections on Contemporary Travel Writing*. U of Michigan P, 1998.

Hood, Mary. *And Venus Is Blue*. 1986. U of Georgia P, 2001.

hooks, bell. *Where We Stand: Class Matters*. Routledge, 2000.

Horwitz, Tony. *Confederates in the Attic: Dispatches from the Unfinished Civil War*. Vintage, 1998.

House, Silas. *Clay's Quilt*. Ballantine, 2001.

House, Silas. *The Coal Tattoo*. 2004. Ballantine, 2005.

House, Silas. "A Conscious Heart." *Journal of Appalachian Studies*, vol. 14, nos. 1–2, Spring–Fall 2008, pp. 7–19.

House, Silas. *A Parchment of Leaves*. 2002. Ballantine, 2003.

House, Silas, and Jason Howard, editors. *Something's Rising: Appalachians Fighting Mountaintop Removal*. UP of Kentucky, 2009.

House, Silas, and Neela Vaswani. *Same Sun Here*. Candlewick, 2011.

Houser, Heather. "Knowledge Work and the Commons in Barbara Kingsolver's and Ann Pancake's Appalachia." *Modern Fiction Studies*, vol. 63, no. 1, Spring 2017, pp. 95–115. *Project Muse*, doi.org/10.1353/mfs.2017.0006.

Hsiung, David C. "Stereotypes." *High Mountains Rising: Appalachia in Time and Place*, edited by Richard A. Straw and H. Tyler Blethen, U of Illinois P, 2004, pp. 101–13.

Hubbs, Jolene. "Documenting Hunger: Famineways in Contemporary Southern Women's Writing." *Southern Literary Journal*, vol. 47, no. 2, Spring 2015, pp. 1–19. *Project Muse*, doi.org/10.1353/slj.2015.0000.

Huber, Patrick. "The Riddle of the Horny Hillbilly." *Dixie Emporium: Tourism, Foodways, and Consumer Culture in the American South*, edited by Anthony J. Stanonis, U of Georgia P, 2008, pp. 69–86.

Huddart, David. *Postcolonial Theory and Autobiography*. Routledge, 2008.

Hufford, Mary. "Working in the Cracks: Public Space, Ecological Crisis, and the Folklorist." *Journal of Folklore Research*, vol. 36, nos. 2–3, 1999, pp. 157–67.

Hulme, Peter, and Tim Youngs. Introduction. *The Cambridge Companion to Travel Writing*, edited by Hulme and Youngs, Cambridge UP, 2002.

Humphery, Kim. *Excess: Anti-Consumerism in the West*. Polity, 2010.

Humphreys, Josephine. *Rich in Love*. 1987. Penguin, 2000.

Hurley, F. Jack. *Portrait of a Decade: Roy Stryker and the Development of Documentary Photography in the Thirties*. Louisiana State UP, 1972.

Hutchinson, Colin. *Reaganism, Thatcherism and the Social Novel*. Springer Verlag, 2008.

Hyde, Katherine. "Portraits and Collaborations: A Reflection on the Work of Wendy Ewald." *Visual Studies*, vol. 20, no. 2, October 2005, pp. 172–90. *Taylor and Francis Online*, dx.doi.org/10.1080/14725860500244043.

Inscoe, John C. "'Race and Remembrance in West Virginia': John Henry for a Post-Modern Age." *Journal of Appalachian Studies*, vol. 10, nos. 1–2, Spring–Fall 2004, pp. 85–94.

Inscoe, John C. *Writing the South through the Self: Explorations in Southern Autobiography.* U of Georgia P, 2011.
Iovino, Serenella. "Ecocriticism and a Non-Anthropocentric Humanism: Reflections on Local Natures and Global Responsibilities." *Local Natures, Global Responsibilities: Ecocritical Perspectives on the New English Literatures,* edited by Laurenz Volkmann et al., Rodopi, 2010, pp. 29–53.
Isbell, Robert. *Ray Hicks: Master Storyteller of the Blue Ridge.* U of North Carolina P, 2001.
Isenberg, Nancy. *White Trash: The 400-Year Untold History of Class in America.* Viking, 2016.
Islam, Syed Manzurul. *The Ethics of Travel: From Marco Polo to Kafka.* Manchester UP, 1996.
Jacobson, Matthew Frye. *Roots Too: White Ethnic Revival in Post-Civil Rights America.* Harvard UP, 2006.
Jahanbani, Sheyda. "'Across the Ocean, Across the Tracks': Imagining Global Poverty in Cold War America." *Journal of American Studies,* vol. 48, no. 4, 2014, pp. 937–74.
Jarvis, Robin. *Romantic Readers and Transatlantic Travel: Expeditions and Tours in North America, 1760–1840.* Ashgate, 2012.
Jones, Gavin. *American Hungers: The Problem of Poverty in U.S. Literature, 1840–1945.* Princeton UP, 2008.
Jones, Jacqueline. *The Dispossessed: America's Underclasses from the Civil War to the Present.* Basic Books, 1992.
Jones, Suzanne W. Introduction. *Race Mixing: Southern Fiction since the Sixties,* edited by Jones, Johns Hopkins UP, 2004, pp. xiii–xv.
Jones, Suzanne W., and Sharon Monteith. "Introduction: South to New Places." *South to a New Place: Region, Literature, Culture,* edited by Jones and Monteith, Louisiana State UP, 2002, pp. 1–19.
Jones, Suzanne W., and Mark Newman, editors. *Poverty and Progress in the U.S. South since 1920.* VU UP, 2006.
Kaplan, Caren. *Questions of Travel: Postmodern Discourses of Displacement.* Duke UP, 1996.
Keeley, Karen A. "Poverty, Sterilization, and Eugenics in Erskine Caldwell's *Tobacco Road*." *Journal of American Studies,* vol. 36, no. 1, April 2002, pp. 23–42.
Keillor, Garrison. *Lake Wobegon Days.* Viking, 1985.
Kelsey, Robin, and Blake Stimson. *The Meaning of Photography.* Yale UP, 2008.
Kennedy, Douglas. *In God's Country: Travels in the Bible Belt, USA.* 1989. Abacus, 1999.
Kerridge, Richard. "Ecologies of Desire: Travel Writing and Nature Writing as Travelogue." *Travel Writing and Empire: Postcolonial Theory in Transit,* edited by Steve Clark, Zed, 1999, pp. 164–82.
Kerridge, Richard. "Environmental Fiction and Narrative Openness." *Process: Landscape and Text,* edited by Catherine Brace and Adeline Johns-Putra, Rodopi, 2010, pp. 65–85.
Kerridge, Richard. Introduction. *Writing the Environment: Ecocriticism and Literature,* edited by Richard Kerridge and Neil Sammells, Zed, 1998, pp. 1–9.
Kidd, Stuart. "FSA Photographers and the Southern Underclass, 1935–1943." *Reading Southern Poverty between the Wars, 1918–1939,* edited by Richard Godden and Martin Crawford, U of Georgia P, 2006, pp. 25–47.

Kidd, Stuart. "Visualizing the Poor White." *A Companion to the Literature and Culture of the American South*, edited by Richard Gray and Owen Robinson, Blackwell, 2007, pp. 110–29.

Killingsworth, M. Jimmie, and Jacqueline S. Palmer. "Ecopolitics and the Literature of the Borderlands: The Frontiers of Environmental Justice in Latina and Native American Writing." *Writing the Environment: Ecocriticism and Literature*, edited by Richard Kerridge and Neil Sammells, Zed, 1998, pp. 196–207.

Kingsolver, Barbara. *Flight Behaviour*. Faber and Faber, 2012.

Kingsolver, Barbara. *Prodigal Summer*. HarperCollins, 2000.

Kirby, Jack Temple. *Mockingbird Song: Ecological Landscapes of the South*. U of North Carolina P, 2006.

Klein, Naomi. *No Is Not Enough: Defeating the New Shock Politics*. Allen Lane, 2017.

Klein, Naomi. *This Changes Everything: Capitalism vs. the Climate*. 2014. Penguin, 2015.

Knoblauch, Loring. "Susan Lipper, Grapevine 1998–1992 @Higher Pictures." *Collector Daily*, 15 Dec. 2016, https://collectordaily.com/susan-lipper-grapevine-1988-1992-higher-pictures/.

Kopple, Barbara, director. *Harlan County USA*. First Run Features, 1976.

Kozloff, Max. *The Privileged Eye: Essays on Photography*. U of New Mexico P, 1987.

Kristeva, Julia. *Powers of Horror: An Essay on Abjection*. Columbia UP, 1982.

Kunzru, Hari. "*Hillbilly Elegy* by JD Vance Review: Does This Memoir Really Explain Trump's Victory?" *Guardian*, 7 Dec. 2016, https://www.theguardian.com/books/2016/dec/07/hillbilly-elegy-by-jd-vance-review.

Kwapis, Ken, director. *A Walk in the Woods*. Entertainment One, 2015.

Lauder, Tracy. "Southern Identity in *Southern Living* Magazine." *Journal of Geography*, vol. 111, no. 1, 2012, pp. 27–28. *Taylor and Francis Online*, doi.org/10.1080/00221341.2011.584348.

Leask, Nigel. *Curiosity and the Aesthetics of Travel Writing, 1770–1840*. Oxford UP, 2002.

Lee, Harper. *To Kill a Mockingbird*. 1960. Minerva, 1991.

LeMahieu, Michael. "An Interview with Dorothy Allison." *Contemporary Literature*, vol. 51, no. 4, Winter 2010, pp. 651–76. *Project Muse*, doi.org/10.1353/cli.2011.0002.

Lewis, Anne, director. *Justice in the Coalfields*. Appalshop, 1995.

Lewis, Ronald L. "Industrialization." *High Mountains Rising: Appalachia in Time and Place*, edited by Richard A. Straw and H. Tyler Blethen, U of Illinois P, 2004, pp. 59–73.

Lifson, Ben. Afterword. *Portraits and Dreams: Photographs and Stories by Children of the Appalachians*, edited by Wendy Ewald, Writers and Readers, 1985, pp. 117–23.

Lipper, Susan. *Grapevine*. Cornerhouse, 1994.

Lipper, Susan, and Frederick Barthelme. *Trip*. Dewi Lewis, 2000.

Lipsitz, George. *The Possessive Investment in Whiteness: How White People Profit from Identity Politics*. Temple UP, 2006.

Lisle, Debbie. *The Global Politics of Contemporary Travel Writing*. Cambridge UP, 2006.

Littler, Jo. *Radical Consumption: Shopping for Change in Contemporary Culture*. Open UP, 2009.

Lloyd, Christopher, and Jessica Rapson. "'Family Territory' to the 'Circumference of the Earth': Local and Planetary Memories of Climate Change in Barbara Kingsolver's *Flight*

Behaviour." *Textual Practice*, vol. 35, no. 5, pp. 911–31. *Taylor and Francis Online*, //doi.org/10.1080/0950236X.2017.1323487.
Logue, John, and Gary McCalla. *Life at Southern Living: A Sort of Memoir*. Louisiana State UP, 2000.
Lovan, Dylan. "After Decade, Still Signs of Coal Slurry Spill." *Washington Post*, 17 Oct. 2010, http://www.washingtonpost.com/wp-dyn/content/article/2010/10/15/AR2010101507010.html.
MacCannell, Dean. *The Tourist: A New Theory of the Leisure Class*. 1976. U of California P, 1999.
Madden, David. "The Cruel Radiance of What Is." *Southern Quarterly*, vol. 22, no. 2, Winter 1984, pp. 5–43.
Maharidge, Dale. "Close Enough to Hurt: Dale Maharidge on *Let Us Now Praise Famous Men*, by James Agee, and the Importance of 'Living' Journalism." *Columbia Journalism Review*, January–February 2005, pp. 54–57.
Maharidge, Dale, and Michael Williamson. *And Their Children After Them*. Pantheon, 1989.
Maharidge, Dale, and Michael Williamson. *Journey to Nowhere: The Saga of the New Underclass*. 1985. Hyperion, 1996.
Maharidge, Dale, and Michael Williamson. *Someplace Like America: Tales from the New Great Depression*. U of California P, 2011.
Mann, Sally. *Deep South*. Bulfinch, 2005.
Marazzi, Christian. *The Violence of Financial Capitalism*. Semiotext(e), 2011.
Martin, Andrew W. "Review: America's New Underclass and (the Absence of) Class Mobilization." *Contemporary Sociology*, vol. 41, no. 3, May 2012, pp. 304–7.
Martinez-Alier, Joan. *The Environmentalism of the Poor: A Study of Ecological Conflicts and Valuation*. Edward Elgar, 2002.
Marx, Karl, and Friedrich Engels. *The Communist Manifesto*. 1848. Penguin, 2015.
Matthews, Scott L. "Protesting the Privilege of Perception: Resistance to Documentary Work in Hale County, Alabama, 1900–2010." *Southern Cultures*, vol. 22, no. 1, Spring 2016, pp. 31–65.
Maus, Derek C. *Understanding Colson Whitehead*. U of South Carolina P, 2014.
Mayer, Brian, Katrina Running, and Kelly Bergstrand. "Compensation and Community Corrosion: Perceived Inequalities, Social Comparisons, and Competition Following the Deepwater Horizon Oil Spill." *Sociological Forum*, vol. 30, no. 2, June 2015, pp. 369–90. *Wiley Online Library*, //onlinelibrary.wiley.com/doi/10.1111/socf.12167/full.
Mbalia, Dorothea Drummond. *Toni Morrison's Developing Class Consciousness*. Susquehanna UP, 1991.
McCarthy, Cormac. *Child of God*. 1973. Picador, 1989.
McChesney, Robert W. Introduction. *Profit over People: Neoliberalism and Global Order*, by Noam Chomsky, Seven Stories, 2007.
McGurty, Eileen Maura. "From NIMBY to Civil Rights: The Origins of the Environmental Justice Movement." *Environmental History and the American South: A Reader*, edited by Paul S. Sutter and Christopher J. Manganiello, U of Georgia P, 2009, pp. 372–99.
McIntyre, Rebecca Cawood. *Souvenirs of the Old South: Northern Tourism and Southern Mythology*. UP of Florida, 2011.

McLaurin, Tim. *The Acorn Plan*. W. W. Norton, 1988.

McNeil, Bryan. *Combating Mountaintop Removal: New Directions in the Fight against Coal*. U of Illinois P, 2011.

McNeil, Bryan. "Global Forces, Local Worlds: Mountaintop Removal and Appalachian Communities." *The American South in a Global World*, edited by James L. Peacock, Harry L. Watson, and Carrie R. Matthews, U of North Carolina P, 2005, pp. 99–110.

Michaels, Walter Benn. *The Beauty of a Social Problem: Photography, Autonomy, Economy*. U of Chicago P, 2015.

Michaels, Walter Benn. *The Trouble with Diversity: How We Learned to Love Identity and Ignore Inequality*. Henry Holt, 2006.

Middleton, Nick. *Ice Tea and Elvis: A Saunter through the Southern States*. 1999. Phoenix, 2000.

Millichap, Joseph R. *The Language of Vision: Photography and Southern Literature in the 1930s and After*. Louisiana State UP, 2016.

Mirzoeff, Nicholas. *The Right to Look: A Counterhistory of Visuality*. Duke UP, 2011.

Morris, Willie. *North toward Home*. Houghton Mifflin, 1967.

Morrison, Toni. *Beloved*. 1987. Vintage, 1997.

Moss, Barbara Robinette. *Change Me into Zeus's Daughter: A Memoir*. Simon and Schuster, 2000.

Moss, Barbara Robinette. *Fierce: A Memoir*. Scribner, 2004.

Mulvey, Laura. *Fetishism and Curiosity*. Indiana UP, 1996.

Murphy, Patrick D. "Anotherness and Inhabitation in Recent Multicultural American Literature." *Writing the Environment: Ecocriticism and Literature*, edited by Richard Kerridge and Neil Sammells, Zed, 1998, pp. 40–52.

Murphy, Patrick D. "Pessimism, Optimism, Human Inertia, and Anthropogenic Climate Change." *Interdisciplinary Studies in Literature and Environment*, vol. 21, no. 1, Winter 2014, pp. 149–63. *Oxford Academic*, //doi-org.ezproxy.uwe.ac.uk/10.1093/isle/isu027.

Naipaul, V. S. *A Turn in the South*. Alfred A. Knopf, 1989.

Nelson, Megan Kate. "The Okefenokee Swamp (Georgia/Florida)." *Southern United States: An Environmental History*, edited by Donald E. Davis, ABC-Clio, 2006, pp. 221–34.

Nixon, Rob. *Slow Violence and the Environmentalism of the Poor*. Harvard UP, 2011.

Obermiller, Phillip, and William Philliber, editors. *Too Few Tomorrows: Urban Appalachians in the 1980s*. Appalachian State UP, 1987.

O'Connor, Alice. *Poverty Knowledge: Social Science, Social Policy, and the Poor in Twentieth-Century U.S. History*. Princeton UP, 2001.

O'Connor, Flannery. "Some Aspects of the Grotesque in Southern Fiction." *Mystery and Manners*, edited by Sally and Robert Fitzgerald, Farrar, Straus and Giroux, 1961, pp. 36–50.

Offutt, Chris. *The Good Brother*. 1997. Secker and Warburg, 1998.

Olney, James, editor. *Autobiography: Essays Theoretical and Critical*. Princeton UP, 1980.

Packard, Vance. *The Waste Makers*. 1960. Longmans, 1961.

Pancake, Ann. *Given Ground*. Middlebury College P, 2001.

Pancake, Ann. *Me and My Daddy Listen to Bob Marley: Novellas and Stories*. Counterpoint, 2015.

Pancake, Ann. *Strange as This Weather Has Been.* Counterpoint, 2007.
Patell, Cyrus R. K. *Negative Liberties: Morrison, Pynchon, and the Problem of Liberal Ideology.* Duke UP, 2001.
Payne, Daniel G. *Voices in the Wilderness: American Nature Writing and Environmental Politics.* UP of New England, 1996.
Peach, Linden. *Toni Morrison.* Macmillan, 1995.
Peacock, James L. *Grounded Globalism: How the U.S. South Embraces the World.* U of Georgia P, 2007.
Peacock, James L., Harry L. Watson, and Carrie R. Matthews, editors. *The American South in a Global World.* U of North Carolina P, 2005.
Petro, Pamela. *Sitting Up with the Dead: A Storied Journey through the American South.* Flamingo, 2001.
Pimpare, Stephen. *A People's History of Poverty in America.* New Press, 2008.
Pratt, Mary Louise. *Imperial Eyes: Travel Writing and Transculturation.* 1992. 2nd ed., Routledge, 1997.
Raban, Jonathan. *Hunting Mister Heartbreak.* Collins Harvill, 1990.
Raban, Jonathan. *Old Glory.* Collins, 1981.
Rabinowitz, Paula. *They Must Be Represented: The Politics of Documentary.* Verso, 1994.
Ramsey, William. "An End of Southern History: The Down-Home Quests of Toni Morrison and Colson Whitehead." *African American Review,* vol. 41, no. 4, Winter 2007, pp. 769–85.
Rand, Ayn. *Anthem.* 1938. Penguin, 2008.
Rash, Ron. *Eureka Mill.* Hub City Writers Project, 1998.
Rash, Ron. *The World Made Straight.* 2006. Picador, 2007.
Ray, Janisse. *Ecology of a Cracker Childhood.* Milkweed, 1999.
Ray, Janisse. *A House of Branches.* Wind Publications, 2010.
Ray, Janisse. *Pinhook: Finding Wholeness in a Fragmented Land.* Chelsea Green, 2005.
Ray, Janisse. *The Seed Underground: A Growing Revolution to Save Food.* Chelsea Green, 2012.
Ray, Janisse. *Wild Card Quilt: The Ecology of Home.* Milkweed, 2003.
Rea, Robert. "The Art of Grit Lit: An Interview with Tom Franklin and Chris Offutt." *Southern Quarterly,* vol. 50, no. 3, Spring 2013, pp. 79–94.
Rebein, Robert. *Hicks, Tribes, and Dirty Realists: American Fiction after Postmodernism.* UP of Kentucky, 2001.
Richards-Shuster, Katie, and Rebecca O'Doherty. "Appalachian Youth Re-envisioning Home, Re-making Identities." *Transforming Places: Lesson from Appalachia,* edited by Stephen L. Fisher and Barbara Ellen Smith. U of Illinois P, 2012, pp. 78–91.
Rieger, Christopher. *Clear-Cutting Eden: Ecology and the Pastoral in Southern Literature.* U of Alabama P, 2009.
Rieger, Christopher. "The Pickup Truck in the Garden: Larry Brown's *Joe.*" *Mississippi Quarterly,* vol. 63.3, no. 4, 2010, pp. 679–94.
Rigney, Barbara Hill. *The Voices of Toni Morrison.* Ohio State UP, 1991.
Roberts, Diane. "Afterword: The South of the Mind." *South to a New Place: Region, Literature, Culture,* edited by Suzanne W. Jones and Sharon Monteith, Louisiana State UP, 2002, pp. 363–73.

Roberts, Diane. "Living Southern in Southern Living." *Dixie Debates: Perspectives on Southern Culture*, edited by Richard King and Helen Taylor, New York UP, 1996, pp. 85–98.

Robertson, Sarah. "Gothic Appalachia." *The Palgrave Handbook of the Southern Gothic*, edited by Susan Castillo Street and Charles L. Crow, Palgrave Macmillan, 2016, pp. 109–20.

Robertson, Sarah. "Junkyard Tales: Poverty and the Southern Landscape in Janisse Ray's *Ecology of a Cracker Childhood*." *Poverty and Progress in the South*, edited by Suzanne Jones and Mark Newman, VU UP, 2006, pp.167–75.

Robertson, Sarah. "Memorializing Southern Poor White Men's Labor in Rick Bragg's Memoir Trilogy." *Journal of American Studies*, vol. 47, no. 2, May 2013, pp. 459–74.

Robertson, Sarah. "Poor Whites in Recent Southern Fiction." *Literature Compass*, vol. 9/10, 2012, pp. 631–41.

Robertson, Sarah. "Poverty and Progress." *The Cambridge Companion to the Literature of the American South*, edited by Sharon Monteith, Cambridge UP, 2013, pp. 104–15.

Romine, Scott. "God and the MoonPie: Consumption, Disenchantment, and the Reliably Lost Cause." *Creating and Consuming the American South*, edited by Martyn Bone, Brian Ward, and William A. Link, UP of Florida, 2015, pp. 49–71.

Romine, Scott. *The Narrative Forms of Southern Community*. Louisiana State UP, 1999.

Romine, Scott. *The Real South: Southern Narrative in the Age of Cultural Reproduction*. Louisiana State UP, 2008.

Rosler, Martha. "In, Around, and Afterthoughts (on Documentary Photography)." *The Contest of Meaning: Critical Histories of Photography*, edited by Richard Bolton, MIT P, 1989, pp. 303–41.

Salsi, Lynn. *The Life and Times of Ray Hicks: Keeper of the Jack Tales*. U of Tennessee P, 2008.

Salstrom, Paul. "The Great Depression." *High Mountains Rising: Appalachia in Time and Place*, edited by Richard A. Straw and H. Tyler Blethen. U of Illinois P, 2004, pp. 74–87.

Satterwhite, Emily. *Dear Appalachia: Readers, Identity, and Popular Fiction since 1878*. UP of Kentucky, 2011.

Scanlan, John. *On Garbage*. Reaktion, 2005.

Schuweiler, Suzanne. "Sally Mann's South." *SECAC Review*, vol. 16, no. 3, 2013, pp. 325–36.

Scott, Clive. *The Spoken Image: Photography and Language*. Reaktion, 1999.

Shaw, Gareth, and Allan M. Williams. *Tourism and Tourism Spaces*. Sage, 2004.

Shugerman, Emily. "Donald Trump Claims Republicans 'Essentially Repealed Obamacare' with Tax Bill." *Independent*, 20 Dec. 2017, www.independent.co.uk/news/world/americas/us-politics/donald-trump-tax-bill-obamacare-pass-healthcare-trumpcare-republicans-congress-a8120856.html.

Skaggs, Merrill Maguire. *The Folk of Southern Fiction*. U of Georgia P, 1972.

Sleipness, Ole Russell. "Consuming Nature: Paradoxes of 'Green' Development in the Rural Southern Appalachian Mountains." *Landscape Journal*, vol. 33, no. 1, 2014, pp. 37–58.

Smith, Bernard. *European Vision and the South Pacific*. 1960. Yale UP, 1985.

Smith, Dina. "Cultural Studies' Misfit: White Trash Studies." *Mississippi Quarterly*, vol. 57, no. 3, Summer 2004, pp. 369–87.

Smith, Jon. "Toward a Postpolitical Southern Studies: On the Limits of the 'Creating and Consuming' Paradigm." *Creating and Consuming the American South*, edited by Martyn Bone, Brian Ward, and William A. Link, UP of Florida, 2015, pp. 72–94.

Smith, Jon, and Deborah Cohn, eds. *Look Away! The U.S. South in New World Studies*. Duke UP, 2004.

Smith, Lee. "Mountain Voices." *Appalachian Portraits*, by Shelby Lee Adams, UP of Mississippi, 1993, pp. 13–22.

Smith, Neil. *Uneven Development: Nature, Capital and the Production of Space*. 3rd ed., Verso, 2010.

Smith, Sidonie. "Memory, Narrative, and the Discourses of Identity in *Abeng* and *No Telephone to Heaven*." *Postcolonialism and Autobiography*, edited by Alfred Hornung and Ernstpeter Ruhe, Rodopi, 1998, pp. 37–59.

Smith, Sidonie, and Julia Watson, editors. *Getting a Life: Everyday Uses of Autobiography*. U of Minnesota P, 1996.

Smith, Stephen. *Myth, Media, and the Southern Mind*. U of Arkansas P, 1986.

Sontag, Susan. *On Photography*. Penguin, 1977.

Sorkin, Adam J. "Introduction: Politics and the Muse; Voices and Visions at the Crossroads." *Politics and the Muse: Studies in the Politics of Recent American Literature*, edited by Sorkin, Bowling Green State UP, 1989, pp. 1–9.

Spangler, Bes Stark. "Tim McLaurin: Universality from Rural North Carolina." *Rough South, Rural South: Region and Class in Recent Southern Literature*, edited by Jean W. Cash and Keith Perry, UP of Mississippi, 2016, pp. 41–49.

Starnes, Richard D., editor. *Southern Journeys: Tourism, History, and Culture in the Modern South*. U of Alabama P, 2003.

Stewart, Kathleen. *A Space on the Side of the Road: Cultural Poetics in an "Other" America*. Princeton UP, 1996.

Stoler, Ann Laura. "Imperial Debris: Reflections on Ruins and Ruination." *Cultural Anthropology*, vol. 23, no. 2, May 2008, pp. 191–219. *JSTOR*, www.jstor.org/stable/20484502.

Stoll, Steve. *Ramp Hollow: The Ordeal of Appalachia*. Hill and Wang, 2017.

Stone, Oliver, director. *Wall Street*. 20th Century Fox, 1987.

Strangleman, Tim. "'Smokestack Nostalgia,' 'Ruin Porn' or Working-Class Obituary: The Role and Meaning of Deindustrial Representation." *International Labor and Working-Class History*, no. 84, Fall 2013, pp. 23–37.

Strasser, Susan. *Waste and Want: A Social History of Trash*. Henry Holt, 1999.

Suter, Scott Hamilton. "Nature, Place, Religion in Silas House's Crow County Trilogy." *Rough South, Rural South: Region and Class in Recent Southern Literature*, edited by Jean W. Cash and Keith Perry, UP of Mississippi, 2016, pp. 182–90.

Sutter, Paul S. "Introduction: No More Backward Region; Southern Environmental History Comes of Age." *Environmental History and the American South: A Reader*, edited by Paul S. Sutter and Christopher J. Manganiello, U of Georgia P, 2009, pp. 1–24.

Tagg, John. *The Burden of Representation: Essays on Photographs and Histories*. Macmillan, 1988.

Tam, Henry. *Communitarianism: A New Agenda for Politics and Citizenship.* Macmillan, 1998.

Taylor, Helen. *Circling Dixie: Contemporary Southern Culture through a Transatlantic Lens.* Rutgers UP, 2001.

Tettenborn, Éva. "'A Mountain Full of Ghosts': Mourning African American Masculinities in Colson Whitehead's *John Henry Days.*" *African American Review*, vol. 46, nos. 2–3, Summer–Fall 2013, pp. 271–84.

Theroux, Paul. *Deep South: Four Seasons on Back Roads.* Hamish Hamilton, 2015.

Thompson, Charles D., Jr. "Review of *A Walk in the Woods: Rediscovering America on the Appalachian Trail*, by Bill Bryson." *Appalachian Journal*, vol. 26, Fall 1999, pp. 72–75.

Thompson, Michael. *Rubbish Theory: The Creation and Destruction of Value.* Oxford UP, 1979.

Tice, George. Foreword. *The Face of Appalachia: Portraits from the Mountain Farm*, by Tim Barnwell, W. W. Norton, 2003, p. 11.

Toffler, Alvin. *Future Shock.* 1970. Pan Books, 1971.

Turnbull, Gemma-Rose. "Surface Tension: Navigating Socially Engaged Documentary Photographic Practices." *Nordicom Review*, no. 36, 2015, pp. 79–95, http://www.nordicom.gu.se/en/node/35942.

Turner, Daniel Cross. Introduction. *Hardlines: Rough South Poetry*, edited by Daniel Cross Turner and William Wright, U of South Carolina P, 2016, pp. 1–9.

Twelve Southerners. *I'll Take My Stand: The South and the Agrarian Tradition.* 1930. Louisiana State UP, 1977.

Vance, J. D. *Hillbilly Elegy: A Memoir of a Family and Culture in Crisis.* William Collins, 2016.

Volkmann, Laurenz, Nancy Grimm, Ines Detmers, and Katrin Thomson, editors. *Local Natures, Global Responsibilities: Ecocritical Perspectives on the New English Literatures.* Rodopi, 2010.

Walker, Alice. *The Third Life of Grange Copeland.* 1970. Phoenix, 2004.

Walley, Christine J. "Trump's Election and the 'White Working Class': What We Missed." *American Ethnologist*, vol. 44, no. 2, May 2017, pp. 231–36. AnthroSource, //doi-org.ezproxy.uwe.ac.uk/10.1111/amet.12473.

Walls, Jeanette. *The Glass Castle.* 2005. Virago, 2006.

Walls, Jeanette. "Jeanette Walls Was Warned Her Memoir, 'The Glass Castle,' Might Be Hollywoodized on Film; What Happened Was Just the Opposite." *Los Angeles Times*, 3 Aug. 2017, www.latimes.com/entertainment/movies/la-ca-mn-glass-castle-jeannette-walls-2017803-story.html.

Wanat, Matt. "Dislocation, Dismemberment, Dystopia: From Cyperpunk to the Fiction of Wendell Berry and Ann Pancake." *Journal of the Midwest Modern Language Association*, vol. 38, no. 1, Spring 2015, pp. 147–70. JSTOR, www.jstor.org/stable/43549875.

Watkins, James. "Contemporary Autobiography and Memoir." *The History of Southern Women's Literature*, edited by Carolyn Perry and Mary Louise Weaks, Louisiana State UP, 2002, pp. 447–54.

Watkins, James. "Drinking Poisoned Waters: Traumatized Masculinity and White Southern Identity in Contemporary Family Memoirs." *White Masculinity in the Recent South*, edited by Trent Watts, Louisiana State UP, 2008, pp. 220–33.

Watkins, James. "'The Use of *I*, Lovely and Terrifying Word': Autobiographical Authority and the Representation of 'Redneck' Masculinity in *A Childhood*." *Perspectives on Harry Crews*, edited by Erik Bledsoe, UP of Mississippi, 2001, pp. 15–28.

Watson, Jay. "Economies of a Cracker Landscape: Poverty as an Environmental Issue in Two Southern Writers." *Mississippi Quarterly*, vol. 55, no. 4, Fall 2002, pp. 497–513.

Welch, Barbara A. "Curiosities and Reflections: British Travelers on the Continent in the Eighteenth Century." *Modern Language Studies*, vol. 10, no. 2, Spring 1980, pp. 10–25.

Weldon, Amy E. "'When Fantasy Meant Survival': Writing, Class, and the Oral Tradition in the Autobiographies of Rick Bragg and Harry Crews." *Mississippi Quarterly*, vol. 53, no. 1, Winter 1999–2000, pp. 89–110.

Welling, Bart. "'This Is What Matters': Reinhabitory Discourse and the 'Poetics of Responsibility' in the Work of Janisse Ray." *The Bioregional Imagination: Literature, Ecology, and Place*, edited by Tom Lynch, Cheryll Glotfelty, and Karla Armbruster, U of Georgia P, 2012, pp. 118–31.

"When a Flow Becomes a Flood." *Economist*, 22 Jan. 2009, www.economist.com/node/12972083.

White, Richard. "'Are You an Environmentalist or Do You Work for a Living?' Work and Nature." *Uncommon Ground: Rethinking the Human Place in Nature*, edited by William Cronon, W. W. Norton, 1995.

Whitehead, Colson. *John Henry Days*. 2001. Fourth Estate, 2002.

Williams, Raymond. *Marxism and Literature*. Oxford UP, 1977.

Williams, Val. "Susan Lipper: Collisions of Experience." *Photoworks*, no. 12, 2009, pp. 56–63.

Williamson, Jerry W. *Hillbillyland: What the Movies Did to the Mountains and What the Mountains Did to the Movies*. U of North Carolina P, 1995.

Williamson, Joel. *The Crucible of Race: Black-White Relations in the American South since Emancipation*. Oxford UP, 1984.

Winders, Jamie. "White in All the Wrong Places: White Rural Poverty in the Postbellum US South." *Cultural Geographies*, no. 10, 2003, pp. 45–63.

Wray, Matt. *Not Quite White: White Trash and the Boundaries of Whiteness*. Duke UP, 2006.

Wray, Matt, and Annalee Newitz. Introduction. *White Trash: Race and Class in America*, edited by Wray and Newitz, Routledge, 1997, pp. 1–12.

Wray, Matt, and Annalee Newitz. "What Is 'White Trash'? Stereotypes and Economic Conditions of Poor Whites in the U.S." *Minnesota Review*, vol. 47, Fall 1996, pp. 57–72. *Project Muse*, //muse.jhu.edu.ezproxy.uwe.ac.uk/article/438717/pdf.

Young, Stephen T. "Wild, Wonderful, White Criminality: Images of 'White Trash' Appalachia." *Critical Criminology*, vol. 25, no. 1, March 2017, pp. 103–17. *SpringerLink*, //link-springer-com.ezproxy.uwe.ac.uk/article/10.1007/s10612-016-9326-7.

Younge, Gary. *No Place Like Home: A Black Briton's Journey through the American South*. Picador, 1999.

Yousaf, Nahem. "Regeneration through Genre: Romancing Katrina in Crime Fiction from *Tubby Meets Katrina* to *K-Ville*." *Journal of American Studies*, vol. 44, no. 3, 2010, pp. 553–71.

Zamalin, Alex. *African American Political Thought and American Culture: The Nation's Struggle for Racial Justice*. Palgrave Macmillan, 2015.

Zandy, Janet. *Hands: Physical Labor, Class, and Cultural Work*. Rutgers UP, 2004.

Zanes, Warren. "Primitive Myths: Photography and the American South." *Afterimage*, vol. 25, no. 4, January–February 1998, pp. 10–12.

Žižek, Slavoj. *Trouble in Paradise: From the End of History to the End of Capitalism*. 2014. Penguin, 2015.

Zwerdling, Daniel. "Poverty and Pollution." *The Progressive*, vol. 37, 1973, pp. 25–29.

Index

Acorn Plan, The, 109–11
activism, xi, 26, 58, 111, 114–17, 121, 128–31, 134–42, 144–45
Adams, Shelby Lee, 41–48, 52
Adams, Timothy Dow, 54–55
Adorno, Theodor, 132
Affordable Care Act, 147
Agee, James, 8, 31–33, 35, 59
Aid to Families with Dependent Children (AFDC), xx, 75
Allen, Barbara L., 119–20
Allison, Dorothy, xv, xvii–xix, 54–55, 63, 65–66, 68–69, 75, 82, 85, 125–28, 148–49
All Over but the Shoutin', xviii, 56, 65, 72, 75–77, 84, 123
Almost Heaven, 3
Alston, Philip, 147, 151
American Hungers, xiii
ancestry, 66–68
And Their Children After Them, 32
And Venus Is Blue, 129–30
Appalachia, 3, 5, 11, 19–20, 36–54, 66, 73–75, 81–82, 100, 103, 127, 130–31, 134–45
Appalachia: A Self-Portrait, 39, 42
Appalachian Legacy, 42
Appalachian Lives, 42, 44–47
Appalachian Portraits, 42, 44–45
Appalshop (Community Film Workshop of Appalachia), 38–41
Aronowitz, Stanley, xviii
Aronson, Ronald, 118, 151
"Arsonists," 131–34
Asen, Robert, 75, 78, 83, 86, 88
Ashcroft, Bill, 64
Atlanta, GA, 7–8, 13, 26
Atlas Shrugged, 91
Aubert, Didier, 55

authenticity, xii, 10–12, 71–74, 85, 89–90, 100, 119
Ava's Man, 56–57, 68, 72
Azoulay, Ariella, 30–31, 39

Baichwal, Jennifer, 43, 45–46
banking crisis of 2008, 23, 25–26, 59, 91, 103, 108, 149
Barca, Stefania, 115
"Barn Burning," xviii–xix
Barnwell, Tim, 48–49, 52
Barret, Elizabeth, 37–39
Barthelme, Frederick, 52
Bartley, Numan V., xix
Bartling, Hugh, 117
Bastard Out of Carolina, 65, 125–28
Bell, Daniel, xxii
Beloved, 91–95, 98, 109
Benjamin, Walter, 29, 132
Benson, Melanie, 105–6, 126–27
Bergstrand, Kelly, 119
Berry, Wendell, 117
Best Cook in the World, The, 56, 72, 74
"Beyond the Pale," 17
Bhabha, Homi K., 16
Biguenet, John, xiii, 96–98, 106
Billings, Dwight, 42–43, 46
Bolstad, Paul, 143
Bonds, Judy, 138
Boorman, John, 3
Bourke-White, Margaret, 9, 31, 48
Boym, Svetlana, 58
Bragg, Rick, xvii–xix, 56–57, 63–66, 68–69, 71–77, 84–86, 123
Brenden, Martin, 12
Brinkmeyer, Robert, xv
Brown, Larry, 121, 123–25, 128–29, 135

Bryant, David, 48
Bryson, Bill, 18–22
Buell, Frederick, 107
Buell, Lawrence, 117, 143
Bullard, Robert D., xx, 145
Bundrum, Charlie, 56–57, 72
Byrd, William, 5

Cabbagetown, 26
Caesar, Terry, 3
Caldwell, Erskine, 9, 16, 31
Cameron, Ardis, 38
Campkin, Ben, 124
capitalism, xii, xviii–xix, 4, 6, 8, 12, 23, 37, 61, 71, 74–75, 78–79, 85–87, 91–92, 95, 104–5, 108, 119, 127–28, 132–33, 135, 137, 149–50
Carpenter, Brian, 89–90, 111
Carr, Duane, 16
Carson, Rachel, 117
Carswell, Simon, xvi
Carter, Jimmy, xv, 7
Cash, Jean W., 89–90
Cash, W. J., 66–67
Cather, Willa, 116
Catledge, Oraien E., 26
Chambers, Deborah, 54
Change Me into Zeus's Daughter, 55, 75–76
Charbonneau, Stephen Michael, 38
Childhood, A, 65
Child of God, 121
Chomsky, Noam, xi, 74, 91–92, 114
Church, Kate, 49
Churner, Rachel, 50
civil rights movement, xiii, 27–28, 65, 115–16
Civil War, 27, 67–68
Clark, John, 98
Clark, Timothy, 136
Clarke, Joni, 145
Clay's Quilt, 138–39
Clean Air Act, 113
Clinton, Bill, xx–xxi, 75, 81
Clinton, Hillary, xvi
Coal River Mountain Watch (CRMW), 137

Coal Tattoo, The, 138–39
Cobb, James C., 67
Cohn, Deborah, xiii, 4
Cole, Dewayne, 40
communalism, xxii, 93–94, 148–49
Communist Manifesto, The, 104
communitarianism, xiii, xxii, 63, 73, 79, 86, 92–96, 109, 111, 117–18, 134, 137, 148–50
community, 66–70, 73, 78, 83, 87–88, 92, 101, 104, 109, 114–16, 121, 123, 128, 136–37, 139–40, 142–43, 145, 148–49
Community Film Workshop of Appalachia (Appalshop), 38–41
Complex, NC, 14–17
Confederates in the Attic, 5, 7–9, 67–68
Cook, Sylvia Jenkins, 147–48
Cornwell, Rupert, 13
cosmopolitanism, 5, 18, 21, 93, 136
counternarratives, 28, 32, 38, 41, 75, 88, 116
Cox, Rosie, 124
Crane, Stephen, 55
Creasman, Boyd, 144
Cretton, Destin Daniel, 69–70
Crewes, Harry, 65
Cunningham, Charles, 30

Davis, David A., 63, 137
Davis, Fred, 72, 74
Dean, Jodi, xx–xxi, 78–79, 87, 149
Deep South, 7, 9–10, 23, 47
Deliverance, 3, 16, 18
"Delta Autumn," 7
Dickey, James, 3, 16
Dix, Andrew, 93
Douglas, Mary, 122–23
Drutt, Matthew, 52
Duck Dynasty, xiv
Dugan, Ellen, 27
Duke, David, 141–42
Dumping in Dixie, 145

Eagleton, Terry, xi–xii
Earth Day, 113

Ecology of a Cracker Childhood, 64, 66, 79, 88, 118, 121, 123
education, xiii, xvii–xviii, xx, 33, 36, 38, 45, 56, 75, 91–92, 104–5, 107–8, 111, 139
Eisenstein, Zillah, 90
Engels, Friedrich, 104
environmentalism, xi, 25, 40, 58, 64, 73, 87–88, 96, 98, 101–7, 111, 113–46, 149
Environmentalism of the Poor, The, 115–16
Ethridge, Robbie, 96
Eureka Mill, 150–51
Evans, Walker, 8–9, 26, 30–33, 45, 47, 59
Ewald, Wendy, 38–42

Face of Appalachia, The, 48
Farm Security Administration (FSA), 9–10, 29–32, 37, 47, 55, 61
Faulkner, William, xviii–xix, 7
Fay, 124
Fierce, 75–78, 85
financial capitalism, xi–xii, xiv–xvi, xix–xxii, 11, 23, 25, 67, 74, 78, 80–81, 85–87, 90–92, 95, 103–4, 106, 108–9, 111, 114–15, 118, 120, 128, 132, 134, 146, 148–50
Fletcher, Martin, 3, 7, 11, 13
Flight Behavior, 101–8, 111, 134
Flynt, Wayne, 66, 76
foodways, 72–75, 79–80
Ford, Richard, 26
Fraley, Jill, 144–45
Franklin, Tom, xiii, 89, 149
Frederickson, Mary E., xix
Freud, Sigmund, 122
From Tobacco Road to Route 66, 147–48
Frost, Robert, 116

Gallagher, Catherine, 65
Gates, Henry Louis, Jr., 65
Gaventa, John, 135
Gekko, Gordon, 91
gender, xi, xiii, xvi–xvii, xxii, 93, 98, 134
Giardina, Denise, 53–54, 138, 140–42
Gilmore, Leigh, 64

Given Ground, 142–44
Glass Castle, The, 69–70, 77
globalization, xii, 4, 10–12, 22, 67, 136–37
Global North, xii–xiii, 119–20
Global South, xiii, xix, 116, 119–20
Goad, Jim, xiv
Goldberg, Vicki, 44
Goldstein, Alyosha, xx
Gone with the Wind, 89
Good Brother, The, 149
Gordon, Avery, xvi–xvii, 132–33, 150–51
Gragson, Ted, 143
Grapevine, 50–51
Great Depression, 27, 29, 32, 68, 72, 74, 147
Great Society, xx, 36
Greenblatt, Stephen, 65
Greeson, Jennifer, 23
Griffiths, Gareth, 64
Grit Lit, xiii, 69, 89–90, 111, 149
Grit Lit: A Rough South Reader, 89
Guattari, Félix, xxii, 128, 137–38, 148
Guinn, Matthew, 68
Gusterson, Hugh, xvi

Hall, Louise, 45
Hands in Harmony, 48
Hanna, Stephen P., 38
Hannah, Barry, xiii
Harding, Wendy, 94
Hardlines, 89
Harrington, Michael, 27, 36, 81
Harris, Eddy L., 21–24
Hartigan, John, Jr., xiv
Harvel, Sherri, 60
Harvey, David, xix, 6, 11–13, 28, 71–72, 86, 90–92, 106, 120, 128, 134–35, 148, 150
Harvey, Dennis, 43
Haug, W. F., 26
Hawkins, Gary, 90
healthcare, 46, 59, 80, 84, 147
Henninger, Katherine, 29, 53, 70, 127
Here Comes Honey Boo Boo, xiv
Herzog, Mary, 19–20

Hicks, Orville, 11–12
Hicks, Ray, 11–13
Hillbilly Elegy, 81, 83–85
Hirsch, Marianne, 53, 57
Hobson, Fred, xiii
Holland, Patrick, 13, 17
Hood, Mary, 129–30
hooks, bell, xi, xiv, xxii, 27, 92–93
Horwitz, Tony, 5, 7–9, 67–68
House, Silas, 138–40
Houser, Heather, 134
Howard, Jason, 138
Hubbs, Jolene, 74–75
Huber, Patrick, 12
Huggan, Graham, 13, 17
Hulme, Peter, 4
Humphery, Kim, 136–37
Humphreys, Josephine, 71
Hunting Mister Heartbreak, 3
Hurley, Jack, 30
Hurricane Katrina, 23, 95–98
Hutchinson, Colin, 91
Hyde, Katherine, 39

identity, 68, 75, 107; class, 63; communal, 66; community, 83; cultural, xi; local, 12, 110; national, 127; personal, 64, 67; politics, 88, 94, 96, 98, 116; southern, 29, 127
I'll Take My Stand, 69
immigrants, xv, xxii, 25, 29–31, 140
Independent, 13
individualism, 67, 75, 90–92, 149
industrialization, 25–26, 58, 87, 148
In God's Country, 9, 14
Inscoe, John, 100
"Invocation," 150–51
Iovino, Serenella, 120
Irish Times, xvi
Isenberg, Nancy, xiv–xv
Ison, Hobart, 37

Jackson, Andrew, 64
Jahanbani, Sheyda, 36–37

Jarvis, Brian, 93
Jastrow, Joseph, 9
Jenner, Paul, 93
Joe, 121, 123–25, 128–29, 135
John Henry Days, 22, 98–101
Johnson, Lyndon B., xx, 36, 38
Jones, Gavin, xiii
Jones, Jacqueline, xix, 10
Jones, Suzanne, 67
Journal of Appalachian Studies, 19
Journey to Nowhere, 26, 32, 59–60

Katz, Stephen, 19–21
Keeley, Karen, 63
Keillor, Garrison, 139
Kennedy, Douglas, 9, 14–18, 24
Kennedy, John F., 36
Kerridge, Richard, 117, 135–36
Kidd, Stuart, 9, 30
Killingsworth, Jimmie, 120
Kingsolver, Barbara, 101–9, 111, 134, 148
Kipling, Rudyard, 17
Kirby, Jack Temple, 115
Klein, Naomi, xi, xxi, 146
Knoblauch, Loring, 50
Kozloff, Max, 49
Kristeva, Julia, 122
Ku Klux Klan, 18, 50–52
Kunzru, Hari, 85
Kwapis, Ken, 19

labor, xi, xx, 10, 51, 115, 128–35
Lake Wobegon Days, 139
Lange, Dorothea, 30–31
Langman, Charles, 6
Lauder, Tracy, 71
Leask, Nigel, 15
Lee, Harper, 27–28
Lee, Robert E., 68
LeMahieu, Michael, xvii, 65, 85
Let Us Now Praise Famous Men, 8–9, 31–32, 35–36
Lévinas, Emmanuel, 95

Life at Southern Living, 71
life-writing, xii, 61, 63–88, 147
Lifson, Ben, 40, 42
Lipper, Susan, 48, 50–52
Lisle, Debbie, 5, 17–19, 21
literature, xii–xiii, xvii, xxii, 7, 16, 89–111, 114–15, 117, 120–21, 128, 136–37, 147, 149–50
Littler, Jo, 114
Lloyd, Christopher, 107
localism, 4, 58, 72–73, 87, 116–17, 119
Logue, John, 71
Look Away!, xiii, 4
Los Angeles Times, 70
Lost Continent, The, 18
Lyson, Thomas A., xxi

MacCannell, Dean, 4, 10, 13
Madden, David, 27, 29, 43–44
Maharidge, Dale, 26, 32–36, 59–61
Mann, Sally, 47–48
Marazzi, Christian, xii, 25, 90, 103–4, 108, 148–50
Martin, Andrew, 60
Martin, Jacky, 94
Martinez-Alier, Joan, 115–16, 145
Marx, Karl, 104
Massey Energy, 142
Matthews, Scott L., 32
Maus, Derek C., 98
Mayer, Brian, 119
Mbalia, Dorothea Drummond, 94
McCalla, Gary, 71
McCarthy, Cormac, 121
McChesney, Robert W., 111
McCurry, Steve, 10
McGurty, Eileen, 113
McIntyre, Rebecca Cawood, 6
McLaurin, Tim, 109–11, 148
McNeil, Bryan, 137
Me and My Daddy Listen to Bob Marley, 131–34
Meiselas, Susan, 39

Michaels, Walter Benn, xi, 30, 59, 98
Middleton, Nick, 3, 6–8
"Migrant Mother," 30–31
Millichap, Joseph, 31
Mind of the South, The, 66
Mirzoeff, Nicholas, 28, 61
Mississippi Solo, 21–22
Mold, 96
Monteith, Sharon, 67
Moonshiners, xv, 11
Morris, Willie, 7
Morrison, Toni, xiii, 91–95, 98, 106, 109, 148
Moss, Barbara Robinette, 55–56, 75–79, 84–85
Most They Ever Had, The, 56, 84–85
"Moths," 129–30
mountaintop removal (MTR), 131, 133–34, 137–40, 142, 144–45
Mulvey, Laura, 16
Murphy, Patrick D., 103–5, 135
Mydans, Carl, 32

Naipaul, V. S., 4–6, 10–11, 13, 21–22, 24
Native Americans, 64, 120, 143–44
neocolonialism, 5, 17–18, 20, 32
neoliberalism, xi–xii, xiv–xvi, xix–xxii, 11, 23, 25, 67, 74, 78, 80–81, 85–87, 90–92, 95, 103–4, 106, 108–9, 111, 114–15, 118, 120, 128, 132, 134, 146, 148–50
Newitz, Annalee, xiv, 67
New Orleans, LA, 95–98
New South, xiii, xix, xxi, 4, 7–8, 10–11, 13, 33
Nixon, Rob, 116–19, 138, 145
Nolte, Nick, 19
Nordan, Lewis, xiii
North American Free Trade Agreement (NAFTA), xxi, 81, 86
North toward Home, 7
nostalgia, xii, 4, 13, 21–22, 25–26, 42, 46–47, 49, 58, 67–68, 71–74, 83, 89, 106

Obama, Barack, 140
O'Connor, Alice, xvii, xx, xxii, 77–78, 81–82

O'Connor, Flannery, 43
O'Connor, Hugh, 37
O'Doherty, Rebecca, 39
Office of Economic Opportunity (OEO), 38
Offutt, Chris, xiii, 149
Old Glory, 3
Old South, xix, 5, 8
Omnibus Budget Reconciliation Act of 1981 (OBRA), xx
On Earth's Furrowed Brow, 48–49
Oraien Catledge: Photographs, 26
Other America, The, 36

Palmer, Jacqueline, 120
Pancake, Ann, xiii, 130–34, 136, 142–45
Parchment of Leaves, A, 138
Patell, Cyrus, 93
Patton, George S., 83
Payne, Daniel, 120
Peach, Linden, 95
Peacock, James, 117
Perry, Keith, 89–90
Petro, Pamela, 3–8, 11–13, 21–22
photo-narratives, xii, xxi, 9–10, 25–61, 147
Picturing the South, 27
Pimpare, Stephen, 151
Pinhook, 118, 143
pollution, 102, 113–14, 119–22, 135
Portraits and Dreams, 38–41
postcolonialism, xii, 64, 116, 135
postmodernism, 30, 64–65, 150
President's Appalachian Regional Commission (PARC), 36
Prince of Frogtown, The, 56, 64
Prodigal Summer, 103

Raban, Jonathan, 3
Rabinowitz, Paula, 37, 53
race and racism, xi, xiii–xiv, xvi, xviii, xxii, 3, 17–18, 21–22, 24, 28, 51–53, 66–67, 70–71, 74, 85, 92–99, 105–6, 111, 115–16, 120, 145–46, 151
Ramsey, William, 98
Rand, Ayn, 91, 149
Rapson, Jessica, 107
Rash, Ron, 150–51
Ray, Byard, 49
Ray, Janisse, xiii, 58, 60, 64, 66, 69, 73, 79–80, 87–88, 117–19, 121, 123, 143, 148
Rea, Robert, 89
Reagan, Ronald, xv, xix–xx, 32, 77–78, 83, 91, 134
realism, 28, 30, 42, 50, 144
Rebein, Robert, xiii
Redford, Robert, 19
Redneck Manifesto, The, xiv
Reedus, Norman, xiv
regionalism, 32, 63, 73, 87–88, 98, 117
Richards-Shuster, Katie, 39
Rich in Love, 71
Rieger, Christopher, 125, 128
Right to Look, The, 28
Rising Water Trilogy, The, 96
Riss, Jacob, 25, 29
Roberts, Diane, 67
Romine, Scott, 5, 10–11, 66, 71, 74, 100, 149
Roosevelt, Franklin, 30
Rosler, Martha, 32
Rough South, xiii, 69, 89–90, 109, 111, 149
Rough South, Rural South, 89
Running, Katrina, 119

Salt and Truth, 42, 45–47
Same Sun Here, 139–40
Sanders, Bernie, xxi
Satterwhite, Emily, 139
Scanlan, John, 121–22
Schuweiler, Suzanne, 47
Scott, Clive, 29
Seed Underground, The, 88, 117–18
segregation, 3, 17–18, 47, 78
sharecroppers and sharecropping, 9, 31, 36, 47–48, 150
Shaw, Gareth, 12
Shepherd, Allen, 40

Shotgun, 96–98
Sitting Up with the Dead, 3, 6–7
slavery, 3, 28, 47, 91–96, 99, 109, 150
Slow Violence and the Environmentalism of the Poor, 116
Smith, Jon, xiii, 4
Smith, Lee, 44
Smith, Neil, 127
Smith, Sidonie, 64–65
Smonk, 149
social class, xi–xiii, xvi–xvii, 11, 13, 46, 67, 70, 90, 93–96, 99, 101–2, 114, 122–28, 136, 145–46, 148, 151; boundaries, xviii–xix, 64, 74, 77–78, 82, 111; inequality, xi–xxii, 105; prejudice, 85, 98; structure, xvii–xviii, 27–28; struggle, 90–92; tensions, 68; working class, 63, 84, 89, 94–96, 109–11, 115
Someplace Like America, 26, 59–60
Something's Rising, 138
Sontag, Susan, 28, 31
Sorkin, Adam, 149
southern exceptionalism, xiii, 22, 44, 117–18
Southern Living, 71–73
South of Haunted Dreams, 21–22
South to a New Place, 67
Spadaro, Jack, 138
Spangler, Bes Stark, 110
Springsteen, Bruce, 60–61
stereotypes, xiv, xvii, 5, 12, 14, 16–20, 22, 35, 38, 41–45, 47, 51, 53–54, 58, 70, 76, 89, 98–100, 120, 123, 137, 142, 148
Stevens, J. C., xvii–xviii
Stewart, Kathleen, 75, 125
Still Life in Harlem, 24
Stoler, Ann, 136
Stone, Oliver, 91–92
Storming Heaven, 140–41
Strange as This Weather Has Been, 130–31, 134, 136, 142, 144–45
Stranger with a Camera, 37–38
Strasser, Susan, 122
Stryker, Roy E., 29–30

Suter, Scott, 139
Sutter, Paul, 117

Tagg, John, 30
Tam, Henry, xxii
Tax Cuts and Jobs Act (TCJA), 147
Taylor, Helen, xiv
Temporary Assistance for Needy Families (TANF), xx
Thatcher, Margaret, xix, 90, 134
Theroux, Paul, 7, 9–10, 23
Third Life of Grange Copeland, The, 27–28
Third World, xxi, 22–23, 59–60, 103, 119
Thompson, Charles, 19
Thompson, Michael, 113–14
Thoreau, Henry David, 116, 117
Tice, George, 48–49
Tiffin, Helen, 64
Tobacco Road, 16
Toffler, Alvin, 122
To Kill a Mockingbird, 27–28
tourists and tourism, 4, 7, 10–13, 20–21
travel writing, xii, xxi, xxii, 3–24, 147
Trip, 52–53
True Meaning of Pictures, The, 43
Trump, Donald, xi, xv–xvi, xxi, 81, 85, 147, 151
Turnbull, Gemma-Rose, 37–38
Turner, Daniel Cross, 89
Turn in the South, A, 6
Two or Three Things I Know for Sure, 54–55

unemployment, xx–xxi, 81, 90, 109, 139
unions, xx, 10, 51, 134, 137, 142
Unquiet Earth, The, 140–41

Vance, J. D., 81–86, 149
Vaswani, Neela, 139–40
violence, xxii, 3, 6, 22, 41, 44, 51, 55, 64, 67, 69, 75, 84, 89, 92, 104, 107, 109, 126–27, 129, 141–42, 144, 150

Walker, Alice, 27–28
Walking Dead, The, xiv

Walk in the Woods, A (movie), 19
Walk in the Woods, A (novel), 18–19, 21
Walley, Christine J., xvi
Walls, Jeanette, 69–70, 77
Wall Street, 91–92
Wanat, Matt, 136
War on Poverty, xx, 36–37, 55, 61
waste, 78, 113, 120–28, 133–34, 145
Waste and Want, 122
Watkins, James, 63
Watson, Jay, 120–21, 128
Watts, Darlene, 40
welfare system, xiii, xix–xxi, 25, 40, 74–84, 90, 95, 108, 114, 139, 147–48, 151
Welty, Eudora, 31
West, Don, 141–42
White, Richard, 114
Whitehead, Colson, 22, 98–101, 106
White Trash, xv
Wild Card Quilt, 58, 60, 73, 87
Williams, Allan, 12
Williams, Raymond, 90–91
Williams, Val, 50–51
Williamson, Joel, 18
Williamson, Michael, 26, 32–34, 36, 59–61
Works Progress Administration, 30
Wray, Matt, xiv, 67
Wright, William, 89

You Have Seen Their Faces, 9, 31
Youngs, Tim, 4
"Youngstown," 60–61
Yousaf, Nahem, 96

Zamalin, Alex, 94–95
Zandy, Janet, 41, 94
Zanes, Warren, 31–32
Žižek, Slavoj, xii, 23, 80, 91
Zwerdling, Daniel, 113, 135

Credit: Rob Umphray

About the Author

Dr. Sarah Robertson is a senior lecturer in American literature at UWE Bristol. Her research focuses on class, economics and environmentalism in southern writing, and she has written extensively about southern poor whites. Her other publications include a monograph on Jayne Anne Phillips, and various articles and book chapters on writers such as William Faulkner, Katherine Anne Porter, Rick Bragg, and William Gay.

www.ingramcontent.com/pod-product-compliance
Lightning Source LLC
Chambersburg PA
CBHW030623230426
43661CB00053B/2120